Praise for
Possibility Unleashed
and Marc Harrison, MD

A great book by an extraordinary leader, medical professional, tri-athlete (with whom I've been privileged to cycle), and cancer survivor. *Possibility Unleashed* recounts a remarkable, beautifully written story that readers will find to be equal parts inspirational, challenging, informative, and instructive. The insights Marc Harrison provides are of universal value and applicability, making this book one that should be on everyone's reading list!

> **—General David Petraeus,** US Army (Ret.), former Commander of US Central Command, former Commander of the International Security Assistance Force (ISAF), and former Director of the CIA

Possibility Unleashed is a classic. Full of wisdom and heart, this book offers lessons on ethical leadership for us all. Harrison's journey—transforming hospitals and creating breakthrough innovations in healthcare—illuminates a path forward for all of us seeking to live our best lives. It's a singular work, a leadership book for our times.

> **—Dave Isay,** founder of StoryCorps

Harrison shares his journey of embracing market disruptions and bringing excellence to organizations. By telling insightful and compelling stories as well as revealing his own vulnerabilities, Harrison underscores the importance of seeking understanding and diversity of opinions while embarking upon change. In doing so, he offers a compelling road map for leaders and an infectious optimism for what lies ahead for those seeking to improve people's lives.

—David J. Shulkin, MD, former Secretary of the
US Department of Veterans Affairs

Drawing on decades of experience as a healthcare system leader and clinician, Marc Harrison provides a wealth of practical advice in this insightful and fast-paced book about how to lead change and unleash innovation in large organizations. I especially appreciate Marc's emphasis on always putting patients' interests first, on rewarding interventions based on the health outcomes they produce, and on focusing health systems on preventing rather than simply treating disease.

—Robert Bradway, Chairman and CEO of Amgen

Marc has written a playbook for leadership, teaching us all to embrace change and the conflict that comes with it, to lead with empathy and, most important, to take action. Passionate and thoughtful, Marc will inspire readers to lead with courage and create "good trouble."

—Caryn Seidman Becker, Chairman and CEO of CLEAR

I feel incredibly fortunate to have Marc as a friend, mentor, and training partner. During many of our backcountry adventures on foot, bikes, or skis I've benefited immensely from Marc's approach to unleashing the talent of others. This book makes his humane leadership philosophy available to all people—without all the early mornings and sore muscles.

—Billy Demong, US Olympic gold medalist in Nordic combined

POSSIBILITY
UNLEASHED

POSSIBILITY
UNLEASHED

PATHBREAKING LESSONS FOR MAKING CHANGE HAPPEN IN YOUR ORGANIZATION AND BEYOND

MARC HARRISON, MD

NEW YORK   CHICAGO   SAN FRANCISCO   ATHENS   LONDON
MADRID   MEXICO CITY   MILAN   NEW DELHI
SINGAPORE   SYDNEY   TORONTO

1 2 3 4 5 6 7 8 9   LCR   28 27 26 25 24 23 22

ISBN   978-1-264-64670-8
MHID   1-264-64670-4

e-ISBN   978-1-264-64682-1
e-MHID   1-264-64682-8

McGraw Hill books are available at special quantity discounts to use as premiums and sales promotions or for use in corporate training programs. To contact a representative, please visit the Contact Us pages at www.mhprofessional.com.

McGraw Hill is committed to making our products accessible to all learners. To learn more about the available support and accommodations we offer, please contact us at accessibility@mheducation.com. We also participate in the Access Text Network (www.accesstext.org), and ATN members may submit requests through ATN.

This book, like anything of substance
that I do, is dedicated to
MC, Alex, Martin, and Settie.
Your good hearts inspire me,
and your love sustains me.

CONTENTS

INTRODUCTION

I n 2009, I was diagnosed with bladder cancer. I was preparing for my seventh Ironman triathlon—I participated in my first triathlon in 1982 and had been doing at least one a year ever since. But this time around, the training wasn't going so well, and during the race itself, I began to urinate blood. That's when I knew something was seriously wrong.

I received aggressive surgical treatment, which thankfully did its job. A month after the procedure, my surgical pathology showed that I was cancer-free. And yet, I knew the battle had just begun. My prognosis wasn't particularly reassuring: only 40 percent of patients survived for five years. That and the physical pain I experienced because of my treatment left me with a deeper empathy for patients and a new awareness that life is short and our fortunes unpredictable. I had always wanted to have a positive impact on the world—that's why I'd become a doctor and more recently a physician leader. Now, I realized, with greater urgency, time was ticking. I had to take bold steps *right now* to make my organization and the broader healthcare system much better than it currently was.[1]

TACKLING THE SEEMINGLY IMPOSSIBLE

I was working at Cleveland Clinic at the time, and my determination to drive far-reaching change led me in 2011 to accept a role overseeing the construction and launch of Cleveland Clinic Abu Dhabi, a world-class hospital that was the first of its kind in the Arabian Gulf. Over a five-year period, and despite the tremendous challenges of operating in a cultural context that was very different from my own, my team and I made what was initially just a bunch of steel planks jutting out of the ground into a gleaming, state-of-the-art facility with patients from more than 70 countries and 3,500 staff.[2] When it was complete, the hospital revolutionized medical care across the region, providing residents with access to cutting-edge treatments.

In 2016, I accepted an opportunity to become CEO at Intermountain, Utah's largest health system with $6.1 billion in revenues, 22 hospitals, and some 1,400 physicians and advanced practice clinicians.[3] I knew this organization well: decades earlier I had completed a pediatric residency and pediatric critical care fellowship there. I believed strongly in the organization's mandate to serve as a model healthcare system for the country, as well as in its mission of "helping people live the healthiest lives possible."[4] Now I would have a chance to lead a daunting evolution of this famed healthcare system.

I say daunting because Intermountain had a sterling reputation nationally for delivering excellent care and also for delivering that care to *everyone*, even those who couldn't afford it. Given that the organization also had a strong culture and was in great shape financially, some inside Intermountain assumed that leadership's greatest priority should be to sustain established practices and ways of operating, not develop new ones. Interestingly, this thinking belied what was actually quite a long history of innovation at Intermountain. The organization had been one of the first health systems in America to establish an insurance company, to create a medical group, and to move toward electronic medical records. Nevertheless, a belief had taken hold in parts of the organization that fundamentally transforming Intermountain at this point in our evolution would be misguided, even dangerous.

I saw it differently, as did Intermountain's board of trustees and its previous leadership. As much as Intermountain had already accomplished, an opportunity existed for the organization to do even more, ratcheting up its innovation and in the process leading much-needed change across the entire healthcare sector. Despite decades of talk about reforming healthcare, our industry was still mired in an outdated, inefficient, and less compassionate fee-for-service model. It was a familiar system that the industry couldn't seem to escape. Under this model, key metrics such as patient experience, quality, and safety lagged, and caregivers focused on taking care of people once they got sick, not on preventing them from getting sick to begin with.

Newer, value-based care models rewarded healthcare systems for delivering better quality care, not just a larger quantity of it. One of these models, population health management, went further and compensated healthcare systems for taking care of patients on a per capita basis for a period of time rather than only for providing discrete "episodes" of care. Using this approach, we would essentially share the risk of taking care of patients. Insurers would pay us a certain amount per patient to provide for their care. If we could provide care for sick patients at lower cost, and if we could keep patients healthier to begin with and minimize their need for expensive healthcare interventions when they got sick, both patients and the healthcare system would benefit. Instead of receiving payment based on the specific services we provide, we would receive compensation based on health *outcomes* we deliver for a given population of patients. Such arrangements would incentivize us to keep people well, not just care for them once they became sick.

These newer models are the future of healthcare, poised to displace the older fee-for-service models. The latter models were bankrupting America even as they compromised the health of its citizens. Since healthcare providers under fee-for-service got paid based on volume, they benefitted financially by seeing more patients and performing more procedures, not by improving what they did. They had little incentive to innovate in ways that would allow them to operate more efficiently, improve the quality and safety of the care they provided, make care more pleasant and convenient for patients, or help keep patients well and out of hospitals.

Given how unsustainable the existing model was, Intermountain prior to my arrival had already begun a bold transition toward value-based care and population health. Since 2011, movement toward these models had been a C-suite priority and board-level goal. We had established an entire department and team dedicated to the transition and to pushing the deeper changes it entailed inside the organization. These efforts had borne fruit. By the time I arrived, 20 percent of our revenue derived from outcome-based payments under the population health model—far more than at most other leading health systems, and a testament to our efforts in this area.

And yet, we needed to do far more. As members of our board and others at Intermountain saw it, government policy would increasingly depart from the fee-for-service paradigm, putting pressure on big healthcare systems to adapt. New players in healthcare were also beginning to nibble away at the business of healthcare systems, finding new and better ways to deliver specific services. Observing the appearance of nimble startups, it seemed clear to us that most healthcare providers operating under fee-for-service, including Intermountain, were like Kodak, BlackBerry, or Blockbuster Video—

big lumbering incumbents that would become easy prey in the years to come. The choice was ours: Adapt now, or consign ourselves to an early death. Disrupt ourselves, or wait to be disrupted.

My cancer diagnosis left me with an even greater sense of urgency. After what I'd been through, waiting was not an option. Although some leaders at Intermountain were already bought in and excited to innovate, I perceived that as an enterprise we had only begun to transform our operations, offerings, and payment arrangements so that they supported value-based care and population health. I wanted us to accelerate decisively and proactively toward these newer models. Over the long term, we would stay on the strongest possible financial footing by becoming the "Tesla of healthcare," seeking out value- and population management–based payment arrangements and deploying new technologies, approaches, and initiatives that would allow us to thrive.

Reinventing ourselves as an innovation machine, we could deliver higher-quality and more proactive care, and do so more compassionately, at lower cost, and at scale. Some healthcare organizations had experimented with population health management and had invested in promising areas such as genomics, prescription drug reform, and at-home care or telehealth, but they hadn't unrolled these innovations to large populations. We wanted to go all in. By fully embracing value-based care and population management, we'd effect a revolution inside Intermountain and inspire change across the industry.

Guided by this vision and drawing on the collective efforts of our 42,000 employees, we've kicked off an ongoing, far-reaching transformation at Intermountain. Our work commenced in 2017 with a reorganization that formed an internally competitive health system into One Intermountain. We also adopted an operating model that, by underpinning a culture of continuous improvement across the organization, mobilized our entire workforce to help drive change.

That was just the beginning. We reorganized and revamped our medical group to become more integrated, allowing us to standardize care and coordinate it more effectively and, in the process, improve quality and reduce cost. We unveiled a host of clinical initiatives and ventures, including Civica Rx, a company that provides patients with more affordable generic drugs; HerediGene, the world's largest population genomics study; an array of new telehealth services and capabilities, including an entire virtual hospital; and much more. We launched numerous pilot programs related to the social determinants of health, such as a behavioral health project that increases access to care for vulnerable populations. We created an impact investing function that bets on ventures poised to contribute to better health in the communities we serve. And the list goes on.

Underlying and facilitating all of this change has been a wide-ranging cultural shift across the organization and in our leadership team. We've learned to move quickly to execute on our strategies. To more honestly assess our shortcomings so we can begin to fix them. To partner with outside organizations rather than thinking we can do it all ourselves. To listen to one another and work through tough issues together. To monitor our ongoing performance and hold ourselves more accountable. And, of course, to embrace loftier, industry-shaking goals.

Over the past five years, we've become one of the first major health systems to make the shift to population or value-based health—it now accounts for half of our revenue, up from 20 percent in 2016. As part of that shift, we've delivered on our social mission, dramatically improving quality, safety, and patient experience, which were already strong. We've expanded on Intermountain's longstanding commitment to increase access to care and improve the health of the diverse populations we serve. We've worked to lower the suicide rate in Utah, reduced the number of opioid pills our caregivers prescribed by 40 percent, provided more than $1.1 billion in free care for low-income patients from 2016 to 2020 for medically necessary services, and earmarked $120 million for impact investing. At the same time, our financial fortunes are better than ever. Not only have we grown rapidly, but we've doubled our revenues and expanded our operations to Idaho and Nevada in addition to Utah. We've also done so in a fiscally sustainable way, achieving the top bond ratings of any US healthcare system.

This work has been immensely rewarding. Leaders sometimes presume that organizations can't deliver better for consumers and achieve social objectives while also growing and delivering strong financial results. We've proved they can.

OVERCOMING THE CONFLICT CULTURE

As you might expect, unleashing this kind of change is immensely challenging. Many of our actions sparked a passionate response among employees fearful for their jobs, as well as a political backlash in the community. But Intermountain's leadership was determined not to let the divisiveness beyond our walls infect our culture. From the front lines to our executive team, we've persevered, attempting to stay true to our organization's founding charge of serving as a model healthcare system and attempting to work creatively to find common ground with many skeptics. Instead of just mustering the usual determination and focus that strong leaders show, we've sought to lean into deep-seated tensions and conflicts, both within the organization and beyond. Rather than avoiding conflict or seeking to ram through it, we've accepted it as a fact of life and attempted to manage it adroitly and compassionately on behalf of progress.

Navigating conflict to ignite change is, I've come to see, a leadership discipline of its own, one that requires special intensity, attentiveness, and skill. On the one hand, and perhaps most notably, leaders must work to avoid the unnecessary and excessive conflict that, in our harshly polarized society, all too often prevents change. It only adds friction, slowing much-needed progress. Departing from a command-and-control mentality and deploying empathy, curiosity, and other "soft" skills, leaders must bring people and organizations together to drive change, creating new and productive collaborations with business partners, customers, employees, community members, and even competitors.

But leaders seeking to unleash their organizations on behalf of progress must also be willing at key moments to *incite* conflict to productive ends. Mindful of their ethical purpose and the organization's mission, they must take meaningful stands on behalf of their beliefs and in the service of progress. On an ongoing basis, they must prod people to embrace change even when they don't necessarily want to. Of course, there's a balance to be struck. At all times, leaders must take care not to go too far but to behave compassionately, empathetically, and respectfully toward others with differing perspectives.

To date, we've succeeded because we've worked creatively to find common ground with many skeptics. One of our community health program managers, a liberal, Harvard-trained healthcare leader, partnered with a leading gun rights advocate in one of America's most conservative states to make progress on firearm-assisted suicides. Likewise, we addressed the problems of high prices and drug shortages by working with competitors to found a nonprofit generic drug company.

Communities struggle with poverty, crime, and other seemingly nonmedical issues. That's not normally seen as a healthcare crisis, but Intermountain views it through that lens because we're following the evidence upstream. So we're investing millions to address these issues, recognizing that they in turn profoundly affect people's health.

It's not just Intermountain that has grown and evolved. I have, too, as have my relationships with caregivers and leaders in the community. Early critics have become good friends, while a good number of skeptical employees are buying into the radical and ongoing changes we've undertaken. I should emphasize that I've learned valuable lessons from them. I've seen leaders and caregivers deploy ideas and strategies on the front lines that I never would have imagined. And I've marveled at how teams of people have unleashed *themselves* to make a difference of their own, pushing me to be a better leader, a better listener, and a better human being.

My urgent need to drive change hasn't wavered. On the contrary, it has only intensified. If cancer doesn't fire you up to try to do the seemingly impossible, I don't know what will. Unfortunately, there's more to that story. In 2018, I received a second tough diagnosis, this time of multiple myeloma, a blood cancer. Educating myself about this condition, I kept running up against the word "incurable," and it haunted me. New treatments were allowing more patients to live with the disease and manage it as a chronic illness, and I was determined to be one of them. More than ever, I couldn't take anything for granted. If I wanted to make an impact with the possibly limited time I had left, I knew I had to push myself and our organization even harder.

In 2019, a key treatment I underwent—a bone marrow transplant—failed, and my condition quickly deteriorated. It seemed that my time really was running out. We scrambled, and I underwent a novel immunotherapy called CAR T-cell therapy.[5] My body's killer T cells were removed, souped up using genetic engineering to better fight the cancerous cells, and then returned to my body. The treatment works for about 70 percent of patients, and so far, I've been one of them.

I don't know how long this treatment and others I might try will contain my disease, so I'm not wasting a minute. Every day, I wake up more committed than ever to pursue the path we've been on and push change forward, regardless of the challenges. Despite what we've accomplished, we're nowhere near ready to declare victory. As I've found, life and business are always evolving, a work in relentless forward progress. We're determined to keep going, continuing to unleash possibility inside our organization and improve the quality, safety, and cost of the care we provide.

ABOUT THIS BOOK

I've written *Possibility Unleashed* to share what we've learned by driving change at Intermountain. I want you to take *your* organization and industry to new heights by unleashing your people's power to innovate. To that end, the book introduces you to a new and perhaps iconoclastic perspective on leadership, one that I find to be not merely innovative but pragmatic, results oriented, collaborative, and healing.

My argument is simple: leaders can have a far greater impact on society than we realize while also building strong, economically healthy organizations where people love to work. The key is to focus not on scoring political points or even behaving "sustainably," as many leaders today strive to do, but on taking personal and organizational responsibility for solving broader social problems and working together to make it happen. Leaders must muster courage on multiple levels. They must recognize the limits of their own authority and seek solutions from frontline employees and external partners. They must set aside political and cultural differences and find common ground. And they must not merely tolerate diversity but draw on it to power breakthrough innovation.

I've written *Possibility Unleashed* in hopes of exposing executives, managers, students, and entrepreneurs to the insights, mindsets, and practical tools that we've mobilized to disrupt a troubled industry and heal ailing communities. In the chapters that follow, I'll elaborate on a set of principles related to the challenge of leading change in fractious times. In the first two chapters, I lay foundational principles—empathy and the welcoming of outsiders—and then cover themes related to organizational transformation (Chapters 3–5), strategy (Chapters 6–9), and stakeholder communications (Chapters 10–11). In each chapter, I'll push into the complexity, exploring the inevitable tensions leaders must surmount and the balancing acts they must sustain to solve big problems. You won't hear just from me. Having had the honor of knowing or working with distinguished leaders in healthcare and beyond, I've woven in stories and lessons of theirs that have helped me to learn and grow as a leader.

As you read this book, I invite you to hold up a mirror to your own leadership and reflect on what it will *really* take in the coming years to bring meaningful change and stay ahead of disruption. The chapters ahead will cover challenging topics such as the importance of talking to your "enemies"; walking in the shoes of the underserved; navigating the land mines of identity politics while acknowledging and leveraging cultural differences; pushing others in your organization into a healthy state of discomfort; and breaking out of your habitual domains to solve problems.

I'll also invite you to ponder what growth in an organization is really all about; whether you have the right business model and offerings to allow for true innovation; whether you're willing to be hated (we must be if we want to do anything truly disruptive and meaningful); and whether you've been honest with yourself about the state of your organization. I hope to approach these themes not with abstractions or platitudes but with heartfelt meditations rooted in real experience. As I'll reveal, a dedication to the difficult and ongoing process of collaborative problem-solving at Intermountain has saved lives, transformed communities, and built a thriving, industry-leading organization.

Many leaders are scouring the horizon for new ways of operating, not least because customers, employees, and investors are clamoring for leadership that is focused on driving progress rather than making a political point. Yet all too often, leaders fail to take bold action and to galvanize others to do the same. We're beset not just by inertia, but by a conflict culture that makes any bold move seem perilous and even impossible. By reflecting on experimentation and change-making, I hope this book will inspire you to set aside conventional thinking, seek out unlikely partnerships, pursue them in productive ways, and get the job done.

The time has come to get serious about change. We all know this. We also know that the polarization and divisiveness in our society has gotten out of hand. So let's stop the grandstanding and the bickering. Let's step up, take responsibility, and work with and through our differences to make change happen. We must become not just innovators in our domains or evangelists for our ideals but pragmatic healers and problem solvers for all of society. Let's unleash possibility in ourselves and our organizations, so that we might move together toward a healthier, more prosperous future.

POSSIBILITY
UNLEASHED

1

WALK IN OTHERS' SHOES

*This is what I learned from spending time
shadowing patients—and being one myself.*

In 1990, when I was a 26-year-old pediatrics intern fresh out of medical school, I had the privilege of working at Intermountain's Primary Children's Hospital for a big, gentle bear of a man named Marty Palmer. Marty was the first child protection pediatrician in the Intermountain West, as well as a bishop for the Church of Jesus Christ of Latter-day Saints. He was an exceptional person and a real role model to me—smart, tremendously accepting of diversity, a master clinician. Doctors would send him their most difficult patients and ask if he could figure out what was wrong with them. Marty also seemed to mentor the most challenging (read: pain-in-the-ass) residents at his continuity clinic. When I inquired about that, he didn't hesitate to mention that I fit right in, especially the pain-in-the-ass part.

One day, a woman in her thirties who had several kids showed up late for her appointment with me. Not just a little late: when I looked at the clock, she was 20 minutes late, then 25, then 30. We had a rule then that if a patient came 30 minutes late for an appointment, the doctor could cancel the appointment entirely, leaving it up to the patient to reschedule if they wished.

My schedule then was challenging: every third or fourth day, I would work all night in the hospital and then head over to an out-patient clinic to see patients. Tired and stressed, I canceled the woman's appointment and announced to everyone within earshot that I was going home to sleep. No sooner had I done so when the woman walked in. "I'm still going home," I said to Marty. "She's 35 minutes late."

"Oh, no, you're not," he replied.

I was taken aback—this woman seemed pretty clearly out of line. Nevertheless, I fought through my fatigue and saw her. When her appointment was over, Marty had another piece of news for me: he wanted me to go visit this woman and her children in their home and then trace the exact steps she took to get to our clinic. I wasn't sure what this little exercise was supposed to accomplish, given all the demands on my time, but I did it. The experience was life changing.

I got on a bus and rode clear across town, got out, waited, and transferred to a second bus. The whole trip might have taken me 20 minutes if I'd driven, but on public transportation it took 90. The woman lived on the second floor of a bleak low-rise building. She let me in and graciously showed me to a living area crammed with boxes and personal items. As we chatted, I noticed for the first time how weary she looked. She was not much older than I was, but given the lines on her face, the bags under her eyes, and her old clothing, one might have thought her in her forties.

As this woman told me, she was a single mom and lived in this tiny two-bedroom apartment with her kids as well as several other adults and children. With no access to a car or childcare, she had to take her kids with her to medical appointments and everywhere else using public transportation. Reflecting on these circumstances, I realized that the very fact she had made her appointment at all was little short of a miracle. I was ashamed of myself for having treated her so poorly and acted so selfishly.

Like many physicians, I pursued medicine to help people. I sought to show kindness and compassion, especially to those who came from difficult circumstances. My father was a general surgeon who dedicated himself to caring for everyone, rich and poor. "Rich people will do fine," he'd say, "but poor people, they really need us, because the odds are stacked against them."

And yet, I had never really been exposed in a visceral way to what it meant to live in poverty. I had grown up in a middle- to upper-middle-class family in Pittsburgh, and we always had enough money for the basics as well as extras like private school and summer camp. Now that I had taken the time to witness difficult living conditions up close, at least for a couple of hours, I was determined not only to treat patients kindly but to venture beyond my own narrow perspective and show real empathy and compassion. I wanted my actions to match my personal beliefs.

EMPATHY'S MOTIVATIONAL POWER

Most leaders who seek to drive change are smart and well-intentioned. They aim to achieve strong business results and do right by their customers, employees, and communities. But there's a difference between having good intentions and really understanding what customers, employees, partners, community members, and others are experiencing. In healthcare, and I suspect in most other industries and endeavors, empathy—the ability to walk in others' shoes, to truly grasp life from their perspective—is foundational to any attempt to drive change, not least because of the impact it has on your own perspective and priorities. As researcher Brené Brown teaches, empathy is "the brave choice to be with someone in their darkness—not to race to turn on the light so we feel better."[1] By bringing the struggles of others to life, empathy ignites a fire deep within you to make change happen.

The lesson Marty taught me changed my life, but it was hardly the only experience that cued me into patients' struggles. My cancer diagnoses did, too, but one other experience stands far above even these in helping me cultivate empathy. In 2011, I was in Pittsburgh, sitting at my brother's kitchen table, when I received a call from a foreign number that I didn't recognize. It was my son Alex's friend Diana, phoning from Tübingen, Germany. Alex, then 19 years old, was visiting her in that quaint medieval city. Apparently, he was out at night when he fell down a set of stone steps and suffered a potentially catastrophic brain injury. A stranger found him unconscious and called EMS, who took him to the emergency room. According to Alex's friend, the situation was dire. He could pass away at any time.

Sitting there at the kitchen table, I felt as if my world had just collapsed. As a pediatric ICU doctor, I had often cared for kids with traumatic brain injuries. Now, half a world away from Alex, I felt the terror and helplessness that I'd seen in so many of my patients' families. Still, I managed to spring into action. I called the hospital in Germany, told my wife, Mary Carole, the devastating news (she was in Abu Dhabi at the time), and arranged for the two of us to meet with our other two children in Germany. While preparing to board a flight to Europe, I called the neurosurgeon caring for Alex and consulted on his care, urging aggressive action (removal of pieces of his skull) to save his life.

The next three weeks were absolutely brutal—far more painful than anything I've experienced in the course of my own health challenges. I stayed at Alex's bedside 24-7, monitoring the smallest details of his care—every ventilator breath, every medication. At a number of points, it seemed unlikely that he would make it. But Mary Carole helped us to stay strong, telling us, "OK, he's made it through another hour. Now, the next hour. Then the next." Ten years later, simply recalling these moments brings tears to my eyes and a sick feeling to my stomach.

Perhaps the most difficult time occurred three to four days into it, as I waited for the results of a CT scan that would offer clues to the extent of the brain damage Alex had sustained. Sitting with the radiologist, waiting for the scan to appear on the monitor, I wondered if my son would ever be able to walk again, or speak, or smile. That is to say, if he lived. And if he didn't live, or if he couldn't live a meaningful life, I wondered how our family would survive it. Frankly, I wasn't sure that we would.

The waiting was nauseating. Fortunately, the scan was positive. If Alex's condition stayed stable, there was at least the prospect of a meaningful recovery. And even if he couldn't live anything like his previous life, Mary Carole and I decided that we would make the best of it. At least we'd still have our son.

Little by little, Alex managed to pull through. In a twist of fate, he received a ride back home from Germany on a medically equipped plane operated by Cleveland Clinic's intercontinental critical care transport team, a business that I'd started during my time at the Clinic. He spent months in inpatient and then outpatient neurological rehab and has since made a full recovery. He went on to finish college and has graduated from medical school and is a resident in obstetrics-gynecology.

Living through the experience of almost losing a child has deepened my empathy for patients, lending it a new fierceness. Ever since then, if I hear that caregivers are not taking care of patients well or are behaving egotistically, I take it personally and become absolutely fired up to fix it. *Nothing* annoys me more than a disregard for patients and their experience. I simply can't abide it. And that's because I know what it feels like to suffer as a patient's loved one.

More broadly, my personal experiences on the patient's side have left me aware of how privileged I am as a wealthy white male doctor and CEO to have access to high quality, affordable care. Although so many patients receiving a bone marrow transplant are forced to relocate, at great expense and inconvenience to their families, I was able to go to Intermountain's transplant unit, located just a couple of miles from our house. Instead of having to stay for weeks at a hotel, my wife could come home every night and sleep in our own bed. Likewise, some months after receiving my CAR-T treatment at the University of Pittsburgh Medical Center, I received a bill for $587,000 in the mail. It was sent to me in error—I received that treatment free of charge as part of a clinical trial. But as I held that unexpected bill in my hand and recovered from the initial shock of receiving it, I could only imagine the terror it would strike in the heart of someone who knew they *would* have to pay.

My awareness of my own privilege inspires me to work hard every day to remedy the inequities in our system, and to do it as quickly as possible. Further, being a patient has left me with a clearer sense of what *all* patients share in common. No matter who we are, where we come from, or what ails us, when we become patients, we all want to be heard. We want to be helped to the full extent possible. We want to be treated with dignity. We want clarity, honesty, and genuine concern from our caregivers. And in the United States at least, we want reassurance that our care won't break us financially.

Understanding these desires as well as the utter helplessness patients feel when they receive a serious diagnosis, I'm more determined than ever to help my organization deliver extraordinary care that is safer, of higher quality, more affordable, more compassionate, and more equitable. I'm also more determined to create a model system at Intermountain, pushing the boundaries of what's possible in healthcare to eventually bring systemic change.

Empathy is so powerful that it often doesn't only motivate the person who feels it to act—it unleashes others who witness that action. As a young doctor teaching and serving as a staff neurologist at the University of Western Ontario, John Noseworthy was asked to drive to the airport to pick up a medical school professor from Mayo Clinic who would deliver a lecture to the staff the following day. Noseworthy was excited: he would have a chance to spend time with this professor, who had an international reputation and would receive an award from the university the following day.

When the professor's plane arrived, he wasn't on it. Noseworthy was puzzled—nobody had called to say the professor had canceled. Eventually, Noseworthy went home, wondering what had happened, disappointed that he wouldn't be able to meet this luminary.

The next day, the professor called to apologize. He had missed his flight but had taken another, later one, arriving early that morning. "May I ask what happened?" Noseworthy inquired.[2]

"Oh," the professor said, "I was with a patient and couldn't make the flight."

Noseworthy was stunned. As he knew, few specialists with international reputations would miss their flight to receive a big award simply because they were with a patient who needed their attention. But this doctor would—and did. "It was like a two-by-four hit me in the forehead," Noseworthy recalls. "It was an extraordinary situation, and I've never forgotten it."

This doctor had so much empathy for the patient's suffering—not to mention personal integrity and humility—that he was willing to put himself second and his patient first. Observing him, Noseworthy was inspired to behave similarly. He became drawn to Mayo Clinic, seeing it as a place that fostered such empathy and dedication and encouraged staff to act on it. When an opportunity arose to work at Mayo and drive change there, Noseworthy didn't hesitate. Years later, he ended up becoming Mayo's CEO.

BUILD BRIDGES; DON'T BURN THEM

As important as empathy is for motivating change, it also unleashes people to drive change by easing conflicts and helping build more productive, trusting relationships. We might not achieve all our objectives in the short term, but we open the way for more long-term progress because we keep potentially fruitful dialogues open. Empathizing with others leads them in turn to empathize with us, laying a foundation for future collaboration, even when times are tough.

For a glimpse of this dynamic at work, consider our challenges in Utah to address the new coronavirus pandemic. Covid-19 pushed communities across America to the breaking point as medicine and politics became hopelessly intertwined. Healthcare professionals advocated for lockdowns, mandatory masking, and other public health measures, while government officials and private citizens in many cases pushed back, mindful of the massive economic toll these measures would take and fearing encroachment on their liberties.

During the summer of 2020, as Covid-19 cases in Utah were starting to rise and strain our resources, citizens and political leaders in some parts of Utah questioned whether the pandemic was really as bad as we were saying it was. After then-governor Gary Herbert issued a mask mandate for kids returning to school in the fall, some local parents were terribly upset and spoke out publicly in protest.[3] "Covid is a hoax. It's a lie. It's a political stunt," one woman said.[4] Others objected to masks on constitutional grounds, regarding the mask mandate as an attack on individual rights.[5] The protests that summer drew national attention, with some observers ridiculing the protesters.[6]

In this context, it would have been convenient for us to disparage anti-maskers as well in our attempts to lobby for what we regarded as evidence-based, medically necessary masking policies. We did, of course, speak out forcefully about the importance of masks, and we continue to do so. But rather than take a hard line and criticize leaders for being slow to adopt the public health measures we wanted, we took a more collaborative approach, inviting a handful of key political leaders—including the governor, lieutenant governor, and legislative leaders—to visit one of our intensive care units. We wanted them to see firsthand the toll taken by the pandemic on both patients and our frontline providers and caregivers.

In organizing this event, we empathized with political leaders, many of whom thought differently about Covid and how to respond to it than we did. We respected their thoughtful and well-meaning perspectives. Although they might have disagreed with us, they, too, wanted to see our community thrive—they just had different ideas about what that meant in these circumstances. We understood, too, that the pandemic had forced them to make impossible decisions between public health and economic well-being. We appreciated the pressure leaders were under from groups that vehemently resisted masking. Given the tensions that existed in Utah, we knew these leaders were taking a political risk—not to mention a risk to their health—simply by donning protective clothing and visiting our facility.

If we had lectured to these leaders, we would have irritated them, likely causing them to harden their resistance to our ideas and making future cooperation less likely. So, we simply sought to show them the facts on the ground of which they might otherwise not be aware. We let them see patients who were all alone in an ICU bed struggling to breathe. We let them speak with our nurses, constituents of theirs who recounted helping patients have final conversations with loved ones over FaceTime. To enhance the intimacy and authenticity of the event and to show respect for our patients, we didn't publicize it or invite the media to cover it. Our hope was that exposure to the sheer humanity of what was happening would spark more dialogue so we could listen to one another and understand our respective positions.

That's exactly what happened. Although we've continued to articulate different viewpoints from those of some political leaders and others in our community over the Covid response, including testing and the role of vaccination, the leaders who visited our facility were able to empathize more fully with our caregivers and the pressures they were under. The resulting feelings of trust opened up new possibilities for change and collaboration going forward. Political leaders on the other side of some public health issues know that I will hang in there with them and try to work collaboratively. I know that about them as well.

You might wonder if it's really possible to empathize with others with whom you disagree, given how deeply you might feel about an issue or a position. I think it is. I couldn't believe more strongly in masks and vaccinations than I do. Weakened by multiple myeloma, my immune system doesn't respond as well to vaccines as most people's do. For me, the decision of others to mask up is a matter of life or death. Yet I still understand the motives and impulses that lead citizens and public officials to different conclusions. They're responding to the truth as they see it, doing their best to safeguard values that are just as important to them as mine are to me.

My friend, former Nebraska governor and senator Bob Kerrey, recalls how during the Vietnam War era he hated Richard Nixon because he, Kerrey, had gone to war in 1969 and blamed Nixon for ensnaring the country in that horrible conflict. Kerrey had been wounded in the war and earned a Medal of Honor while serving as a Navy SEAL. Some 18 years later, when Kerrey was in Santa Barbara, California, teaching a class on the war, he went for a walk on the beach and felt moved, once and for all, to forgive the former president. Staring into the waves, feeling empathy for the former president, regarding him as a fellow human being with both flaws and noble qualities, Kerrey shouted, "I forgive you, Richard Nixon!"[7]

Kerrey also recalls how in 2019 he served as the grand marshal at the Veterans' Day Parade in New York City. Breaking with the presidential tradition of laying a wreath at Arlington National Cemetery, former President Donald Trump decided to speak at the parade, a move that some felt politicized the event. "I went to the parade prepared to be angry at him for doing it," Kerrey said. "And I watched him while he was speaking, and I felt empathy for him. I saw a human being up there. It doesn't mean I voted for him. I didn't. It doesn't mean I like his policies. In most cases, I didn't. It doesn't mean I embraced his behavior. In many instances, I didn't. But I saw him as Donald J. Trump, human being."

With enough time and discipline, all of us can feel empathy, even for our opponents or people we strongly dislike. When an issue becomes politicized, we create barriers between people, lumping them into groups or camps or parties. But while those distinctions might be grounded in truth, in the end we are all human beings who share needs, concerns, and qualities in common with one another. It takes work, and it might not be possible all at once, but when we open our hearts and make that imaginative leap, we lower the psychological barriers that separate us from others. We increase the odds that others will lower their barriers as well.

GOING SLOW TO GO FASTER

When our attempts to lead change cause conflict to arise, our natural inclination can be to become impatient and try to ram through our agenda. *We* know the right course of action (or think we do). We desperately want to take an idea to reality. I'm as guilty of this as anyone—I like to move fast. But as I've come to understand during my time at Intermountain, we have so much to gain by resisting our impulse to act and instead slow down, ask questions, and take time to listen and empathize. In my own development as a leader, I've focused on pausing and letting others have a chance to think through issues rather than forcing a quick decision. I know that I might not win everyone over to our cause. But if I take my time, I'll usually be able to engage a broader group of people to collaborate and push change forward. Solutions will prove more durable, relationships among team members will strengthen, and my team will have a more active hand in running the organization.

During the spring of 2020, in the aftermath of George Floyd's murder, I sought to accelerate change at Intermountain in the area of diversity, equity, and inclusion (DEI). Believing intensely in DEI's importance, I was thinking like an ICU doctor confronted with a patient in respiratory distress: rather than stand around, I wanted to jump in, intubate the patient right away, and put them on a ventilator. Fortunately, several members of my team urged me to slow down the process lest I come across as just another arrogant white male leader. With their help, I realized that if we didn't take time to listen and empathize, we would fail to galvanize our people, and our change efforts would lose steam. Well-intentioned leaders do this all the time, taking bold action only to see progress falter as people become distracted or leave the organization.

Resisting the urge to promulgate action from on high, my leadership team and I embarked on a listening tour that extended over a period of about six to eight weeks. We convened groups of frontline caregivers, inviting diverse groups of people to participate. We included clinical and nonclinical staff, people at all levels in the organization, and a full spectrum of identities (ethnic, religious, gender, LGBTQ+, and so on). Holding sessions on Zoom, we asked participants to share their personal perspectives on what it felt like to work in our culture and how we might improve.

I knew we had work to do in this area, but what I heard stunned, saddened, and humbled me. One Black nurse-midwife recounted how she always had to wear her stethoscope so that patients and colleagues would accord her a modicum of professional respect. Another caregiver told us of a nurse from New York City, who had come temporarily to help us care for Covid patients, who was called the N-word by a patient within her first 12 hours of working at Intermountain Medical Center. Still other caregivers described being passed over for promotions or fielding a constant barrage of microaggressions on the job.

Our chief clinical information officer, a Kenyan native named Seraphine Kapsandoy, made a particular impression on me, describing how "exhausting" she found it to operate in what she experienced as an uncomfortable work environment. "I have to work twice as hard to show my worth and gain access to the same opportunities as others," she said.[8] In fact, she found it demoralizing just to have to sit down again with leaders to talk about her travails as a Black woman. The organization had promised in the past to improve equity but failed to make any headway. Why should she believe it would be any different now?

Years earlier, when she worked as a nurse on our transplant unit, a patient called her the N-word and refused to allow her to take care of him. In situations such as these, she had tried to work with managers and human resources but found she couldn't get the support she needed. "I just learned to absorb it, go home, talk with my family, but come back the next day and just keep working," she said. She could count several talented colleagues who decided not to put up with it and who subsequently left the organization.

Consulting with employees like Seraphine, we assembled a far-reaching plan to drive equity deep into our organization. Working with a broad group of leaders across Intermountain, we revised our Fundamentals of Extraordinary Care statement, the bedrock upon which we define our goals, including a plank on equity that compels us to "eliminate disparities and create opportunities for caregivers, patients, members, and communities to thrive."[9] We adopted equity as a value, proclaiming our intention to "embrace diversity and treat one another with dignity and empathy." We created an ombudsman so employees had recourse when our HR systems didn't work properly to resolve equity-related issues. Finally, we invested in the implementation of projects—50 of them across the organization thus far—to help us make our patient and employee experiences more equitable. For instance, we've changed our stroke care and the way we help new moms with breastfeeding to ensure that everyone achieves the same great outcomes. As we've done this work, we've also strived to show empathy for our white employees, some of whom are feeling displaced, disoriented, and fearful as we implement policies or statements emphasizing equity.

We have been able to set ourselves on this more sensitive and I think more successful path to change in part because we had the support of more conservative-minded leaders inside our organization who were all-in because they now had a visceral sense of what diverse employees were experiencing and could empathize with them. It hasn't been comfortable having conversations about equity, and we're still just beginning our journey, but by taking time to listen, we were able to normalize the conversation and build momentum to initiate real, meaningful reform. We're not yet a national leader in DEI, but in our particular social, cultural, and political context, we've made important strides—relentless forward progress, as I like to call it.

MORE NUANCED SOLUTIONS

When we take time to listen and empathize, we not only get more buy-in—we also often wind up moving toward a more thoughtful handling of issues than we would have had if we'd simply imposed our own views. I've seen this happen as my own team has struggled to handle vexing, highly politicized issues that cut to the core of their own personal belief systems.

As an example, consider our formulation of policies around Covid-19 vaccinations. In our area and nationally, well-meaning citizens harshly disagreed with one another about vaccination and the ability of government and private organizations to mandate it. Some supporters of vaccination wanted to vaccinate as many people as possible as quickly as possible and felt that public health concerns justified the imposition of mandates. Those who opposed the Covid-19 vaccine mandate distrusted vaccines for a whole slew of reasons, some of which I felt were legitimate and others less so, and they saw mandates as little more than tyranny and an attack on individual rights. The debate very quickly became toxic, with people on each side vilifying the other.

We had a lot of work to do on vaccination. By May 2021, only 45 percent of people in Utah were fully vaccinated, and only about 65 percent of Intermountain caregivers.[10] We desperately wanted to get our caregiver numbers closer to 100 percent. But how? Other organizations took a hard line, imposing mandates. The results were mixed: yes, more people became vaccinated, but by forcing employees to receive vaccination or risk losing their jobs, these measures hardened the views of opponents and alienated them from the system, arousing discontent and paving the way for greater tension later.

Our leadership team was conflicted about how to proceed. We all believed wholeheartedly in the medical value and safety of vaccinations. Some of us advocated for a mandate at Intermountain, while others were less enthusiastic, fearing blowback and even the departure of staff at a time when we were experiencing a labor shortage.

I will admit that I initially was too strident in my own support for vaccination. As some of my colleagues continue to remind me, I tended to dismiss anti-vaxxers in harsh terms as "crazy" or "nuts." Thankfully, members of my team with different viewpoints helped me to soften my stance somewhat. After my chief of staff, Katherina Holzhauser, conveyed her own hesitancy around the Covid-19 vaccine, I gained more understanding and compassion for anti-vaxxers. My empathy further grew after others shared stories of a nurse in our organization who felt terrified of getting the vaccine because she had lost three pregnancies already and feared that the vaccine would jeopardize her current efforts to finally become a mom. Even if the science indicated that the vaccine didn't pose as much danger as this nurse and others believed, people had other concerns that mattered to them, and I needed to respect that. As much as I still favored vaccination, I had to remain keenly aware of the damage caused when we alienated people by mandating a health measure they so strongly opposed.

We wound up taking a more nuanced approach. We held off on issuing a mandate for as long as we could, giving people the choice as to whether or not to get vaccinated. At the same time, we offered members of our SelectHealth insurance system $100 cash rewards for getting the vaccine, a measure that resulted in nearly 30,000 additional vaccinations. Through that and the spread of messaging that encouraged vaccination, we were able to get about 75 percent of our employees fully vaccinated, with another 10 percent partially vaccinated. To further protect patients and staff, we also made sure to outfit our staff with the protective clothing they needed and put strict protocols in place to limit transmission. To our knowledge, no patient has ever been infected with Covid by an Intermountain staff member, a result that makes us proud.

In October 2021, we eventually did issue a mandate, but only because we had no choice: the Biden administration issued mandates that would greatly limit our ability to serve Medicare, Medicaid, and other patients if we didn't comply. Even though our decision was forced on us and we offered exemptions in compliance with the law on religious or medical grounds, our mandate touched off a firestorm of criticism from opponents on Twitter and Facebook.

Our initial policy wasn't perfect, but we got the vast majority of people in our system vaccinated while providing choice, dignity, and ongoing education. We did our best to listen to people and respect them, and the result was a more nuanced policy that evolved over time and got the best results possible without exacerbating tensions in our community any more than we had to.

Individuals inside Intermountain noticed this outcome and appreciated it. In the wake of the announcement of our mandate, a centrist-minded member of my leadership team issued a text message to our group that will stay with me for a while. "Proud of the professional approach," they said. "The chips will inevitably fall where they may, but you have all done a very professional job in an incredibly challenging, divisive, and difficult environment." Like other tough issues we've faced, this one might have broken our team. Instead, it brought us closer together.

FOSTERING EMPATHY

There are many tactics leaders can deploy to foster more empathy in ourselves and our teams. Some of my favorites include accompanying customers (in our case, patients) during their purchase and consumption process, asking personal questions at every meeting, holding information roundtable discussions on a periodic basis at which anyone can raise any topic, and starting every meeting by recounting a powerful experience someone in the organization had with a customer.

A common denominator underlies these and similar techniques. Becoming more empathetic entails cultivating genuine *curiosity* about others—including and especially those who think differently than you do—and devoting time and effort to satisfy that curiosity. For some of us, curiosity comes naturally. In my case, it goes to the core of who I am—I am constantly motivated to experimenting and exploring. Not long ago, in fact, when I was desperately ill with multiple myeloma and wondering if the end was near, the prospect of continued learning actually brought me some solace. Mary Carole and I found ourselves discussing what might lie on the other side of death. "Well," I said, "I guess that might be my next adventure—to find out." I really do intend to learn up until the very end, and maybe even afterward. For me, a great day is one filled with big ideas, interesting people, a chance to learn, do something different, or make a difference.

Whether or not you are naturally empathetic, I encourage you to fuel your understanding of others by unleashing your curiosity to the fullest. If the demands of leadership have caused you to push curiosity aside, then put it back front and center. Doing so can be as simple as pausing when you're tempted to issue a directive or give an answer, and instead ask other people what they think. John Noseworthy remembers a pivotal moment when another leader at Mayo Clinic pulled him aside to give him some career-enhancing advice. "When people ask questions," this leader said, "Why do you always give an answer? Why not instead use the question as a conversation starter to get others to contribute *their* ideas?"

So often as leaders, we assume we must know everything. We don't. It's usually best to let our curiosity lead us and extract what others think. Not only does it bring new ideas to the surface, it allows us to feel more empathy for others and build relationships with them, opening the way to change.

It's so important for leaders to try their best to walk in other people's shoes. Others might behave in ways that anger or annoy you, but their behavior takes on different meaning when you remember that everyone has some problem they're dealing with and is bringing unique life experience to the table. Assuming the best and treating others generously is not only the right thing to do, it fuels our passion for change, and it enables us to resolve tensions and arrive at mutually satisfying solutions with customers, colleagues, and external stakeholders. Before you can unleash others, you must first take the time to understand them, whether you agree with them or not, especially when emotions run high.

QUESTIONS FOR REFLECTION

1. When you look around your leadership table, virtual or physical, what different points of view do you see represented? If tensions exist between you and other members of your team, have you taken the time to empathize with them and engage constructively around the issue?

2. What biases do you harbor that might prevent you from empathizing with certain stakeholders, including employees, customers, and community members?

3. Have you ever taken time out to literally walk in the shoes of your customers? If so, what did you learn? If not, what are you waiting for?

4. When confronted with complaints from unhappy customers, do you tend to react defensively, or do you truly make an effort to understand their life and perspective?

5. How good are you at recognizing your own emotions and when they might be impeding your ability to empathize? Further, how good are you at managing these emotions and understanding where they originate? When you become upset or angry, how do you handle it?

6. How skilled is your leadership team in addressing complex and combustible issues? Are you able to slow down, take time to listen, understand one another's viewpoints, and come to a more thoughtful, nuanced solution? Do you make a practice of going around the room and making sure that everyone has expressed their opinion? Do you probe to get at important concerns or feelings that team members might not be vocalizing?

7. Are you able to empathize with your enemies and perceive them as imperfect human beings just like you? Do you find yourself building bridges over time with your opponents, or do you remain stuck in your deeply entrenched positions?

2

EMBRACE AN
OUTSIDER'S PERSPECTIVE

*Committing to change means immersing
yourself in different cultures and embracing
an outsider's perspective.*

Why in the world would a Jewish guy from Pittsburgh want
to move to the United Arab Emirates to run a hospital? I'm
sure some people wondered that in 2011, when I became CEO of
Cleveland Clinic's large multispecialty facility in Abu Dhabi. Four
other CEOs had come and gone over the previous five years. As I like
to joke, I got offered the job because there were no other leaders at the
Clinic left to ask.

And yet, having recently overcome bladder cancer, I wanted a
challenge, and this was a big one. When I first arrived in Abu Dhabi,
the massive, three-million-square-foot facility was in the early stages
of construction. The administrative offices had only just been moved
out of a trailer and into something more permanent. Over the next
several years, we'd have to complete the building, hire 3,500 peo-

ple, construct the hospital's systems, purchase all the necessary equipment, and implement processes that would render our medical operations safe and effective.

Critically, I'd have to lead all of this while operating as an outsider. I'd never been to Abu Dhabi before, and the language, culture, religion, and politics of the region were new to me. This posed an incredible challenge. Because I didn't know the social etiquette in this culture, I constantly worried about saying something awkward or offensive to my local colleagues and partners. Outside of work, I struggled with simple tasks like buying groceries or ordering in restaurants, as so many of the foods were unfamiliar. Lacking a social network, I was lonely, especially for the first few months until my family arrived. I also felt overwhelmed and isolated. The accommodations I'd been given were perfectly comfortable, but they were located in a hotel across the street from our project. Every window looked out on the construction site— an unsubtle reminder of the enormous task before me.

Despite my initial trepidation, I stayed in the job for five years, overcoming numerous crises and occasional sleepless nights. At one point about a year in, I became so frustrated with the organizational politics that I nearly quit. I can't convey how hard it was for our team to finish this mammoth project on time and on budget—with the Arab Spring going on, no less—and how challenging it was for me to lead our team while also living eight time zones away from home. And yet, as I became acclimated, I found living and working in Abu Dhabi to be an incredible experience. Despite my many mistakes and stumbles, my Emirati colleagues treated me well, and we developed strong working relationships. My outsider status proved to be a benefit, allowing me to bring a unique perspective to my work and lead the organization in ways that might have been more difficult for insiders.

It's fashionable today—and absolutely necessary—to call for more diversity in organizations and to understand its business benefits. But when it comes to supercharging an organization's poten-tial for innovation and growth, that conversation is incomplete. To unleash an organization and its people to drive change, leaders must embrace outsider perspectives more broadly. In addition to pushing diversity and inclusion as one of their top business priorities, leaders should accept that it's OK for them and other leaders at every level not to belong. They should physically put themselves in the outsid-er's role, as I did by accepting the Abu Dhabi assignment and later by coming in from Cleveland Clinic to lead Intermountain. And they should bring outsider perspectives—and actual outsiders—into their ranks with the deliberate purpose of shaking things up.

Let's be clear: it's critically important to recognize the invaluable contributions of strong leaders from within the organization and to draw upon the strengths of these individuals. In many cases, insiders can themselves serve as powerful change agents within organizations if given the chance. But leaders have much to gain from drawing on outsider perspectives to help drive progress. The point of promoting outsider viewpoints isn't to displace insiders. Rather, it's to unleash all of us—including the organization's existing leaders—as a powerful force for innovation by helping us to see with fresh eyes.

GIFTS OF THE OUTSIDER

In 2017, we at Intermountain brought in a consummate outsider, making a hire that raised eyebrows and sparked curiosity within Intermountain and in the healthcare industry. We appointed Kevan Mabbutt, formerly global head of consumer insight at Disney, as our chief consumer officer with a mandate to revolutionize our consumer experience. To my knowledge, nobody in healthcare had thought to hire an executive from a big consumer brand to run their marketing function. But I believed Mabbutt was exactly the kind of leader we needed to innovate Intermountain's already strong offerings, accelerate our evolution into a platform company, and instill a more intense consumer focus and discipline across our organization.

In addition to working at the world's preeminent consumer-focused company, Mabbutt's personal profile didn't fit that of the typical Intermountain leader: he had been born in the United Kingdom, was raised in Zambia, had worked at the BBC and Discovery Channel, and was a fan of safaris and Formula 1 racing.[1] These outsider attributes, I thought, coupled with his inherent creativity and empathy for consumers, would help us break from the status quo and drive aggressive change.

Mabbutt was hardly the only external hire we've brought into the C-suite to help accelerate change. Besides myself, our leadership team includes our chief operating officer Rob Allen, who worked at Intermountain early in his career and subsequently occupied posts in Wyoming, New Jersey, and Massachusetts; chief nursing officer Sue Robel, who built a successful 34-year career at Geisinger Health prior to joining us; and Marti Lolli, CEO of our SelectHealth insurance plan, who grew up in rural Montana and had built her career at an organization in Michigan.[2] We also count outsiders in clinical and management roles throughout the organization. We absolutely treasure the excellent leaders in Intermountain who have grown up in the local area and built their careers inside the organization. At the same time, we've found that individuals from other geographies and industries and from diverse backgrounds can enrich our collective thinking, furthering our efforts to drive change. The ability to fit into an organization and grow with it over a period of years or decades is tremendously valuable, but not belonging has its benefits, too. Organizations need both perspectives.

Outsiders tend to fuel progress in four primary ways. First, *they are uniquely alert to an organization's blind spots.* Outsiders can cut through some of the rigid bureaucratic rules that impede change, precisely because they spot dysfunctional or subpar features of the organization that insiders may not perceive as clearly. When Kevan Mabbutt joined us, we were all set for a deal with a company that would help us create a digital front door. This firm had developed a digital platform, and we were planning to buy their services. I was impatient to get started with this work, and when Kevan arrived I made it clear: I wanted to get this deal done. To my surprise, he advised that we blow up the deal. The services we were contracting for lacked consumer relevance and were too expensive in his view, and he also harbored concerns that the company wouldn't be able to deliver everything they were promising. Although we had scrutinized this deal backward and forward, he hadn't been part of this years-long process, and so could look at it with fresh eyes and spot flaws we couldn't see and that I in particular hadn't recognized. I listened to him, and good thing: the company has since failed and had to reinvent itself under new leadership.

Kevan's bold action leads me to a second benefit: *outsiders often take more risks on behalf of change than insiders do*, in part because they're not as invested in the status quo. Insiders may shrink from change, attempting to safeguard "how we've always done it." Outsiders may not know about traditional practices or policies, and if they do know, they might not feel the same need to conserve them. Outsiders may also harbor more of a growth mindset that inclines them to take risks, trying out new ideas or arrangements and potentially failing in hopes of learning and developing. Insiders often perceive and resist any change as "too risky," while outsiders more often see equal or greater risk in adhering to the status quo.

Consider again my experience in Abu Dhabi. In the Emirates, as in other places I've lived, long-running family alliances and disagreements influence professional and business relationships. Colleagues belonging to families with centuries-old histories of enmity can't easily forge relationships with one another. Simply trying to do so could prove risky. But as an outsider, I didn't hold any family allegiances. Instead, I came in respecting this diversity and worked to bridge these kinds of divides, bring people together, and make progress happen. By the end of my four-and-a-half-year tenure, we had our 3,500 people from 70 countries working seamlessly together to make people in the region healthier, transcending gender, ethnicity, and religion. My experience confirmed what I've long known: that our shared humanity transcends any differences that separate us.

A third reason outsiders help to drive change is that *they introduce new knowledge and best practices*. People inside large organizations can sometimes navel-gaze, precisely because they've already achieved some measure of success. Drinking their own Kool-Aid, they can lose sight of the outside world and think that their processes and norms are automatically better than anyone else's. The general specialization of professional and academic life only fuels such narrow thinking. Quoting an "internationally renowned scientist," the journalist David Epstein writes that, "increasing specialization has created a 'system of parallel trenches' in the quest for innovation. Everyone is digging deeper into their own trench and rarely standing up to look in the next trench over, even though the solution to their problem happens to reside there."[3] The presence of outsiders challenges such navel-gazing, introducing new ideas, assumptions, and practices.

In helping us to construct My Health+, our digital front door, Kevan didn't limit himself to technologies or formats already present in the organization. Instead, he very deliberately looked outside rather than inside healthcare and found inspiration from other industries. My Health+ offers digital functionality in three key areas: finding the right care, managing care, and paying for care. To develop capabilities in each of these areas, Kevan used his expertise to identify best practice leaders. In the case of finding and booking appointments, he and his team looked to the airline industry and their proficiency in scheduling flights. For managing care, he and his team looked to Disney and other hospitality brands adept at helping consumers navigate complex experiences. And when it came to creating a simple, relatively pain-free path for processing payments online, they looked to Amazon.[4]

In addition to introducing new best practices, outsiders can help organizations ramp up accountability by introducing new standards for assessment. One reason my team succeeded in Abu Dhabi is that we didn't hold our facility to local operational standards, comparing us to other hospitals in Abu Dhabi. We had determined that we wanted to build a facility to deliver quality, safety, and patient experience that was every bit as good as what patients can access at Cleveland Clinic's main campus. Having those external standards and holding people accountable for achieving them made a big difference in our success. As I'll recount in the next chapter, we have done something similar at Intermountain. Recognizing that we had been assessing our performance by focusing on our own internal metrics, we introduced external benchmarking, a move that allowed us to spot hidden weak areas and improve them.

A fourth reason outsiders help fuel change inside organizations is that *they have a catalyzing effect*, inspiring and emboldening insiders to change as well. You don't even have to hire outsiders per se to see this effect in action—just inviting them in for a visit can do the trick. Later in this book, I'll describe how we reinvented our primary care model, paying providers salaries and tasking them with keeping people well, as part of a value-based care model that includes a fixed amount of prepaid revenue per covered member. A pioneer in this area was Dr. Rushika Fernandopulle, cofounder and CEO of a venture-backed company called Iora Health. Fernandopulle and his team had operationalized the model at a small scale, achieving great success keeping people well.

In 2017, we invited Fernandopulle to speak with Intermountain's community-based care group, which oversaw primary care. We dangled the possibility of bringing him in to disrupt our primary care model. We wanted Fernandopulle to visit and for people to know that he was there. If they did, we thought they might feel a little anxious—enough to take change more seriously.

Our gambit worked. Following Fernandopulle's visit, a group of very talented Intermountain leaders approached me to express enthusiasm for reimagining primary care. They wanted to build a new primary care model themselves. They rose to the occasion in impressive fashion. Today, between Intermountain and Castell (a company we launched), we care for more than 500,000 patients under the prepaid model, with exceptional gains in quality, customer experience, and caregiver satisfaction. Exposure to an outsider was just the boost this group of leaders needed. As this story demonstrates, insiders who open their hearts and minds to an outsider perspective can drive change, too.

These four mechanisms allow outsiders to serve as change agents inside organizations, not necessarily opposing the status quo at every turn, but questioning it and breaking with it when necessary or helpful. They allow the rest of us to operate at our very best and to envision new possibilities. Kevan is a case in point. Not only has he spearheaded a range of consumer innovations inside Intermountain; he also injected a respect for and interest in consumers into the organization from an entirely new perspective. He helped us develop a modernized social media strategy. He helped us rethink our approach to marketing, enabling us to evaluate in terms of the economic and reputational value we create, not just the number of impressions we make through our advertising efforts. He took marketing from a reactive service function to a strategic driver of our mission and business objectives by focusing relentlessly on consumer relevance and influence. And the list goes on and on.

MAKING GOOD TROUBLE

In remarks delivered in 2020, civil rights icon and political leader John Lewis exhorted listeners to, "Get in good trouble, necessary trouble, and help redeem the soul of America."[5] Driving change in any kind of business organization ultimately boils down to the creation of "good trouble." It requires a willingness to question the status quo, not in the spirit of egotism or belligerence, but out of a genuine desire to spur progress. Because outsiders are more inclined to reveal blind spots, take risks on behalf of change, introduce novel practices, and galvanize others, they are often well positioned to create "good trouble," unleashing others inside an organization to join them as well.

But of course, good trouble is still trouble. It sparks conflict, unsettling people accustomed to the status quo and prompting them to push back against change. Outsiders introduce ideas that might alter how decisions are made, how responsibilities are divided, how the organization will invest its time and energy, and much more. If they are to succeed, they must minimize and manage the resistance their very presence naturally provokes.

When I arrived in Abu Dhabi, a project manager who felt threatened by my presence did his best to scuttle my efforts, subjecting me over the course of months to what I can only describe as hazing. He did everything he could to cause problems for me, raising the same bureaucratic roadblocks he'd used to impede the previous CEOs. I never encountered anything of this sort at Intermountain, but I know that my arrival and the subsequent moves I made rattled some people in the organization who pined for "the way we've always done things." Eventually, some relented, while others left the organization. And some continue to harbor misgivings, perceiving me as an outsider taking Intermountain astray. I deeply respect these individuals and know they want what's best for the organization. I hope that with time they'll come to view me and my decisions differently.

If we're going to adopt the outsider role ourselves or bring in others to do so, we must expect resistance and become comfortable with it. I've been rattling cages since childhood, much to the horror of my more conventionally minded mother, so I'm about as used to it as anyone can be. In elementary school, my teachers constantly sent me to the principal's office—the bench outside it basically had my name on it. In high school, if there was a student protest going on, I was involved. I got suspended from Sunday school for advocating for Palestinian civil rights. (My line was: "How can an oppressed people like the Jews systematically oppress others?") I suppose that setting off a smoke bomb under my Sunday school teacher's car didn't help my cause. In short, I've been pushing against the status quo in one way or another ever since I can remember. I've grown a tough shell and have learned not to take it personally when people push back. I've also realized that an outsider perspective doesn't mean I always get it right. It simply widens my gaze and opens my ears.

This last insight leads me to a broader point about making good trouble as an outsider: you can't simply thumb your nose at insiders and hope to succeed. Part of the challenge you face isn't just to withstand resistance but to actively and genuinely engage with insiders who might harbor different ideas than you do. Insiders are often correct in their judgments, and their perspective is equally critical in helping an organization to drive meaningful progress. Further, insiders can help outsiders themselves learn and grow—something I've experienced firsthand at Intermountain. If you enter with an I-know-best mentality, you'll miss out, and the organization will, too. It's far better to hear out what insiders have to say, acknowledging that their intentions are likely very good, even if you don't agree on how to achieve the desired results. It's far better, in other words, to practice the kind of intense empathy described in Chapter 1, giving way where you can and staying strong where you must.

Kevan Mabbutt's arrival and our decisive movement toward a more consumer-centric orientation sparked intense resistance among some inside Intermountain. Many caregivers expressed disapproval, arguing we were damaging the sacred doctor-patient relationship by even referring to patients as customers or consumers. Patients aren't customers, some caregivers told us. They're patients. And healthcare isn't just another business. It's a sacred calling. If we start thinking about patients as customers, we risked compromising the intimacy and integrity of our relationship with them, thinking about them strictly in economic terms.

These were legitimate concerns. As a physician, I deeply care about the integrity of the doctor-patient relationship. And I also believe that thinking of patients as customers doesn't compromise that integrity; on the contrary, it enhances it. Traditionally, our organization and healthcare companies generally were designed around providers and their needs—not patients. Patients bore the brunt, suffering needless waits, scheduling difficulties, and other inconveniences. Putting patients and their needs first for a change—treating them as customers—was fully in keeping with an elevated, servant-oriented mindset. It also was a practical necessity. Times had changed, and consumers wanted better treatment. If we didn't offer them healthcare to fit their needs, others would. To prepare for the future and avoid disruption of our business, we would fundamentally change our operating model to put patients first and implement digital technologies.

I and other like-minded leaders in the organization made these points over and over again in the course of socializing a consumer orientation inside Intermountain. We also did our best (although not always successfully) to forge common ground with those who felt differently, noting that life thrusts all of us eventually into the role of healthcare consumer, even if we're providers. To evoke the need for change, I told stories from my own life that I thought were relatable. There was the time, for instance, when my kids came home for Thanksgiving and one of them needed a haircut. He went online and booked an appointment. A couple of hours later, I asked him when he was going in, and he said, "Oh, I don't know. They'll text me when they're ready." This caught my attention. Rather than have customers wait around for an hour reading boring magazines, as hair salons used to do, this one had devised a technology-based system that minimized waits for customers. Why, I asked our leaders, weren't healthcare systems like us doing that, especially considering that twenty-somethings like my son were poised to become our single largest group of patients?

I also recounted a time when I had a sore neck from running a triathlon and desperately needed a chiropractor to help sort it out. I went to a local chain of chiropractors and arranged for a session. When I handed them my credit card to pay for the appointment, they asked me if I wanted to prepay for the next 10 appointments. They also handed me a little tag with a code on it. The next time I came in, all I had to do was swipe my tag and my patient information would come up. Their system would immediately register me for my appointment and charge my credit card. Now consider healthcare. When you want to see a dermatologist, for example, you may have to wait for five months. When you get there, you have to fill out a paper form and most likely fill one out again each successive visit. You also have to physically hand over a credit card each time. Will you receive a small discount for paying in advance? I don't think so.

Caregivers inside Intermountain could understand these stories because they also booked appointments with professionals outside of healthcare and appreciated how innovations in those contexts made life easier. They could understand intuitively that such innovations might make life easier for our patients, too. It took a couple of years, but the sheer repetition of such stories allowed our organization to assimilate this seemingly outsider philosophy and embrace it as our own. Eventually, most people came to take these ideas for granted. And as they did, our shift toward behaving like a more customer-centric organization gained traction.

As outsiders or advocates of outsider positions, we can't expect others to "get in line" and accept us. We must set our egos aside and do the hard work of bringing others along. Orit Gadiesh, a widely respected businessperson and the chairwoman of the consultancy Bain & Company, recalls the challenges she experienced earlier in her career working with clients in male-dominated industries. Often, as the only woman in a meeting, she faced the challenge of winning over male CEOs who were her clients. Microaggressions, and even bigger ones, were a regular occurrence. "I never took it personally," she says. "I never thought I needed to change the world. If I had a CEO who I could see was uncomfortable with women, I thought it was my job to make him comfortable with me."[6]

Gadiesh used humor to build rapport and looked for opportunities to connect around common interests. She also wasn't afraid to get creative when she needed to. On one occasion, she had an assistant contact her counterparts in the offices of 10 male leaders who were set to participate in a meeting with her team, asking these assistants to inform their bosses in advance that a woman would be attending on the Bain side. That way, Gadiesh would avoid any awkwardness that might ensue if her presence proved surprising. It was a small gesture, but as Gadiesh understood, it would help her to build rapport.

Bringing others along often means not just making a special effort in the moment but doing our homework. We must frame our outsider perspectives skillfully in ways that speak to the concerns and mindsets of insiders. We must take the time to get to know the insiders and what *they* care about so we can hold productive, respectful conversations. As Gail Miller, a highly respected Utah businessperson and former chair of Intermountain's board, notes, "Change is good if it's done correctly. And to do it correctly, you have to study it. You have to understand the lay of the land." This is a task, she suggests, that's even more vital if you're coming in as an outsider, with little or no baseline understanding of the landscape.[7]

Dr. Kathleen E. McKee agrees. A neurologist with Intermountain Neurosciences Institute at Intermountain Medical Center, she is a relative newcomer to Intermountain, having arrived in 2019. She is also an outsider, having done her internship, residency, and fellowship at Massachusetts General Hospital in Boston. Soon after her arrival, she emerged as a change agent, working hard and passionately to further diversity, equity, and inclusion (DEI). The murder of George Floyd and the subsequent burst of national interest and activity related to DEI left her wondering about Intermountain's activities in this area. Observing what she regarded as "radio silence" compared with how other organizations were responding, and discovering that we lacked a chief equity officer, she wrote me a letter in 2020, urging that we adopt equity as one of our fundamentals of extraordinary care, alongside safety, quality, a personalized and caring patient experience, a strong consumer focus, partnership with the community, and engaged caregivers. Afterward, McKee participated in meetings and other activities, sharing what she knew about the history of equity in healthcare and urging more leadership in this area. She also coauthored a paper about our organization's experiences embarking on an ongoing journey toward more equity (described in Chapter 1).[8]

McKee is unsparing—and rightfully so—in her assessment of all the equity-related work that remains to be done at Intermountain. Crucially, though, she has been effective at driving change because she has imbued her advocacy with a genuine respect for insiders and their perspectives. She spent a great deal of time consulting extensively with mentors and colleagues to understand insiders and uncover strategies for engaging with them productively. These conversations led her to realize, among other things, that many of her colleagues admired the late business expert Clayton Christensen. To help her ideas seem less foreign, she has often connected them to Christensen's work, a move she believes has helped to foster dialogue. "You've got to find some common ground first," she says, if you want to engage with people around change. "You've got to find out what matters most and also what's bothering people the most," recognizing that the answers to these questions might not be what you would think at first glance.[9] It's important for all outsiders to realize that teaching and learning goes both ways—insiders and outsiders must help one another do both.

Aside from doing this groundwork, outsiders seeking to make good trouble must shine light on themselves and their own motivations. Insiders sometimes resist change proposed by outsiders because they suspect that ego and opportunism are driving it rather than a genuine desire to improve the organization. In many cases, of course, they're right. Outsiders operate with a whole range of motivations. Further, some might be only dimly aware of their deepest intentions. Outsiders should ask themselves: Are they truly trying to drive change in an area they care about for the organization's benefit? Or are they doing so to gain some kind of advantage for themselves? You can fool an organization at first if you lack the strength of your convictions, but people will sniff out artifice eventually. Conversely, an outsider deeply dedicated to the welfare of the organization, its customers, and the wider world will usually gain credibility as time passes and enlist insiders to their cause.

Outsiders must also take steps to convey their genuine commitment and make it palpable. In 2021, we named Dr. Paul Krakovitz as the region president of Intermountain Healthcare in Nevada. Krakovitz was responsible for overseeing our integration of a large physician group (about 340 physicians and 55 clinics) that we acquired in that state.[10] Krakovitz faced a challenging task. Although this physician group was well-practiced in value-based care, it had focused on caring for a single demographic: patients over the age of 65. As an integrated system, Intermountain cared for patients at every stage of life, and we needed our doctors in Nevada to do that, too. As an outsider coming in from Intermountain's headquarters, Krakovitz had to convince the doctors to follow him in making an array of difficult operational changes. Further, he had to navigate an existing culture in Nevada that was different in some respects from that prevailing in Intermountain's traditional service areas of Utah and Idaho. Since two other organizations had owned this physician group in recent years, Krakovitz also had to contend with skepticism about whether or not he and Intermountain were in Nevada to stay, as well as fear that Intermountain, a much larger organization, would dictatorially assert its will and change everything about the Nevada physician group.

In this environment, Krakovitz worked to win adherents among insiders in Nevada by listening intently to their concerns rather than dictating solutions. "I knew I was doing well," he says, "when I would be in a meeting, and I was telling them what the output felt like, and someone would say, 'I'm doing all the talking, I'm sorry. Next time we meet, I'd like to learn more about you.'"[11] The act of listening proved to insiders in Nevada that he wasn't going to take an aggressive, dictatorial approach. By allowing insiders to express themselves, Krakovitz allowed them to feel confident that their ideas and approaches had merit, even as he was able to soak up knowledge about the organization.

In addition to listening, Krakovitz took other steps to make his commitment to the Nevada organization come alive. First, he relocated to the local area, demonstrating that he was personally all-in as a leader. (I did the same when I accepted the post at Abu Dhabi, and it made a difference.) Second, although the pandemic was still raging, he held as many meetings as possible in person rather than via Zoom—he wanted people to feel his presence and really get to know him. Third, he brought down senior leaders from Intermountain's corporate center to Las Vegas to meet with members of the organization there. He wanted people in Las Vegas to know Intermountain's leaders personally and to understand that these leaders were willing to spend considerable time forging long-term relationships built on trust and mutual respect. He also wanted the physician practice in Nevada to understand that he as a leader was committed to connecting the Nevada operations to Intermountain, ensuring the two organizations would fully integrate with one another.

Krakovitz is already seeing signs that insiders in Nevada are beginning to accept him and feel more comfortable with Intermountain. Building trust will take time, and future challenges will certainly arise, but Krakovitz is optimistic that the integration will succeed. Openly affirming his commitment to the Nevada organization as an outsider allowed him to get a running start and unleash people to pursue change.

INTEGRATING OUTSIDER PERSPECTIVES

To activate the power of outsider perspectives in your organization, take a balanced approach. Don't suddenly throw outsiders or advocates of outsider positions into every key role and ask them to make trouble. We've sometimes gone too far in embracing outsiders, and on these occasions, we've paid the price. In 2017, we sought to enhance how we handled the task of transferring patients from the outside into Intermountain facilities to receive care. We experimented with outsourcing this function, hoping that doing so would allow us to operate more efficiently. It didn't work. We had assumed that the process of transferring patients was straightforward and easily codified, allowing outsiders to step in and perform it well. As we learned, this function relies on quite a bit of insider knowledge; outsiders can't do it as effectively. We reversed course, building from scratch a new internal center for transferring patients that now performs exceptionally well.

I'll say it again: insiders are critically important too in legacy organizations seeking to stay fresh and vibrant. If everyone were a change agent coming from the outside, chaos would ensue. We need cadres of people who understand the organization's history, purpose, and founding principles and can connect novelty and change to this heritage. We need people who understand what already works so the organization can retain these elements, build upon them, and adapt them.

Although we've introduced outsiders like Kevan, Rob, Sue, Marti, Kathleen, and Paul into the mix, our leadership team at Intermountain remains a solid mix of organization veterans and newcomers. The combination allows for a productive tension between old and new to flourish, allowing us to make progress and do so in a way that minimizes unnecessary conflict and disruption to the organization. It also allows our team to model the productive collaborations between insiders and outsiders that we want to see take root across the entire organization.

One practice of ours is to bring in outsiders only after trying and failing to find someone internally who is more qualified and able to drive a desired change. When we were searching for a chief marketing officer, I spent months scanning the entire healthcare industry, and I couldn't find the kind of consumer-centric leader I felt we needed. Only then did I entertain the possibility of bringing in a marketing executive from a leading consumer company. Likewise, we brought an outsider in as our chief nursing officer for the enterprise after I had exhausted possibilities internally. Our previous chief nursing officer was a wonderful spokesperson for the organization and a polished thought leader on safety and quality. She was also a long-time Intermountain employee who was beloved inside the organization. I would have been happy to retain her on our team. Only when it became clear that I couldn't and that nobody else in our organization could fill her shoes did we start to look to hire an outsider.

In addition to bringing in outsiders, seize opportunities to become one yourself. Open yourself to career moves that might put you in an unfamiliar geography or business area. The loneliness and uncertainty that comes with stepping into a new environment is real, but don't fear it—lean into it and learn from it. If you can't step into an unfamiliar environment or hire an outsider, then at least try to seek guidance from people with diverse backgrounds who can push you in new and perhaps uncomfortable directions. In many cases, you can expose yourself to fresh perspectives simply by sitting down with customers and *listening* to them describe their experiences, needs, and desires.

Functioning as an outsider or inviting them into your midst is by no means the easiest path. But it's a vital way of unleashing change in yourself and others. For organizations as well as people, change only comes at times when you challenge yourself. Athletes don't build new muscle by performing the same familiar movements in a relaxing way. They do it by gritting their teeth and putting their muscles under strain so that they work up a sweat. We can all become change athletes, drawing on outsiders to reveal weakness in the status quo, push us into our discomfort zones, and help us to grow and improve.

QUESTIONS FOR REFLECTION

1. If you think back on your career, have you ever operated as an outsider in a team or organization? What results were you able to achieve? Are there any opportunities on the horizon to do it again?

2. How might you help the outsiders in your midst overcome resistance to change?

3. Has your organization tried and failed to drive change in key areas? If so, might bringing in an outsider to lead be the missing ingredient?

4. Do outsiders find the organization a hospitable place? Do they see the opportunity to drive progress? If not, what might you do to change that?

5. Do you send public signals that nonconformism and fresh thinking are positive attributes to be admired, or do you and other leaders send mixed messages?

6. If you're an outsider in an organization, what have you done to show that you're all-in?

3

LOOK IN THE MIRROR

Be honest with yourself
about the state of your organization.

When you were in high school, did you ever walk into an exam thinking you had mastered a subject only to receive a grade that was surprisingly average or even subpar? It's a humbling but also potentially energizing experience—and one that we at Intermountain know quite well.

In 2016, before I became the organization's new CEO, I asked executives on my new leadership team to hire a consulting firm to thoroughly assess our culture and operations. One might have thought this unnecessary: in recent years, *Forbes* had named us in its list of best top employers, and Moody's and Standard & Poor's had given us the highest rating of any nonprofit healthcare system. A number of our hospitals received national recognition for their high quality. The Patient Safety Movement ranked us in the top 3 out of 400 institutions for our work in improving safety in our facilities.[1] Clearly, we were doing something right.

But I had been speaking to leaders and consultants about CEO transitions while also devouring everything I could read on the subject. A recurring theme emerged: for incoming CEOs, especially those entering from the outside, it's important to obtain a clear initial picture of the organization—what it does well and not so well.

A top consulting firm, McKinsey & Company, assessed our organization for us. Some of the results were extremely strong. Intermountain Medical Center ranked at the very top of its peer group—in the ninety-ninth percentile nationally—when it came to the number of patients readmitted within 30 days (in other words, fewer of our patients had to return for unplanned care after leaving our facilities, which is a measure of quality). Our patient experience also ranked consistently above the national average and was tracking upward.[2]

And yet, other results were humbling. While Intermountain was known for delivering some of the highest quality care in the country and for pioneering the standardization of care, our review revealed that we actually scored at or below the median for quality in some areas. For instance, too many of our patients developed potentially serious central line infections. Although we performed better in this regard than Mayo Clinic and Cleveland Clinic, in 2015 we ranked at only about the thirty-fifth to fortieth percentile nationwide—nowhere near where we wanted to be.[3] Also worth noting, we were paying millions each year in penalties under government programs that docked us for lower performance in specific areas.

McKinsey's analysis uncovered other weaknesses in safety, stewardship, patients' ability to access our services, financial performance, and more. Some of the problems seemed small but really weren't. We learned that our 180 health clinics turned off their phones each day at noon so that staff could all have lunch together. That's nice, but what about all the patients who were calling and trying to book appointments?

Reflecting on McKinsey's findings, I concluded that past Intermountain leaders had laid a strong foundation in the form of a financially sound, integrated health system focused on improving quality and lowering costs. We had embarked years earlier on the path toward value-based care, digitization, and more customer focus—a tradition of innovation that had attracted me to Intermountain in the first place. But we also had the opportunity to build on our past accomplishments and innovate in these areas at much greater scale. Healthcare is always aspirational—we must constantly strive to improve and enhance what we do. McKinsey's findings were a clarion call for us to become even better than we already were.

Many of our leaders and employees certainly thought this way. Learning of the findings, they yearned to get to work devising new solutions that would push us further and faster toward our broader strategic goals. But others found the results of our assessment unsettling. "I would say it was a somber and sobering moment for people," says Dr. Shannon Connor Phillips, our chief medical officer for community-based care.[4] My readiness to acknowledge Intermountain's weak spots "challenged people," our chief operating officer Rob Allen remembers. "It was hard, and people felt that the history and legacy of Intermountain were being attacked."[5] On my leadership team, even individuals who were receptive to the data felt anxious about it. As Intermountain veterans, they knew how tough it would be to improve on core quality and safety metrics.

The point of assessing ourselves, registering both our strengths and weaknesses, wasn't to stigmatize ourselves or deflate our egos. It was to galvanize us behind a change agenda. And more specifically, it was to help us address a challenge that often stymies leaders at large, successful organizations. How do you inspire dedicated professionals who are already exceptional achievers to aim even higher? How do you take an accomplished, even iconic organization or team and energize people to advance its mission and live its values in new and exciting ways?

Our experience at Intermountain has taught me that it all starts with developing a common fact base. We must document the existence of problems that need fixing, challenging our people to look at our organization in the mirror and be brutally honest about what we see. We must encourage them to set aside any complacency they might feel and take a more realistic view, seeing the team or organization as outsiders might see it. While we're at it, we must habituate ourselves as leaders to doing the very same thing on the individual level, embracing an ethic of rigorous, ongoing self-assessment and change.

NO MORE NAVEL-GAZING

Some large, successful organizations lose touch with reality when it comes to their performance. When organizational practices, processes, or norms work well already, well-meaning people within a system want to retain and replicate them. Why change what isn't broken? People become invested in the status quo, building identities and careers around them. They feel less inclined to probe for flaws or shortcomings, and they often resist those who do. Over time, flaws can fade into the background and become hard to spot, entrenching the status quo even more.

Some of these dynamics were visible inside Intermountain, though ours was far from an intellectually sterile or stagnant culture. Because our employees cared so deeply about our mission of helping people live the healthiest lives possible, we had been working hard to improve safety, quality, and patient experience, to increase access in our communities, and to address the broader social determinants of health. Teams and groups within our organization were experimenting with innovations such as telehealth and the introduction of continuous improvement methodologies. We also were looking to the future, boldly investing almost $1 billion over the past five years on constructing new facilities.

Nevertheless, McKinsey's analysis left me wondering if we could unleash dynamism, innovation, and an underlying introspection even more. In particular, I suspected that we could fire ourselves up to change by enhancing how we tracked our performance. Prior to my arrival, Intermountain had gained renown for its quality improvement initiatives, and our chief quality officer Brent James had emerged as a leading expert in the field. Applying industrial approaches to process management, we developed standard treatment regimens for medical procedures like delivering babies or caring for people with strokes, asking caregivers to track how well they did in quantitative terms and using that information to fine-tune and enhance the regimens over time. These initiatives were enormously successful, improving patient outcomes and driving down costs.[6]

Our approach also had some important limitations. Rather than comparing the quality of our care to that of other leading institutions (called "benchmarking"), we often tracked progress by comparing our numbers each year to how we performed in the past. We weren't trying to evade accountability or prevent ourselves from changing. On the contrary, we reasoned that the industry in general wasn't delivering strong quality, so we would do well to focus on bettering our own performance year-over-year. We also questioned the science behind some of the comparative quality measurements used in healthcare.

As valid as some of these concerns might have been, our reluctance to measure ourselves against others blinded us to some of our shortcomings. As Scott Anderson, chair emeritus of our board and president and CEO of Zions First National Bank, observed, "You need to compare where you are with the best in the industry. And if there's a gap, you need to sit down then and have that hard conversation of what you need to do, not only to continue to improve but to step up the pace so that, in fact, on a comparative basis with the best in the industry, you are out there with them."[7]

Benchmarking affords organizations tremendous opportunities. It spawns a discipline of improvement, one that, in the words of Dr. Shannon Connor Phillips, "becomes part of what you do every day." Tracking how others are doing, you become curious "to learn who the high performers are and what worked," and you constantly challenge yourself to be better.[8] Since we weren't benchmarking nationally, our improvement efforts in areas like quality and safety lacked some of the energy and insight that come when you compare yourself to high-performing peers. We needed to study the bigger picture, even if it wasn't always flattering, and we had to open ourselves up more to best practices from others. An extra dose of humility and honesty would reignite our curiosity, lend a new intensity to what we did, and hopefully take us to a whole new level.

A NEW KIND OF INTROSPECTION

We've since introduced comparative measurements across Intermountain to underpin our change efforts. With our board's strong support, our first step was to select specific industrywide measures to use in tracking progress and to select companies that would provide us with data about our peers. To help us monitor how well our hospitals were doing, we partnered with the healthcare consultancy Vizient, which collects information from the country's biggest, most advanced hospitals. To help us improve patient experience and caregiver engagement, we partnered with Press Ganey, another organization that collects data from a peer group of organizations and from our own customers.

Not only could we use data from these partners to analyze how we worked; we also could learn the best practices of other institutions. In some cases, we could adopt these best practices, accelerating our progress. In other cases, we could deploy solutions generated by our own improvement efforts (more on that in Chapter 5). We didn't need to arrive at all the answers ourselves. Instead, we needed to ask more questions and look for answers everywhere, not just within the confines of our organization.

With these partnerships in place, we met with teams at our hospitals and other facilities to introduce comparative assessments and discuss the gaps we were seeing in performance. These conversations weren't always easy. Think of times when someone has challenged *you* to achieve even more in an area where you already excelled. It can come as quite a blow. We were asking our operations, medical, and nursing leaders to make themselves far more vulnerable by measuring themselves against our peers. When the data showed opportunities for improvement, we were asking our people to parse the data closely and identify the root causes of problems. We were also asking them to look to other organizations for possible solutions.

When leaders and caregivers pushed back, as they sometimes did, they weren't necessarily wrong. Physicians, hospital operators, and finance professionals are all trained to view data skeptically, and some at Intermountain argued that national benchmarks were flawed— they used data that was old and out of date, they compared systems that differed in important respects, and so on. Still, as Dr. Mike Woodruff, emergency room physician and senior medical director for our Office of Patient Experience, notes, "No measure is perfect. No cohort that you compare yourself against will be exactly appropriate to your circumstances."[9] Even with its flaws, a comparative view allowed us to spot improvement opportunities we'd otherwise miss. Further, consumers were using publicly available benchmarks to evaluate us. We needed to pay attention to these measurements, too, taking any potential inaccuracies into account and improving the measurements going forward.

Our local teams persisted when faced with internal resistance, as did our Office of Patient Experience, which helped to implement quality, safety, and patient experience improvement initiatives, and our human resources team, which did the same with caregiver engagement. I pushed hard, too, stressing what was at stake for our patients and trying to humanize the conversation about abstract data as much as possible. I reminded caregivers that we were treating *people* and potentially hurting or killing them when we didn't do it well. To drill home the point, I used human-like stick figures in my presentations instead of the usual bar charts. Making the point so directly got people's attention. Since we were proceeding from a common fact base and referencing our shared desire to deliver even more completely on our mission, many of the skeptics eventually bought into the improvement initiatives we launched. The combination of approaching measurements comparatively and probing for root causes proved enormously effective, allowing us to uncover improvement opportunities that previously had gone unnoticed.

Consider mortality at Intermountain Medical Center, the largest hospital in our system. Like other health systems, we keep track of how many of our patients admitted for specific conditions end up dying. We compare those numbers to how many we expect will die based on data from our peers nationally. Unfortunately, analysis suggested that our performance lagged that of our peers. It seemed at first that we had a safety issue—more people were dying unexpectedly at our facility than at peer institutions. Although we spotted ways to improve safety and quality by standardizing best practices across our system, closer analysis uncovered a different root cause.

Our numbers ran high not only because of mistakes we were making in our care or inefficiencies in our system but because we were caring for these patients in our intensive care unit (ICU), using advanced technology to try to prolong their lives, rather than transferring them to hospice and focusing on relieving their pain and symptoms. Here's an esoteric fact for you: When health systems provide end-of-life care in hospice, they don't count these patients in their mortality figures; that data is meant to capture *avoidable* deaths. When systems care for these patients in the ICU, they do count, skewing the data unfavorably, even if these patients never had a chance of living. As Woodruff suggests, Intermountain had developed a blind spot in how it cared for people at the end of their lives. "We were geared toward providing the most care. We were rushing patients from the emergency department to the ICU. We put in breathing tubes, put in lines, gave them antibiotics, put them on a bypass machine, gave them all of our technology. We were geared to doing more and more and more for patients, rather than focusing as much as we might have on delivering the *right* care for them and their families."[10]

More care versus the *right* care. Think about that for a moment. American culture often associates more with better, and healthcare isn't immune from that thinking. In fact, more care has long served as healthcare's reigning business model, with facilities piling on the diagnostic tests, procedures, and pills to help patients get better. And yet, as we at Intermountain have long believed, *more* isn't the answer. More care is how many systems boost their profits, often without benefiting patients. The *right* care is compassionate, of the highest possible quality, and often much more affordable for patients, employers, and the country at large.

The standard treatment regimens we developed prior to my arrival aimed to deliver the right care by codifying best practices for caregiving. But opportunities still existed to push this work even further. In this instance, a comparative view coupled with a root-cause analysis led us to be more curious and humbler—to think more expansively about end-of-life than we had before and to uncover important improvement opportunities we had been missing. Reviewing how our high-performing peers approached palliative and hospice care, we found that by adjusting what we did, we could provide end-of-life care more compassionately by keeping more patients out of the ICU. We could determine more quickly when a patient arrives if they are likely to never again leave the hospital alive. We could offer resources more rapidly to patients and their families to help them understand how best to ensure quality of life during their loved one's final days and moments. These changes would reduce our costs (caring for patients in the ICU is expensive), but more important, they would allow us to give patients a more comfortable and meaningful death in hospice, surrounded by their loved ones.

These and similar changes across our system haven't come easily to us. Just like exercising at the gym can make your muscles sore, challenging our caregivers to deliver care in new ways can lead to some sore feelings. And I might have pushed too hard at times as we introduced comparative measurements, perhaps leading some to believe that as an outsider, I felt I had all the answers. I wish I knew the precise amount of pressure to apply at any given time to promote change, but to be honest, I'm learning, too, and inspiring people who are already excellent to achieve even more is an extraordinarily delicate task. We leaders must do the best we can, understanding the sensitivities people feel and respecting them. And we must appeal to a higher calling that we believe in at our core.

Although I was an outsider, I knew that what matters most at Intermountain—what has always mattered most—is providing the best care possible for patients. Although they aren't perfect, comparative measurements enhance our ability to do that. That's the message I worked with other leaders on our team to convey, and it's one that over time inspired us to take a more expansive look at our performance and how we could improve it.

HARD ON ISSUES, EASY ON PEOPLE

More honest and comprehensive introspection isn't just good for organizations. We can also instill it at the team level to unleash our people. As we'll see in Chapter 5, my leadership team and I have embedded introspection deeply into our culture by reimagining how we work. Central to our approach is a system of continuous improvement, where frontline team members surface operational issues and help leaders at all levels scrutinize performance more carefully.

Individual leaders can also take important steps on their own to build cultures of introspection and critical analysis within their teams. Here, they must strike an important balance. While they must set strong expectations that motivate people to do their best, and while they must hold people accountable for meeting those expectations, they must also help team members feel nurtured and respected, so that they are comfortable sharing frank, often difficult feedback.

To sustain this balance, I strive to take an approach I call "going hard on issues but easy on people." I drive performance extremely hard on issues I care about. When results prove disappointing, I don't hesitate to let people know. When we're stuck creatively and having the same conversations on an issue we had three years ago, I'm very direct in observing it and exhorting my team to do better. But I also try to temper this message so that I'm easy on others around me. I don't yell or swear at people. I don't personally impugn individuals who aren't delivering. I don't play politics and speak behind people's backs. I maintain cordial and even friendly relationships with everyone. I'm not perfect—there are times I wish I'd been easier on people. But in general, I try hard to treat people compassionately and with civility.

Let's say I oversee a facility where patients are developing infections from their IV lines—a problem that shouldn't happen. I could raise this issue by ranting and raving, saying, "What the hell is going on? How many times have we talked about this? Don't we give a damn about patients? Who's the leader there? Do they want to keep their job?" A softer, gentler approach might be to say, "Boy, this is disappointing. Have we performed a root-cause analysis? If so, what have we learned that we can share with others? What unit in our system is the best on this? Can we bring them in to share what they know and identify the flaw that's leading to these infections?" If I take an aggressive approach, few people will feel safe raising issues, and they'll go underground. A softer, gentler approach allows me to drill home the issue's importance without antagonizing the very people we rely on to spot problems. Hard on results, easy on people.

Can we leaders treat others compassionately while also driving strong performance? I think so. Don't listen to hard-liners who argue you must crack the whip to motivate your team. Taking a more humane approach reduces unproductive conflict and engenders an environment of civility. In our organization, such civility has persisted even when we've had to usher leaders out of the company. In one instance, a reorganization led to the departure of a leader whom many inside Intermountain regarded as a rock star. The departure led some within the organization to become angry with me. One of the people who wasn't angry, however, was this leader himself. We stayed in touch and remained friends. I've maintained similar relationships with a number of people I've had to fire over the years, precisely because they feel that they've been treated compassionately.

We can take steps to treat people well and adopt standards of civility even as we push hard for the desired results. First, *hold regular group conversations dedicated to honestly but compassionately discussing thorny operational issues.* During the pandemic, Dr. Mark Briesacher, then our senior vice president and chief physician executive, began holding a huddle every two weeks for physicians across Intermountain. Relates Briesacher: "Everyone knows that we'll discuss the most important questions on this call—issues like physician suicide, peer support, unprofessional behavior, and clinical mistakes that teams have made." The point of these conversations is to create a culture in which it's normal to hold a mirror up and honestly gauge our performance, but in a way that is respectful, productive, and never threatening. By leading such conversations, Briesacher also sets an example for the kind of civil but critical discourse he wants other leaders throughout the organization to follow.

We can foster civility by taking a second step: *providing more opportunities for others on the team to become vulnerable with one another.* When I worked at Cleveland Clinic, I once asked my team to go around the table and relate something their colleagues didn't know about them. One leader described how two of his children were severely autistic. Caring for them had become extremely hard on his marriage, and the family had persevered because of its strong faith in God. The story moved everyone in the room. From then on, a new level of intimacy, friendship, and respect bound the team together. It became easier for everyone to show empathy and to engage with one another as human beings. Do you suppose people provided more frank feedback to one another? Do you think the team performed better as a result? Absolutely.

Third, we can *explicitly engage team members to take responsibility for one another's personal improvement efforts.* When I first arrived at Intermountain, we engaged a professional coach to work with our leadership team. This coach interviewed each leader, looking deep into their histories and personalities and probing their individual strengths and weaknesses. We also performed intensive evaluations of one another, with each of us sharing the contents of the resulting reports.

This wasn't an easy exercise. As Briesacher relates, the sharing of direct feedback hasn't always been a dominant part of Intermountain's culture. "Many people in the organization feel that when you're direct with others, you're being unkind." By having members of our leadership team evaluate each other's strengths and weaknesses, I wanted to challenge this cultural norm, building trust among our team members and achieving new levels of candor. I wanted team members to feel mutually accountable for their own growth and development, with each offering direct feedback to others and calling them out when they've failed to address it, and each listening to and acting on feedback from others in turn.

For Briesacher, the impact of this exercise and similar ones we've done since has been profound. "It has been gratifying to hear positive feedback," he observes. "I also learned that I have a tendency to slow down and become more deliberate when I'm under stress. While some of that is good, you can't slow down too much and become paralyzed." Briesacher had long understood this tendency of his, but once he'd received data about it from his peers, he was able to focus on making behavior changes so that stress didn't affect his performance. He was also able to rely on his peers to help him when, despite his best efforts, he was taking too much time making decisions. "We're a team of individuals with strengths and weaknesses and different perspectives," he says. "What we have now is a deep trust, knowing that we'll be direct with one another out of a place of kindness and integrity and in a way that honors our relationship, while also allowing the organization to move forward."

A fourth way we can go hard on issues but easy on people is to *make ourselves vulnerable, too*. I do this nearly every day. I solicit and receive very frank feedback from my team members about my performance, whether it's how I handled a personnel matter, how I ran a meeting, or how well I presented myself during a media appearance. Likewise, when we created those detailed, critical assessments for members of my team, I had one created for me as well. Believe me, it probed deeply into what I did not do well, even as it alerted me to my strengths. I learned that my strengths actually cut both ways, becoming weaknesses at times. Some of my team members appreciated my tendency to speak candidly and call things exactly as I see them, while others found that intimidating and off-putting. My team members appreciated my quick mind—but not when I moved on during a conversation without giving others a chance to say their piece.

Was it easy to hear such feedback? Not so much. Was it helpful? Absolutely. We're now able to talk openly about my difficult tendencies, which tend to pop up most when I'm under pressure. I can explain to others how my unhelpful reflexes—my "least good self," as I call it—might have originated. My team members can understand me better and call me out when my least good self crops up. Meanwhile, I'm able to take steps to moderate my behavior so that I can have more impact as a leader. Over time, my least good self becomes a little bit better.

I have also made myself vulnerable by speaking frankly about my cancer diagnoses. When I was diagnosed with multiple myeloma, I told team members about what this illness meant for me—that it was incurable and that I would need to undergo a bone marrow transplant. I informed them that I would continue to work but I would need their help. I can't be sure, but I suspect this honesty encouraged them to freely disclose their own challenges. The resulting communication made it easier for everyone to provide critical feedback about performance issues when they arose.

A fifth and final way of adopting standards of civility even as we push hard for results is to *avoid triangulation*. You see it all the time in teams: one person goes to the boss and complains about a colleague. The boss gets an ego boost by serving as the mediator, standing above the fray, and enjoying a kind of self-affirming intimacy with both parties. I don't foster this dynamic, nor do I engage in the fruitless politicking that goes with it. When team members confront me with issues they have with colleagues, I nudge them to figure it out themselves. I ask if they've spoken with the others involved, and if not, I encourage them to do so. If they try and fail, I will agree to talk with both of them and help them to resolve the situation.

By encouraging people to have frank and sometimes uncomfortable conversations with one another, I nudge them to confront potentially difficult parts of themselves and in turn to improve their performance. These conversations foster open communication among team members, who over time come to accept one another much more deeply as complex and imperfect human beings who are, in effect, works in progress. Meanwhile, by avoiding the ego boost that one receives at the center of the triangle, I can remain more honest with myself and introspective about my own performance.

Beyond these five actions, I try to model my "hard on issues, easy on people" approach for other leaders in the organization so that they might adopt it. We've instilled elements of this approach across the organization through leadership training that focuses on psychological safety and the holding of difficult conversations. We routinely query our frontline caregivers about how safe they feel reporting issues to their supervisors, and we also rank teams in terms of how healthy and functional they are. When we find teams that are demoralized and disengaged and whose members don't feel safe coming forward with constructive feedback, we provide coaches to the team leaders or, in extreme cases, replace these leaders.

"ARRIVING" IS JUST A FANCY WORD FOR STOPPING

Assessing how well you're doing can leave you complacent and self-satisfied, or it can elicit the humility and curiosity you need to reach the next level. It all depends on how you go about it. At Intermountain, our willingness to observe ourselves in a more honest, uncompromising way has fueled a new intensity around improvement, one that persists to this day. We haven't arrived at our ultimate destination, nor will we—self-analysis and improvement are a constant, never-ending process, and "arriving" as I see it is just a fancy word for stopping. But we have achieved massive performance gains that inspire us to keep going.

In 2016, only 2 of our 12 eligible hospitals earned top marks for quality in nationwide rankings. In 2021, 10 out of 12 did. Our Vizient metrics in mortality, safety, patient experience, effectiveness, and equity improved each year between 2019 and 2021. In 2019, we ranked as a system at the seventy-ninth percentile among our peers nationwide. By 2021, we ranked in the eighty-ninth percentile. As we've improved quality, we've also lowered costs: one analysis found that our pricing for a panel of key services ran 19 to 56 percent below market prices.[11]

I'm proud to say that we've continued to scrutinize our performance and advance our improvement efforts during the pandemic. At times of crisis, it's tempting for organizations and individuals to move into survival mode and give themselves a pass on self-improvement. Pulling together, we've managed to avoid that trap. As a result, we're providing better care today at a lower cost than we were when the pandemic first struck. Although we still haven't met our immediate goal, which is to reside in the top decile of health systems across the board, we're getting much closer.

It's important, I think, to acknowledge such accomplishments, but I find it equally important not to linger on them. If organizations are to continue improving, we leaders must maintain a constant, disciplined focus on imperfections and deficiencies. We must never stop taking stock of them, and we must continue to work as hard as we can to understand their root causes. It's easy to look in the mirror for a time only to begin breathing our own exhaust again once we've achieved a measure of success. We must resist this tendency, staying grounded in reality and confronting the organization ever more fully with it as time passes. When it comes to unleashing and sustaining a revolution, complacency and self-deception get us nowhere. Introspection, inquisitiveness, and a burning determination to remedy our deficits win the day.

QUESTIONS FOR REFLECTION

1. Does your organization tend to look at itself honestly in the mirror, or are you in the habit of believing your own press?
2. When is the last time you had a qualified outside observer perform a comprehensive and objective assessment of your organization?
3. Is a general enthusiasm for growth and change evident in your culture?

4. Are you benchmarking yourself against your peers? When you spot deficiencies, do you avidly look to identify their root causes?

5. When it comes to solving problems, do leaders in your organization insist on developing solutions themselves, or are they willing to swallow their pride and look elsewhere?

6. In your own capacity as a leader, are you hard on issues but easy on people? If not, what might you do to better to couple a performance focus with an atmosphere of psychological safety?

7. Do you make members of your team responsible for one another's growth and development? How might you enhance their accountability to one another?

8. Do you have systems, practices, or processes in place that let you, your team, and your organization stay focused on reality over a prolonged period?

4

FIX WHAT ISN'T BROKEN . . . YET

*Don't shrink from fundamentally reimagining
your organization just because your business
seems to be doing fine right now.*

Large, successful organizations that welcome innovators can be something of a rarity. Even though they're at risk for disruption, these organizations tend to *discourage* people from fundamentally reimagining how work gets done, penalizing them or shutting them out if they go too far.

So imagine how Dr. Cara Camiolo Reddy, then a staff rehabilitation physician at Intermountain, felt one day in the fall of 2018 when she and a colleague, Dr. Rusty Moore, sat down for a meeting with one of our senior administrators. As Camiolo recalls, the administrator, Nannette Berensen, informed her that their agenda was nothing less than reorganizing from top to bottom how Intermountain rehabilitated patients after surgeries, strokes, and other major health episodes. "OK, let's go," Berensen said, a blank legal pad in her hands and a pen at the ready. "Tell me everything you know about rehabilitative care and how we build this."[1] Music to an innovator's ears.

For the next several hours, Camiolo, Moore, and Berensen brainstormed organizational changes that might allow our rehabilitation teams to communicate better and work more smoothly together across our network of facilities. These changes would standardize care, helping our specialists operate more efficiently and ensuring that patients received uniformly great care. Particularly important to Camiolo, Moore, and Berensen was making the experience of receiving care easier and more convenient for patients. If you suffered a stroke or had a traumatic injury and faced a long recovery, Camiolo, Moore, and Berensen wanted you to be able to move seamlessly from the emergency room to an inpatient floor or from the hospital to your home, receiving precisely the care you need at each stage and avoiding bureaucratic delays and red tape.

Camiolo, Moore, and Berensen's thinking was high level, the beginning of a broader change process that would convene rehabilitative caregivers and administrators across Intermountain. Over the next several months, teams of specialists fleshed out specific procedures and collaborative arrangements, forging new links across our facilities and departments. As Camiolo notes, some caregivers initially resisted efforts to standardize care. For decades, rehabilitative medicine at Intermountain had been fragmented, with teams at local facilities enjoying autonomy. Skeptics feared that they would no longer have enough of a voice in how they operated. And as they pointed out, rehabilitative care at Intermountain wasn't by any means broken. We already provided very high-quality care. Why mess with a good thing?

Camiolo, Moore, Berensen, and like-minded colleagues agreed that our care wasn't broken. In fact, Camiolo had come to Intermountain from the University of Pittsburgh, taking on a less senior role in the process, precisely because she'd been impressed by our caregivers' spirit and expertise. But she, Moore, and Berensen noted that opportunities for improvement still existed. A lack of coordination on our part meant we often weren't channeling patients to the care they needed at various stages of their recovery. Patients had trouble accessing this care, even though some of our rehabilitation facilities were only half full, so they went to our competitors. We could serve patients better and see improved business results if we coordinated our efforts in new ways. Wouldn't it be great if our patients could focus more on healing rather than on navigating our bureaucracy?

As the work of redesigning processes and procedures picked up, most of the skeptics became champions of change—they realized the positive difference these changes would make for patients. "I've had rehabilitation caregivers come up to me and say, 'I've worked here for 30 years. This is the best thing that's ever happened to caregivers and their patients,'" Camiolo says. The data suggests they were on to something. Within just one year of standardizing our efforts, over 20 percent more patients were receiving rehabilitative care from us rather than jumping to our competitors—a huge leap forward.

Driving progress usually requires that we reinvent organizations so that they can execute in new ways. How do we do that even before many or even most people appreciate the necessity of change? And how do we stay strong as innovators, even when we know we're stirring up conflict?

These are vital questions in our volatile age. Somehow, leaders must find it in themselves to lean decisively into the task of future-proofing our organizations, with all the struggle and angst that this might entail. As I've learned at Intermountain, a little old-fashioned courage and determination goes a long way. As unpleasant as conflict is, it may be OK to rile people up if we're doing it for the right reason, and if we're also doing what we can to make change as palatable as possible for those affected. As my friend, former Utah governor and current Intermountain board chair Mike Leavitt, likes to say, if you've got 60 percent approval ratings as a leader, that's likely too high and you're probably not trying hard enough.

GO BIG OR GO HOME

Since my arrival as CEO, my team and I have spent quite a bit of time fixing what didn't seem to be broken. We haven't just reimagined a narrow slice of Intermountain—we've brought sweeping change to the entire organization. That's another important lesson I've learned: go big or go home. We can't be afraid to do the big things within our scope of control just because they're scary or we haven't done them before.

I'd had experience steering a startup prior to coming to Intermountain, but I'd never led a full-blown reorganization. That said, I was now ready to. I first came to see the need for fundamental change during my first months as CEO as I familiarized myself with the organization. On one occasion, I met with leaders at one of our hospitals to learn about clinical innovations they were implementing. The work these leaders were doing was amazing, but a part of their presentation caught my eye. In describing their success, these leaders proudly reported that they had grown their business by attracting customers from other Intermountain facilities. That struck me as odd. Although I admired their passion and their drive to succeed, I wondered why teams and facilities at Intermountain were competing with one another. Wouldn't our organization operate more successfully if we thought of ourselves as a single, unified whole, coordinated our efforts, and competed with other systems?

I saw signs that other teams in our organization were competing with one another rather than collaborating and that they didn't always borrow or share best practices. At the time, Intermountain comprised four regions that ran independently of one another. In our northern region, Tim Pehrson, currently CEO of the INTEGRIS health system, had spearheaded a truly impressive continuous improvement process. But the other three regions had decided not to adopt it. As a result, those regions hadn't embedded continuous improvement as fully or effectively as their counterparts in the north had done.

Such fragmentation and a siloed mentality seemed to account for some of the gaps in quality that the initial assessment of the organization revealed. As I've mentioned, we were famous for developing best-in-class clinical protocols to standardize care, but we didn't apply those consistently across our network of facilities—by some estimates, it happened only 40 percent of the time.[2] With our facilities sometimes located hundreds of miles apart, and with clinical programs lacking the authority to mandate that everyone in the system adopted best practices, individual teams often went their own way. Patients received different care—and had different outcomes—depending on where in our system they were seen. Experience at our facilities also varied, thanks to differences in processes and workflows. Many patients didn't even know they were interfacing with Intermountain. Rather, they saw themselves as customers of specific hospitals or clinics.

A lack of coordination wasn't new at Intermountain, nor was it inherently a mark of dysfunction. Our system was created in 1975 when the Church of Jesus Christ of Latter-day Saints donated its 15 hospitals to the community. A secular, nonprofit organization—Intermountain Healthcare—was created to receive the hospitals and charged with establishing a model health system. Although Intermountain's early leaders began to link these hospitals together, the system still operated very much as a federation of autonomous hospitals. As we added more hospitals and eventually a medical group of physicians and clinics, we formed ourselves into regions that remained a loose federation. We made tremendous gains in safety and quality under our regional structure, distinguished ourselves as innovators in patient care, and improved access to healthcare in the communities we served.

Individually, the regions were well led, economically savvy, and focused on the community. Yet new challenges that had appeared on the horizon worried me. The cost of care was rising, those who paid for it—employers, government, and patients—were becoming increasingly burdened, and traditional health organizations were struggling. Although Intermountain was financially healthy, our costs had risen by 22 percent from 2012 to 2017.[3] In 2017 alone, usage of our hospitals had fallen slightly while the number of employees on our team had increased.[4] Customers in Utah were becoming more price conscious, as many of them participated in health plans with high deductibles. Competitors, including Amazon, Walgreens, CVS, Google, and others, were poised to steal market share, introducing offerings that cost less and were more convenient.

To meet these impending challenges, we would have to move more quickly toward the newer business models of value-based care and population health. That in turn would require us to streamline the organization and find new ways to work better together. We could wait to make profound changes until we were on the verge of failure, as the Kodaks and Blockbuster Videos of this world have done. Or we could evolve proactively, restructuring and transforming ourselves to get ahead of the disruption. To me, the answer was clear. Great organizations embark on change when the need for it becomes clear. They don't wait for the situation to become dire.[5]

Of course, preempting disruption through a reorganization would be easier said than done. Research shows that many reorganizations fail and that they also prove stressful for employees.[6] Moreover, we'd be asking people to change at a time when we weren't yet broken. Virtually everything about our organization would be in play, from reporting structures to processes to compensation structures to the way we organized daily work. Looking around the industry and beyond, I saw examples of leaders who had tried reorganizations and transformations only to spark devastating internal conflicts. If we didn't get restructuring right, an initiative intended to bring us together and launch us into the future could tear us apart, leaving us even more vulnerable.

Despite the risks, we moved decisively in 2017 and 2018 to unify the organization, so that *all* of Intermountain moved in sync. With the strong and courageous support of our board, we did away with our regions, forged new links across our local facilities, and restructured ourselves as "One Intermountain" under an aligned reporting structure. We also instituted common ways of working that would keep everybody working together and accountable for achieving results. With these changes in place, we'd be able to spread best practices far more readily across the organization, deploy strategies in a coordinated way, solve problems more quickly, and much more.[7]

In the course of adopting a more unified structure, we created two groups within Intermountain: one dedicated to keeping people well and managing their health, and the other to caring for people once they are seriously ill or injured. This was quite a radical change, one that would help us to move more rapidly toward value-based care and population health. In the group dedicated to keeping people well, we would reward practitioners for finding new ways to manage people's health risks so that they wouldn't need more extensive emergency or hospital care. In the group dedicated to caring for patients once they're sick, we would continue to incent practitioners to deliver high quality care at a more affordable cost. The imperatives underlying this dual structure are complex, but in essence we realized that keeping people well and caring for them when they're sick are very different. We needed to operate these two parts of our business in somewhat disparate ways to drive high performance in each, keep costs low, and make our entire network of facilities work better.

Our restructuring remains very much a work in progress, and it's premature to issue a final verdict on its success. But I'm optimistic. Our restructuring has unleashed a rush of innovation that is reducing costs while improving quality and patient experience. By reimagining manifold facets of the care we provide as well as how we conceive of a healthcare system's role and function, we're not just becoming less vulnerable to disruption than we've been in the past. We're *leading* disruption in ways that would have been unthinkable just a few years ago. We're helping to revolutionize America's broken healthcare system.

TIE IT BACK TO THE MISSION

Between 2003 and 2008, US Army General Stanley McChrystal led an ambitious transformation of the Joint Special Operations Command (JSOC), a force of elite special operations units from across the country's military. He also led a force under JSOC control, the Joint Special Operations Task Force ("Task Force") in Iraq. As McChrystal notes, when he took over its command, the JSOC was at the top of its game: it was "the most elite part of the US military, well-funded, staffed by specially selected people with incredible levels of maturity. Since its founding in 1981, it had gotten better and better," and it had also developed great confidence and pride in its abilities.[8]

By 2003, however, in its battle against Al-Qaeda in Iraq (AQI), the JSOC and its Task Force faced battlefield conditions that were more fluid and unpredictable than anything it had previously encountered. "We had been purposely built to do a certain kind of counter-terrorism, hostage rescue, counter-hijacking, that sort of thing, and do very elegant missions, but not do them very often. So, we could do detailed planning, rehearsals, and execution. Now, suddenly, we were in an environment where we had to operate really fast and constantly adapt, and that wasn't in our habit or psyche."

Like Intermountain, the Task Force would need to fundamentally change if it was going to continue to compete and win. In particular, the Task Force would have to overcome a siloed mindset and learn to cooperate better with parts of the US government that it had previously regarded as competitors, including the Central Intelligence Agency and the State Department.

Initially, some of the JSOC's leaders didn't want to acknowledge the need for change. The reigning mindset was, "We were really good, so why can't the war be how we want it to be?" As reality sank in, members of the Task Force continued to resist the move toward more collaboration and sharing of information, concerned that it would erode the Task Force's operational capacity. "There was a fear that if we change from what we were, where our confidence and our stature was well-established and we had proven excellence in how we operated, we'd be in uncharted territory," McChrystal says. "If we were a football team and started playing basketball, maybe we wouldn't be good basketball players."

To convince the organization to embrace the transformation, McChrystal made a simple but powerful argument: What mattered was that the United States won the war in Iraq. That outcome was the Task Force's ultimate purpose, and it wouldn't happen unless the Task Force adapted to new battlefield conditions quickly and decisively. "The argument I made to the organization was, 'We're going to do whatever it takes to win. If it's stupid and it works, it isn't stupid. And so, we're going to adapt until we figure out what works and we're going to then do more of that.'"

Reverting back to the purpose ultimately proved an unassailable argument. As McChrystal asks, "Who can be against, 'Hey, we're going to do whatever it takes to win?'" The organization came to support the transformation, especially as it began to yield results. In the end, the Task Force saw tremendous operational improvements, notably in the key output metric of the number of raids undertaken. In 2003, the Task Force mounted one raid against the enemy per week. Two years later, it mounted roughly 10 per night—an exponential improvement without increasing the size of the force or significantly enhancing its technological resources.

When attempting to galvanize a large, successful organization around momentous change, especially when the need for it doesn't yet seem dire, tying that change back to the organization's core mission or purpose is essential. It allows us to walk a delicate line, affirming the organization's heritage and tradition while at the same time making a compelling case for undertaking fundamental, proactive change. It also allows us to convince people that they are not compromising the very strengths that made the organization successful but rather drawing on these strengths and safeguarding them for the future.

In presenting our restructuring plans, my leadership team and I linked them to our initial charge of building a model health system and our core mission of helping people live the healthiest lives possible. We did our best to evoke a sense of continuity, explaining how our restructuring, while challenging in the short term, would allow our organization to survive the dramatic changes taking place in our industry, enabling us to continue to deliver on our historic charge. Yes, we were functioning as a model healthcare system now and had every right to feel proud of that. But we needed to ensure that Intermountain could continue to do so in the future.[9]

We further pointed out that Intermountain had long innovated to improve the care we provided and lower its cost. The changes associated with and enabled by our restructuring were simply the latest in a series of measures designed to keep us on the cutting edge.[10] This argument was key. Yes, we were making bold changes. But a capacity and willingness to change has always defined our organization. Rather than taking us off track, change would keep us moored even more tightly to our roots.

Our messaging didn't win everyone over right away. Just as Dr. Camiolo and her colleagues encountered resistance in reorganizing our rehabilitative care efforts, so my own team and I ruffled a few feathers by introducing One Intermountain. Or perhaps more than a few. As Rob Allen, our chief operating officer, remembers, "There were people who were very concerned that the history of Intermountain—the legacy of who Intermountain was—was being thrown out. People had great pride in working for Intermountain Healthcare, and there was this fear that these things that we've held to are gone."[11]

In retrospect, I underestimated the pushback that One Intermountain generated—a testament to my own naivete about the difficulty of change. One employee on Glassdoor described One Intermountain as a "Wack-A-Doo Reorganization Without Adequate Direction."[12] Another told a local newspaper, "I think they've taken a big hit with . . . just how employees feel. There really (are) morale issues across the board."[13] A few of our senior leaders left, with one grumbling that we had destroyed what had been "a high level of trust and mutual respect amongst employees and management."[14]

This response was understandable—some of the changes we made were extremely unpleasant and anxiety-producing. In doing away with our regions, we eliminated hundreds of primarily managerial roles, and at the same time we also outsourced about 100 IT and 2,300 office jobs.[15] More broadly, we were asking people in an organization that had long been stable and highly predictable to accept dramatic changes to roles, our reporting structure, and our ways of working. At one point, 1,000 of our leaders had transitioned into new jobs over a three-month period. Bear in mind, too, caregivers often choose careers in healthcare precisely because they're seeking stability, and the professional training they receive tends to emphasize predictability, order, and regularity.

In retrospect, we also didn't socialize One Intermountain with caregivers and leaders across the organization as well as we should have. What we should have done was involve leaders early in the process, soliciting feedback from them, giving them tools to use in communicating the change to their teams, and trusting them to serve as spokespeople. Instead, we kept an excessively tight lid on information about our restructuring. Our organization only learned key details when we announced them at a public meeting, leaving some within the organization feeling angry and betrayed because we hadn't first confided in them. Since this meeting happened to occur while I was attending the World Economic Forum in Davos, I came across as especially distant and aloof—an uncaring member of the global elite. It was a bungled launch all around, one that made an inherently difficult situation that much worse.

I went on to exacerbate the internal tumult by sometimes failing to communicate the change as adeptly as I might have. On one occasion, I likened our existing model to a Model T and proclaimed that I wanted us to become the Tesla of healthcare. Although that analogy is instructive, it understandably led some to take offense, especially given all the innovation that occurred at Intermountain prior to my arrival. Intermountain has been a leader in innovation and clinical care for decades, and I deeply revere its heritage. The last thing I wanted to do was disparage it. With this analogy, I probably made the case for change too sharply, and the comments became a lightning rod for those opposed to our restructuring.

At the same time, I think many in the organization could tell how intensely I felt about value-based care (which Intermountain was already committed to pursuing), the organizational changes I was advocating, and Intermountain's mission. That's important. As Frans van Houten, CEO of the Dutch multinational Philips, observes, leaders can't simply make rational arguments when communicating big organizational shifts and expect to generate followership. They must feel genuinely passionate about their underlying strategy and convey that energy. In reorienting Philips toward its healthcare markets and driving organizational change to support the strategy, van Houten drew upon a longstanding passion he had for healthcare (his mother was a physician, and in his youth, he had hoped to attend medical school).[16]

Likewise, General McChrystal relates how he became "fanatical" about JSOC's mission of winning in part because competitiveness and an intense desire to win is an important part of his personality. As he says, "I don't think I suddenly became a hugely courageous leader or a brilliant leader. But I did become a leader who was very committed to winning, and I used to talk that way to the organization. It was very, very helpful."[17]

At Intermountain, resistance subsided as our reorganization started to bear fruit, leading to improvements in quality, safety, and patient experience, and as our caregivers began to exercise a voice in continuous improvement under our new operating model (more on this in Chapter 5). The introduction of big change unleashed in our case a fairly big storm, but by staying close to our purpose and sticking to our message, we managed to weather the turbulence and emerge even stronger and more unified—an organization that truly was One Intermountain.

LEAVE SPACE FOR INNOVATION

Once you've begun to generate support for fundamental change to preempt disruption, how do you deepen that support and ensure that it lasts? As we learned, it's vital to give people a meaningful role in reimagining the organization. By their very nature, organizational shifts can create new spaces for innovation by suspending old rules and ways of operating. People at all levels who are interested in advancing progress sense that an opening for progress exists, and they step up. Leaders can open these spaces wider, further galvanizing people to embrace and pursue innovation, by giving teams and individuals autonomy in changing the system.

In transforming the Task Force in Iraq, General McChrystal devolved decision-making authority downward and to the periphery in his organization, a decision he credits with unleashing tremendous performance gains. It was tempting to continue a traditional command-and-control approach, funneling all information from the periphery of the organization to the center. In a global operation such as his (the JSOC operated in dozens of countries), information technology gave leaders unprecedented abilities to track and direct operations. But in a fast-changing, chaotic environment, leaders achieve better results when they cede control to local teams, speed up the flow of information across the organization, and focus more on providing general guidance to shape action. "You have to give more junior, less experienced people general guidance and let them figure things out, because you can't tell them in advance exactly what conditions they'll be facing."

In reorganizing Intermountain, our senior leadership team didn't dictate the details. We left it to several dozen clinical and nonclinical working groups to redesign how we worked across our system with an eye toward efficiency and cost savings.[18] Our goal, as we publicly described it, was to "operate as a system, with local flexibility." This would afford us "scale and consistency, while enabling local leaders the flexibility to meet local needs."[19]

In the short term, the decision to leave the operational details of the restructuring to local groups aroused anxiety in the workforce, as it made for more uncertainty. We often feel more comfortable in times of transition when people in charge tell us what to do. Over the long term, empowering local groups unleashed talent throughout the enterprise, galvanizing frontline caregivers to participate in and lead change. As our restructuring became established and as we launched a range of other initiatives, we saw extraordinary enthusiasm and efforts from literally thousands of people across our system who pulled together in new ways to advance value-based care and our mission.

One of these individuals was Dr. Chad Spain, a primary care physician at one of our Utah clinics. Practicing under the traditional fee-for-service model, he felt constant pressure to cram more patients into his schedule, to the point where he was spending only about 15 to 20 minutes with each one. This bothered Spain: he had gone into medicine to help people, and he felt that he didn't have the time he needed to forge relationships and understand patients' complex medical conditions. "I was very frustrated," he remembers. "Burnout is real, it was there, and it had me questioning my career choice."[20]

In 2017, Spain jumped at a chance to participate in a small pilot initiative we launched called Reimagined Primary Care. As part of the program, doctors would reduce their loads from 1,500–2,000 patients to about 750. Instead of having his compensation pegged to patient volume, Spain would receive a fixed salary. In keeping with a population-health, value-based care model, insurance companies would pay Intermountain a fixed price for his patients' care. If Spain could keep patients healthier and out of the hospital, our costs would go down and the new model would prove economically viable. Patients would benefit, and Spain's own work would be more fulfilling.

We launched this pilot as a prelude to what we hoped would be a broader shift of our primary care physicians to the population health model. To that end, we enlisted participating physicians to help us define and fine-tune the new model of primary care. Every week, Spain and a handful of other doctors met with administrators to discuss issues such as how best to reduce their patient load, how to communicate the changes to their patients, what support staff they needed to improve preventive care for patients, and so on. Although these meetings took time out of Dr. Spain's day, they were "very rewarding because for what seemed like the first time, we as providers were being heard. We'd say, 'Hey, here's what we see are issues in delivering good healthcare,' and administration was taking that back and saying, 'OK, let's see if we can build this system around you.'"

The new model transformed Spain's practice of medicine. At the start of each day, he and other providers in his clinic would meet with a designated caregiver who monitored patient progress, such as whether they were meeting their blood sugar goals or receiving appropriate cancer screening, or how they fared after a recent emergency room visit. Having this caregiver on the team helped to prevent patients from falling through the cracks, as sometimes happened under the fee-for-service model, given the overwhelming patient loads.

During the morning huddle, Spain and his colleagues received an update on patients, allowing them to plan for their care. After the huddle, Spain spent most of his day meeting with patients, taking 30 to 60 minutes with each one instead of 15. "You can imagine the benefit that comes from that," he says. "The more time you spend, the better you get to know them, and the better you can take care of their chronic illness." Dr. Spain also had time blocked off in his day to see patients with acute but non-life-threatening conditions—a flu, perhaps, or a worrisome rash—that would have previously led them to visit an emergency room or urgent care facility. Seeing such patients in a primary care setting is less costly, and we pass the savings along to patients or use it to improve the quality of their care.

Thanks to Spain's efforts and those of other participating caregivers, the Reimagined Primary Care pilot was a breakout success. A year after the pilot's launch, we saw a 60 percent drop in hospital admissions among these patients. The cost to care for an individual patient over a single month dropped 20 percent. Patient experience improved, as did physician satisfaction.[21] We've since moved all primary care providers at Intermountain to some form of value-based care or hybrid model. Although we're by no means done ironing out kinks in the model, the impact has been profound. Spain is eager to see further changes, but he reports that he has grown much happier in his practice of medicine. "I have more time to spend with patients. I can make visits to their homes. Patients feel that if they need me, they have access. And our data proved that we were providing better healthcare and we had a great team to do it."

Our restructuring has opened the way for Spain and thousands of others at Intermountain to drive change. Spain has taken on leadership roles, serving as board president of the Utah Academy of Family Physicians. "They say change is always hard," Spain reflects, "but I don't think in this setting of healthcare that we can be afraid of it. If we want healthcare to change, we need to be willing to make change ourselves."[22]

THE THREATS YOU DON'T SEE COMING

In 2020, health systems across America were sent into disarray by the arrival of the Covid-19 pandemic. Enforced lockdowns meant they couldn't book revenue from noncritical procedures as they had before.

Meanwhile, their costs rose: they had to treat more uninsured people who flocked to emergency rooms, and they also had to shoulder the high cost of outfitting caregivers with personal protective equipment. Operational issues such as staffing shortages and a lack of ICU beds made the situation even more difficult. With financial strains mounting, some facilities buckled. By November 2020, over three dozen hospitals had filed for bankruptcy, and more would follow.[23]

Covid hit our organization hard, but the impact would have been much worse had we not restructured ourselves a few years earlier. Under our old organization, each of our 23 hospitals would have created their own individual plan for handling surges of patients sickened by the virus. Operational functions such as supply chain would have had plans of their own. Some of these arrangements would have responded better than others, and we would have struggled to bring all of the resources available in our system to bear in a coordinated way. Our ability to care for patients in this frightening time would have been greatly impaired.

Under our new organizational structure, we came together to devise and execute one plan for our entire system. As part of our incident command system, teams of leaders huddled regularly to coordinate treatment protocols for patients, infectious disease control, protective equipment, operations, communications, and so on. We were able to collect data systemwide and predictively model Covid volumes at specific locations. We could coordinate patient care across our system, transferring patients between facilities in ways that best served their care. When beds in one local area were full, we could move patients to beds at other facilities.

Critically, we also coordinated our staffing. Instead of local nursing directors making staffing decisions at their locations, our chief nursing executive, Sue Robel, worked with Heather Brace, our chief people officer, to move our 10,000 nurses around to the facilities where we needed them via a central redeployment office. When the virus forced us to shut down elective procedures, we rapidly retrained people and sent them to work in facilities in our system that were seeing a crush of Covid patients.

Like other health systems, we faced severe staffing issues and caregiver burnout. But our staff didn't lose their jobs or see reductions in their work hours or incomes, and we had the flexibility to respond quickly to hotspots as they arose. As Robel reports, "Without nurses moving between our regions, we wouldn't have had enough caregivers to take care of our patients. We wouldn't have been able to open up all of our beds. So, that was a huge, huge benefit for us, to function as One Intermountain."[24]

Taking steps to future-proof an organization can prepare us for disruptions we see coming—and critically, those we don't. Given the increased economic volatility the world is seeing, it really does behoove us all to take a close look at our organizations. Are they really up to the task of preempting disruption? If not, we shouldn't hesitate to reinvent them, even if doing so will arouse resistance. It's less about being popular and more about doing what's right. Restructure the organization to operate better under your present model *and* to align better with powerful new ones. Build support for restructuring and transformation by tying it back to your heritage and core purpose. And foster more autonomy, giving your people space they need to collaborate with you in driving change.

Driving big, systemic changes in an organization isn't for every leader. Some of us are inclined temperamentally to pursue incremental improvements—and that's great. Organizations desperately need these leaders to consolidate gains in times of relative stability. But in less stable times, we as leaders must step up and be capable of driving larger changes for the organization's greater good.

Which kind of leader are you? Do you have the strength, determination, and sheer stubbornness to yank the organization forward, even if that might anger some people? If so, it's time to do it. When we see a significant problem in the organization that needs fixing, we can grit our teeth and get the job done.

I opened this chapter with a quote from former Utah governor Mike Leavitt. He has another saying of which I'm fond: "If you're 5 steps ahead of your organization, you're a leader; 15 steps, you're a martyr." In other words, don't overdo it.

I agree wholeheartedly. It would be a mistake to create tumult in an organization for its own sake or to conflate the presence of conflict with change-making. Change, in the end, must always be purposeful. We should avoid unnecessary, unproductive, harmful conflict, pursuing healthy conflict that moves our organizations forward and enables people to work better together over the long term. It might be hard to restrain from pushing too hard, especially if, like me, you're passionate and impatient by nature. But think of it this way: If we try to make our organizations into something they aren't or can't be, we'll certainly fail. If we challenge them to become a better, more successful version of what they already are, we just might succeed.

QUESTIONS FOR REFLECTION

1. Take an honest look at your organization. In its present state, will it serve to support or impede your efforts to stay ahead of disruption?

2. If you've attempted to reimagine your organization in the past, did you go far enough, given the business challenges you face?

3. How might you change your organization so that it not merely operates better but advances the nontraditional business models you must adopt to thrive in the years ahead?

4. Are you communicating major changes effectively by tying them back to your organization's heritage and core mission?

5. Are you giving your people enough autonomy in executing organizational change so that they can unleash and apply their own talents?

6. Are you by temperament a transformational leader or one who excels at stabilizing organizations and consolidating previous change?

5

UNLOCK THE GENIUS
AT THE BEDSIDE
(OR AT THE FRONT LINE)

Take—and implement—suggestions
for improvement from your workforce.

The last two chapters have described how leaders can lay the groundwork for massive change by reshaping their organizations. But how, practically speaking, do established organizations actually unleash possibility? What's the secret to a company that doesn't simply talk about supercharging its performance, revolutionizing its industry, or saving the world, but actually gets the job done?

The best way I can think to answer this question is to tell you about a tiny newborn named Maci, born 17 weeks prematurely at one of Intermountain's hospitals in 2009 and weighing in at just over a pound. Her young life hung in the balance—babies born so early have less than a 50 percent chance of survival. Even the slightest error on the part of caregivers could have proved fatal. Given her fragile state, you would presume that caregivers would have taken care to keep interventions of all kinds to the absolute minimum. In fact, throughout her stay in our neonatal intensive care unit (NICU), Maci experienced in excess of 1,200 pokes in the form of lab tests, intravenous catheter placements and manipulations, and other procedures, many of which were painful or noxious.[1]

To be sure, we weren't the only ones who were poking newborns a lot. At most hospitals, it remains standard practice for caregivers to subject newborns to frequent needle jabs in order to run various blood tests. That's a lot of pain, and newborns feel it. As studies have found, receiving more than about 70 pokes can injure the brains of babies, resulting in developmental issues that show up by the time these children are in grade school. Frequent pokes also subject babies to increased risk of infection.[2]

As it turns out, a large percentage of these pokes aren't even necessary for the care of babies like Maci. Rather, they result from processes and procedures that have been adopted and become routine over time. In a NICU, caregivers might have established a process to conduct a certain kind of blood test on newborns each Monday. They might have given this test to all patients, not ascertaining for each individual case whether a baby really needed it. Or doctors might be ordering tests that are nice to run but aren't strictly necessary, without considering just how many pokes other caregivers might have to make to obtain necessary blood samples.

A great deal of care happens by force of habit. Caregivers perform tests and other interventions because they were trained to do so, without stopping to ask whether the science really backs up their actions. "We find that vast amounts of care is happening behind the scenes that may or may not actually benefit the patient," observes Dr. R. Erick Ridout, a neonatologist at Intermountain's St. George Regional Hospital. "But if we don't know about it, we can't actually figure that out."[3]

Determined to improve how we care for infants, Ridout in 2008 created a database and an ecosystem of care called POKE (an acronym for "preventing pain and organisms from skin and catheter entry") that allowed team members at his NICU to track every decision they made while caring for patients.[4] For the first time ever, caregivers would have a sense of what care felt like from the patient's perspective, empowering babies who otherwise lacked a voice. Mapping out each step in a care process that included multiple caregivers, they would know the sum total of pokes infants experienced. With that information, they would be able to question existing protocols and devise new ones that, by rendering care simpler and more efficient, minimized pokes.

Analyzing the data, caregivers in Ridout's unit found, in his words, that "the vast majority of things that were occurring in our NICU were not adding value. It wasn't that we were providing bad care. We just were providing care in established ways, and we started questioning it and found that we could eliminate a tremendous amount of it." Little by little, Ridout and his colleagues worked on improving protocols to eliminate unnecessary tests and other procedures and to make care safer. "Each day we tried to get a little bit better, a little bit better, identifying what didn't add value." Success led to more success—a flywheel effect that continues to this day.

Relentlessly assessing whether every care decision added value to each patient resulted in massive reductions in the number of pokes babies experienced—Ridout's NICU eliminated roughly 11,000 per year. Were Maci to come to Ridout's NICU today, she would experience about 1,000 fewer pokes with no adverse effects on her treatment. This more efficient and humane care is also safer. To take but one example, bloodstream infections from central lines are extremely dangerous and almost entirely avoidable. Many NICUs around the country are happy if they go a month without seeing one such infection. Thanks to process improvements made as part of POKE,

Ridout's NICU has gone more than *13 years* without a single infection as of this writing. Eliminating care that doesn't add value also lowers cost. Over a little more than a decade, reducing pokes at Ridout's NICU saved our system almost $3 million.[5]

Maci was one of the first babies whose care experience was tracked so caregivers could aggregate the number of pokes she'd experienced. Today, she's thriving and has come back to visit with Ridout annually at the NICU's Reunion.[6] POKE, meanwhile, has been so successful that we've rolled it out to all of our NICUs. In just a single year, our NICU babies experienced 150,000 fewer pokes. That's a far more compassionate way to care for babies who are already facing challenging health problems. Of course, eliminating so much care that doesn't add value also means forgoing the revenue it would bring in—about $50 million each year once implemented across the Intermountain System.[7] But we decided we simply had to introduce POKE in our other NICUs—it was the right thing to do for patients.

In 2017, inspired by POKE and other local improvement initiatives underway at Intermountain, we introduced a standard, system-wide process for improving how we work as part of our restructuring efforts. Now *all* of our teams could help to improve how they cared for patients. This initiative, which began under my predecessor, has played a huge role in producing our systemwide gains in quality, safety, and patient experience I described earlier. And since we've set specific goals related to the adoption of value-based care and population health, our improvement process has allowed us to move much more aggressively toward a disruptive business model than we would have otherwise. Hearing of our success, organizations from over a dozen countries have visited Intermountain to learn about our system for organizing improvement efforts for our people.[8]

As we've learned, the secret to affecting radical change in an organization is not a particular technology or strategy. It's something far simpler: empowering everyone to make small strides forward each day. As leaders, we should enable frontline teams to reflect constantly on what they're doing, to make incremental changes, and to take responsibility for their results. We must set clear goals, measure performance, and implement a way to improve operations.

Reflecting on POKE, Dr. Ridout notes that, "We're not doing anything novel. We're just doing it. That's the difference." It is indeed. Most leaders in healthcare and beyond know about continuous improvement, and they also know about specific methods like lean, Six Sigma, or the Toyota Production System that originated in industrial settings. This all sounds like fancy business school or corporate lingo that can make eyes roll. But the heart of it is simple. How do we do better together? Many leaders don't embed such methods as deeply as they might in their own companies—a failure that is also a significant opportunity.

If you haven't made continuous improvement a central focus in your organization, I hope you will. Organizations that are constantly striving to improve are simply better places—nimbler, more energetic, more innovative—because they've unlocked their greatest resource, the genius and passion of their people.

REVOLUTIONIZE THE CULTURE

As we've seen, an emphasis on improvement unleashes workforces in the first instance by *embedding a strong culture of improvement*. Rather than take for granted how work gets done, people learn to spot flaws, look for root causes, and make changes. They develop a critical perspective regarding improvement as a core part of what they do, the pathway to potentially massive accomplishments over the long term. They come to feel more comfortable speaking up and welcoming the contributions of their peers.

This was certainly the case with POKE. As Dr. Ridout relates, the essence of the program wasn't the database. It was the practice of "evaluating every single decision we make, action we take, resource we utilize from a patient's perspective, and if it doesn't add value, then we're going to stop it."[9] Embedded in this practice was a shift in cultural values, with a new emphasis on putting patients first, tracking performance, probing for failures rather than ignoring them, feeling deep respect for frontline caregivers and their contributions (more on this in a moment), cultivating an atmosphere of psychological safety so caregivers and family members can raise issues, and striving for excellence.

Similar values have marked the culture of improvement at Intermountain generally. As Guido Bergomi, executive director of our Office of Patient Experience, remarks, teams at Intermountain increasingly have begun to move away from a culture of competitiveness and ego toward one of "caring and learning." They are aiming to reach "a much better place of talking about our processes and what could or did go wrong, asking how do we prevent it from going wrong again."[10] Dr. Mike Woodruff, an emergency room physician and senior medical director for our Office of Patient Experience, agrees, describing our emerging culture as one of "Ownership, accountability, and transparency, with the vulnerability and the curiosity to say, 'What are we doing wrong here? And what can we learn to get better?'"[11]

Instilling an improvement-focused culture and all that comes with that is not easy, whether in healthcare or other domains of performance. Wes Johnson, veteran coach and the US Olympic Committee's 2019 Paralympic Coach of the Year, finds that his elite athletes do much better when they focus not on some big performance goal but rather on making small tweaks to what they do on an ongoing basis. And yet, he notes that some athletes don't like the incremental approach. Rather than starting small and chipping away at a challenge, they want to charge in and tackle what they perceive as their biggest challenges.

Athletes can also struggle with the idea that improvement isn't always a linear process. "On the quest for progress, there're a lot of hard days," Johnson says. "We're just very up front with athletes about that and making sure that they understand that that's part of the process, that it's not going to be easy, and there are going to be some failures along the way."[12] Athletes must begin to see failures in a more positive light—as opportunities for growth. They must learn to trust the process, understanding that if they stick with it, small improvements really will deliver big results in the end. Some athletes can't make this shift, and in those cases, Johnson has had to let them go. But many can and do.

The bottom line is simple. We want to create a culture where people are curious to learn more, have the tenacity to do better, and grow from failure.

I first discovered the strains and stresses that come with embracing an improvement-focused culture during the early 2000s when I introduced an improvement initiative at Cleveland Clinic. Many doctors resisted, perceiving it as both overly bureaucratic and a challenge to their status as experts. They protested that we were a health system, not a factory, so we shouldn't import industrial process improvement methods and expect them to work.

The name "continuous improvement" does sound somewhat formulaic and cold—especially in a setting that is all about caring for people. Further, improvement methods go against the grain of medical education. During their training, most young doctors serve as apprentices to established physicians in their field, doing the grunt work in exchange for a chance to learn under a master practitioner's watchful eye. Young doctors usually don't learn how to troubleshoot a system that isn't working well—the emphasis isn't on challenging existing practice and improving it but on respecting one's elders and copying what they do.

More recently, the introduction of continuous improvement at Intermountain prompted resistance from some administrators at our local facilities who felt that we were imposing a way of working upon them. Protective of their autonomy, they didn't like that we were going to closely measure performance and hold them accountable for achieving specific goals.

There is no shortcut to dealing with such resistance. We must push through as compassionately as we can. My team and I have done that, preaching the gospel of continuous improvement as well as its underlying goal, providing the safest, highest quality care to patients at the lowest appropriate cost. To remedy gaps in medical education, we've invested heavily in training physician leaders throughout Intermountain to nurture improvement efforts by staying alert to problems, staying humble, and driving toward relentless forward progress.

This ongoing effort has paid off. Over time, resistance has receded, and our desired culture has taken hold. In general, leaders and teams across Intermountain have learned to treat failures as learning opportunities and work together every day to make incremental process changes. When queried, individuals on most of our teams report feeling safer than they had in the past to bring issues to light. The shift in mindset has been, in Woodruff's estimation, nothing less than "a revolution for Intermountain."

AN ORGANIZATION OF PLAYERS, NOT TOURISTS

What were you doing at the age of 17? Hanging out with your friends? Working at a minimum wage job? Bain & Company chairwoman Orit Gadiesh was watching senior military and political officials wage war in one of the world's most volatile regions. Reporting for mandatory military service in her native Israel, she was assigned to assist the deputy to the chief of staff of the Israeli Defense Forces (IDF). In this capacity, she attended meetings of the country's top brass in their war bunker during Israel's so-called "War of Attrition" with Egypt and other Arab countries during the late 1960s. Her job duties were menial: serving coffee and passing out documents. But the opportunity to observe the country's most senior military and political officials in action was invaluable.

As she recounts, one leadership lesson she learned stands out above the rest: the importance of consulting with frontline soldiers and understanding their reality when making operational decisions. Senior leaders, including the IDF's chief of staff and minister of defense, huddled often with frontline soldiers to exchange ideas. Officials also led troops themselves on the front lines rather than staying sequestered in their bunkers. "People always say that that's the way armies should operate," she relates. The Israeli Army actually did so, and it gave them an operational advantage. It was also "one of the reasons that so many high-ranked officers have been killed in the various wars. They really are up on the front lines."[13]

In gleaning knowledge from frontline soldiers, the leaders Gadeish observed weren't micromanaging. Although they expressed their opinions and gave advice, they let the frontline commanders make final operational decisions, even though these commanders ranked much lower than they did in the chain of command. "That's a lesson you never forget," Gadeish says. "I learned this pragmatism. It's not about lofty things. It's about doing what really needs to get done in order to be successful in the next thing we have to do." To help an organization execute well, leaders must check their egos at the door and trust the judgment of frontline personnel. They might weigh in, but they must give the front line a certain amount of autonomy to adapt strategies to the operational realities on the ground.

Methods for improving how work gets done also empower front-line employees, another way that they unleash workforces to execute big changes. In driving improvement programs, leaders set their egos aside, respecting the judgment and expertise of frontline personnel and truly listening to them, just like the Israeli generals did. Rather than micromanaging changes to how work gets done, they adopt a servant-oriented mindset, seeking to support improvement processes in which employees themselves generate the solutions.

In Dr. Ridout's words, leaders under the POKE approach "massively invest" in frontline caregivers "every single day by valuing what they say, empowering them, and oftentimes implementing the care they recommend." They also give caregivers the tools they need to capture the voice of patients, such as the POKE database. There is "genius that exists at every bedside across our organization," Ridout says. With continuous improvement, leaders seek to leverage and unleash that intellectual power.

Since 2017, Intermountain's systemwide improvement efforts have served to unleash the genius of frontline caregivers as well. To engage caregivers in daily improvement, we've instituted a system of morning frontline huddles across our organization. These are quick, 15-minute meetings in which caregivers report data from the past 24 hours and alert their colleagues to problems that have arisen, bearing on safety, quality, access to care, and our stewardship of resources. If a local team can resolve a problem on its own by making an operational change, great. Otherwise, the local team escalates the issue to managers and leaders.

Every day, we hold more than 3,100 huddles of frontline employees across Intermountain. These quick meetings are highly productive, generating tens of thousands of ideas for improvement each year.

Our teams and organizational leaders don't just sit on these ideas. They take action. When caregivers think they know how to solve a problem they've identified, they enter them into an online ideas system. Then they think through their idea with their teams. If the idea has merit, they work to implement it on an experimental basis. Once ideas are proven to work, we share them across Intermountain.

We implement more than 50,000 ideas from our caregivers each year.[14] Some of these are relatively minor process changes to remedy problems such as medication errors, delays admitting patients, or even just an exit sign that's hard for patients to see. Other ideas are bigger process changes that improve how caregivers across our system do their work. For example, physicians might suggest ideas for changing how medications are administered or how we treat patients with particular ailments.

It's tempting to focus on the bigger, higher-impact ideas, but the much more numerous smaller changes implemented year after year are really what drive progress the most. Every now and then, a breakthrough idea will emerge, and of course we run with those. But as our vice president of continuous improvement Dr. Matt Pollard notes, the whole point of our huddles and idea collection system is to "aggregate all of the collective intellect, energy, and heart and soul of our employees in this system. That's the magic."[15] Pollard would "rather have a million small improvements than one massive one," and so would I (although the massive ones are nice, too).

In cascading daily huddles across Intermountain, I had hoped that caregivers would come away feeling more respected, empowered, and happier with their jobs, since they would have more of a voice in how they deliver care. Consultations with people across our organization and our own data so far suggests that they do. As one of our analyses found, Intermountain teams that implemented more ideas tended to have higher engagement scores than those that implemented fewer ideas. Observing the sheer number of ideas we generate systemwide each year, Pollard surmises that "not only are our caregivers excited about improving the work, but they want to improve the work for their patients, they see the benefit of coming together as teams and rooting out the waste in their processes, and solving it themselves instead of someone else coming in and telling them exactly how to solve their problems."[16]

Empowering frontline teams to improve how they work ties back to the cultural change described earlier, as it fosters greater openness to bigger changes organizations might be attempting. When Frans van Houten, CEO of the Dutch multinational Philips since 2011, set about to turn around the ailing company, he realized that he had to invest in improvement as part of the company's shift from a lumbering conglomerate to a more customer-focused provider of comprehensive healthcare solutions.[17] Philips had a long tradition of innovation, but it lacked the discipline to actually execute in ways that wowed customers. Implementation of continuous improvement across the organization would allow Philips to "be very disciplined in perfecting execution, as opposed to inventing the next thing."[18]

Critically, continuous improvement would also allow Philips to rally its workforce behind the company's transformation. As van Houten notes, leaders often struggle to galvanize employees behind big changes, with many preferring to stand by passively rather than help push change along. They become "tourists" who are along for the ride or even "prisoners" who are dragged against their will, not active players in the company's future success.

Continuous improvement would allow frontline employees to play an important and active role in pushing Philips forward. With a structured way of working that included daily tracking of performance, problem solving, root-cause analysis, and empowerment to make improvements, members of the rank and file could "actually become a contributor to the overall journey" of the company in line with its larger purpose. "You suddenly start unlocking thousands of people to become part of a journey of improvement and change, as opposed to people standing by and saying, 'Well, he's changing the company, and I hate it.'"

Philips trained more than 25,000 members of its 80,000-strong workforce in continuous improvement methods, pulling them out of their ordinary jobs for a week or two at a time. The point was to "get the transformation deep down into the rank and file of the organization to get people involved." The training itself helped turn employees into advocates for change, as it gave leaders an opportunity to describe and explain the transformation. In van Houten's opinion, this extensive effort that unfolded during a two- to three-year period made all the difference in rallying the organization behind the transformation. Had he and his team not mobilized the front line, van Houten doubts whether the transformation would have succeeded to the extent it has—Philips is now one of the world's foremost medical technology firms.[19] The company has become an organization of players, and it shows.

Similarly, improvement enables us to move aggressively toward our new models of value-based care and population health. In general, the ongoing process of adopting new best practices from other parts of the organization instills openness in teams. It leaves them, in Dr. Pollard's words, "always on the lookout for the next best thing that's coming along that's going to help us."[20] Our improvement efforts also facilitate numerous operational changes required to keep people well rather than just take care of them when they're sick.

To take but one example, we know that we can keep elderly patients out of the hospital if we follow up with them on the phone within a week after discharging them, asking them questions about how they're feeling, whether they've filled their prescriptions, and so on. Not long ago, we discovered that we weren't doing a good job of this. Although we were doing fairly well at preventing patients from having to return to the hospital, even here there was room for improvement. We promptly identified the operational snags, created a metric to track this behavior, and worked to implement changes—all because we have a series of structures and tools in place to improve how we work.

We now are much better at following up with these patients. As a result, fewer of them wind up back in the hospital again. It's a small bit of progress, but it pushes us that much further along toward our new, disruptive business model.

THE ANTIDOTE TO ENTROPY

In 2017, as teams at Intermountain were beginning to focus on improving how they work, our frontline huddles turned up some problems with our CT scanners. Clinical teams were finding that their patients had to wait way too long to receive CT scans. Imaging teams at multiple hospitals found that their machines were down for long periods of time due to a lack of replacement parts.

In many organizations, problems uncovered by local teams might go unaddressed because senior leaders never hear about them, or because no mechanism exists for ensuring that leaders can spot problems that recur across teams. At Intermountain we struggled with this. Although many frontline teams performed regular huddles, these weren't connected in any rigorous way. All too often, information about problems stayed with local teams.

As we spread improvement efforts across our system, we didn't limit huddles to frontline teams. We created a system of *tiered, synchronized* huddles that ensured that information flowed up and down the system with great speed. Thanks to this system, senior leaders quickly learned about the recurring problems with our CT scanners and were able to investigate. Looking into the root cause of these issues, it appeared that we were having a systemic problem with a large imaging vendor. Because this vendor's network of warehouses was located primarily in Europe, we had to wait a week or longer for replacement parts.

Once we grasped the problem, we raised it with the vendor, who didn't even know we had been experiencing issues. Since we were a large customer, this vendor agreed to work with us to change their network of shipping and warehouses so that we could get replacement parts more quickly. In fairly short order, our imaging equipment was staying up and serving patients better, and other US-based health systems working with this vendor saw similar gains. As a bonus, we developed a closer relationship with this vendor because we had a chance to work through the problem together.

Yet another way that focusing on improving how we work can unleash workforces is by allowing for greater alignment across an organization. Many organizations are highly fragmented. Even when they aren't formally siloed, as we used to be, information doesn't flow up and down the chain of command. Problems remain buried. Best practices don't spread. Leaders struggle to communicate strategies. Local teams fail to execute them well. Galvanizing people across an organization to improve how they work can solve this lack of coordination. It can help organizations drive progress by ensuring that everyone is pulling together in the same direction.

Our system of tiered, synchronized huddles has allowed for much greater alignment across Intermountain. The huddles work like this: Every morning, all those frontline meetings I told you about take place at 8:45 a.m. If a local team can resolve a problem on its own by making a process change, great. Otherwise, the local team escalates the issue, and it is reported at a series of 9 a.m. huddles of leaders one level up in the organization. If leaders at this level can resolve the problem, great. Otherwise, they escalate it up another level. This process continues all the way up the organization.

All told, we hold about 3,100 daily huddles across seven managerial levels. By 10:15 a.m. each morning, when my team huddles, we're in a position to consider problems that might have arisen with the front line and have escalated up the chain of command over the past hour and a quarter. If a significant problem has arisen and leaders at every level can't address it, we hear about it. And if the same problem has emerged in multiple places across Intermountain, we hear about that, too. Meanwhile, information flows back down—teams at the lower tiers learn about how the organization has handled previous issues that have been escalated and the results of any actions taken.

When our huddles uncover important safety issues, my senior leadership team can quickly identify them as systemwide problems and alert caregivers across the organization. We can keep a closer eye on operations, understanding when we have systemwide shortages of drugs, for instance, or when caregivers require training on a new piece of equipment. Since our local huddles report key metrics relative to safety, we get real-time updates on our safety performance across Intermountain. We can monitor business performance—for instance, whether we're meeting our goal of keeping our clinics open longer or creating more appointment slots for patients.[21]

We use our improvement efforts and system of huddles to deploy strategies across our large and expanding network of facilities. And they also enable us to adapt rapidly to unforeseen disruptions as they arise. Consider our response to Covid. When the pandemic erupted, our system of huddles allowed us to react to a fluid situation on the ground and rapidly make a whole slew of operational changes. These huddles morphed seamlessly into Covid-oriented huddles, handling daily operational tasks like establishing testing sites, monitoring our supplies of personal protective equipment, identifying and addressing future drug shortages, monitoring bed capacity across our facilities, and much more. As the pandemic wore on, frontline caregivers surfaced problems and iterated to solve them, tracking their performance and escalating the problems when necessary so that leaders could devise broader, systemwide solutions.

I can't emphasize enough how important these structured improvement efforts were (and still are) for us in adapting to Covid. If we had not been doing this work for several years already, our efforts would have been well meaning but ultimately uncoordinated and ineffectual. Each individual facility at Intermountain would have been desperately trying to manage the volume of Covid patients. One Intermountain gave us the organizational structure to operate in a synchronized way, and our huddles and improvement methods gave us a common culture and process for taking swift action in a unified way.

The second law of thermodynamics holds that systems tend toward entropy or disorder. That's true of organizations, too. Leave them to their own devices, and they will devolve into chaos. Convening an entire organization to improve how teams work is an antidote to entropy. It allows leaders to keep a better handle on operations, and it keeps teams aligned around common goals. The pandemic, that great sower of entropy, posed an enormous challenge, but we had a way of pushing back against the chaos and maintaining order.

MAKE IT PERSONAL—AND KEEP IT REAL

During the early 2000s, when I served as a frontline physician and later chairman of the Pediatric Intensive Care Unit at Cleveland Clinic Children's Hospital, I noticed that the external vendors we were using to transport critically ill children to our facility were underperforming. Because these vendors didn't know how to care for tiny newborns with congenital heart disease, they couldn't begin life-saving interventions en route. When an infant or child is experiencing a cardiac crisis, every minute counts. Children would arrive at our unit much sicker than they had to be, and as a result, they weren't doing very well.

I felt we needed to do better for these patients, so I took it upon myself to fix the problem. Working with the administrator of our children's hospital, I created a business plan for bringing the transportation of critically ill babies in-house. When a newborn needed specialized care from us, our own specialists would fly or drive over, pick up the patient, and bring them to us, providing them with the lifesaving care they desperately needed on the way.

I wound up presenting this plan to Dr. Floyd Loop, then-CEO of Cleveland Clinic, and his executive team. It was an experience I'll never forget. Dr. Loop had a huge stack of papers in front of him on the table, and as I made my pitch, he proceeded to read papers, sign them, and shuffle them around. I started to wonder if he was paying any attention, but it turned out that he was. When I finished, he looked up at me and muttered, "Why the f*** haven't you done this before?" That was it—the only words Dr. Loop ever said to me.

"Well, sir," I said, "I'll take that as a yes. I'll start working on it straight away." I did, and within a year, our pediatric critical care transport service was a big success, improving quality and helping more babies survive. At the Clinic's request, I created an in-house critical care transport service for adults, a much larger service that included international transport via jet. This business also succeeded and continues to operate today, transporting some 4,500 patients every year under the mantra, "No patient too sick, no patient too far."[22]

Little did I know that this initiative would come to carry deep personal meaning for me. It was this very service that picked up my son Alex in Germany following his devastating brain injury and brought him home to the United States for treatment.

There is no great secret to teams and organizations—or individuals, for that matter—who actually make change happen rather than simply talking about it. We have to *work* at making change, questioning the status quo and pushing hard every day to improve on it. We all have it in us to make change and improve. At Intermountain, we just wanted to create a way that we could all learn from one another and grow as teams each and every day.

By establishing improvement as an organizational imperative and providing teams with the tools and support they need to speak up about problems, implement solutions, and track progress, leaders lay the groundwork for a true culture of improvement to blossom. By empowering frontline personnel to speak up and make decisions, leaders unleash the genius of their people. And by giving everyone across the organization a common language and practices they can use to drive change, leaders align and unify the organization, enabling it to become a powerhouse of change.

You'll notice that I haven't said much about the specific tools we at Intermountain use to structure team discussion in our huddles. That's because in my view the specific improvement methods you use don't matter that much. What's most important is simply that teams have *some* kind of structure in place that focuses them on iterating over time to improve performance. Our system incorporates a variety of methods, including lean, Six Sigma, Total Productive Maintenance, and the Theory of Constraints (let's face it, the naming of these methods could use some improvement, too). I encourage you to explore these and other approaches, crafting an improvement process that works best for your organization.

Don't feel you must have everything figured out before you start. It's better, I find, to begin somewhere, notch some early wins, and proceed from there. Choose a single project that's important to the organization and easy to understand, and work on that. At Intermountain, our huddle process and the commitment of our leadership team to listen to what flowed out of it every single day became the foundation upon which our broader improvement efforts took shape. At Cleveland Clinic, our improvement efforts grew out of a specific initiative I started to optimize how we transferred patients into and out of our facilities.

Personal engagement makes all the difference, too. I first came to understand this at Cleveland Clinic while launching our Abu Dhabi operations. We held daily huddles to organize our work, and I saw how meaningful it was that I made a point of showing up. People understood that improving what we did and aligning ourselves around execution were important priorities of mine. And they took the work seriously.

As improvement efforts progress and bear fruit, it's also important that leaders and our organization retain the purity of intention that hopefully led us to undertake the work in the first place. It can be flattering when, after a period of time, the outside world starts to notice the amazing results we're generating. Industry awards and the like are great. But if we allow improvement to become a vanity project, we'll veer off track. Tune out this noise and allow the organization's animating purpose to continue to power your improvement efforts and your own personal commitment to them.

It might sound corny, but there's a soulfulness that drives improvement at Intermountain. We care deeply about our patients and really do want to provide them with exceptional care. That's why we show up at work each day. And it's why we work each day to get just a little bit better. "In the end," Dr. Pollard says, "It's all about making care better for patients. What's right for the patient? How do we get to that? That's what this is about. We're not going to stand still and pat ourselves on the back and say, 'Intermountain provides the best quality care in the nation.' If there's a single sign that we don't, there's always room for improvement."[23]

My wish for you is that you never stop striving to do better in your own work, and that you instill this mentality of continuous improvement in your organization. Big changes can and sometimes do happen all at once. But most of the time, they happen little by little, day by day, huddle by huddle. Empower your people to drive hard and improve. Help them discover the joy and satisfaction that comes with the ongoing pursuit of mastery. Power your organization forward by tapping its most valuable resource—the genius and energy of employees themselves.

QUESTIONS FOR REFLECTION

1. Do you have systems in place that allow people in your organization to focus on improving what they do? If so, how well are they working? Is improvement deeply embedded in everyday work?

2. What are some of the biggest improvement stories to emerge from your organization in recent years? What cultural elements helped to contribute to those victories?

3. Do honest and productive conversations about improvement opportunities take place across your organization?

4. Are people in your organization active participants in change, or are they mere tourists watching from the sidelines?

5. Are you harnessing the genius of your frontline employees as effectively as you might?

6. How well does information currently flow up and down your organization? Might a standard system for improving work help to improve alignment?

7. If you're currently leading an improvement initiative, what's driving you? Are you becoming distracted by third-party accolades, or are you staying focused on what *really* matters— fulfilling your organization's core mission?

6

ASK "WHAT IF?"

Don't wait for others in your industry
to reimagine how you deliver value.
Fire up your imagination and do it yourself.

In 2020, as Ghana was preparing to hold a presidential election, polling officials in one region faced a difficult situation. With the pandemic raging, personnel manning the polls lacked the masks and protective equipment they needed to stay safe. The polls were scheduled to open in just 48 hours. There was no way that officials could distribute the supplies that quickly by truck to dozens of sites.

Fortunately, the Ghanaian government could turn to a different, nontraditional option: distributing the supplies by autonomous drone. Within those 48 hours, drones had flown over 18,000 face masks and other equipment to 29 sites, making 160 different flights. The polling stations opened on time, with all personnel having the equipment to stay safe.[1]

Ghana's ability to transport medical equipment so quickly owes to the imagination and drive of a brilliant young entrepreneur named Keller Cliffton Rinaudo. During the early 2010s, Keller became fascinated with robotics and automation technology, especially their potential to revolutionize global logistics. Rather than using big, expensive, gas-guzzling trucks to move goods around, he imagined that societies might one day rely on an automated network of battery-operated drones to make deliveries. The result could be "game-changing for humanity," he says, allowing us to move goods far more cheaply and efficiently and with far less environmental impact.[2]

Between 2013 and 2015, Keller and several cofounders of the startup Zipline set about designing such an automated drone network. To maximize their humanitarian impact, they focused at first on the logistical challenge of delivering healthcare products. If you're lucky enough to live in a wealthy part of the world, you can physically access the medications, devices, and other healthcare-related materials you need (affording them is another matter). But due to a wide variety of factors, the largest logistics companies only do a good job serving the wealthier people in developed countries. This inequality amounts to a humanitarian disaster: each year, millions of kids around the world die because they can't access the basic medical products they need.

Consulting with governments in East Africa, Keller and his team convinced Rwanda to allow Zipline to transport donated blood—a vital medical product often scarce in local areas—via drone. Zipline launched its service in 2016 on a limited basis, becoming the world's first medical drone company.

As Keller discovered, he and his team had grossly underestimated the challenges of operating a distribution network for a complicated and perishable product like blood. There were many kinds of blood products, and they had to be stored under different conditions. These products also had different shelf lives. For nine months, the team pulled all-nighters, desperately iterating to get the service working reliably. The plan had been to ferry blood to 21 hospitals around the country, but the team focused at first on getting it reliably to just a single hospital. "The government was very patient with us," Keller says. "What we were doing was totally unprecedented. No one had ever heard of this idea of using autonomous vehicles to deliver healthcare products. And then, one day, it started working."

Rwanda had taken a huge bet on a promising technology as well as on Keller's team of "10 nerdy twenty-somethings." Good thing: today, Rwanda has the world's largest system of commercial autonomous vehicles and is the first country to put each of its citizens within a 15-minute delivery of any essential medical product. Zipline has dramatically expanded its footprint, serving 2,500 hospitals and health facilities across Rwanda, Ghana, and Nigeria.

Taking our lead from Rwanda, Intermountain is now making its own bet on Zipline. As the company enters the US market, we'll be one of the first major health systems to roll out delivery via automated drones. Initially, we'll deliver medications and other products, but in the years to come, we'll expand the service to cover a much broader range of products.[3] Our patients will be able to consult with their doctors virtually and have their medications transported to them in the time it takes their local pizza place to make a delivery—no need to visit a pharmacy. For seriously ill patients or those living in rural areas, this will be a game changer. For all patients, drone deliveries will make healthcare much more convenient, making it easier to stay healthier and out of hospitals.

Skeptics might think we're a little loopy to pursue drone deliveries of medications. We see it differently. Why *not* seek out promising new ways of delivering care in service to our mission? Shouldn't health systems like ours explore emerging technologies that might be relevant and applicable, including not just drones but also artificial intelligence, genomics, blockchain, 3D printing, the metaverse, and more, and take bold risks to pursue them? Shouldn't we be willing to reimagine *every-*

thing about our core offerings to improve quality, reduce cost, and render care more convenient and accessible?

We believe we should, and it's a proposition we'd extend to large, established companies everywhere. As good as our present offerings might be, we should still scour every facet of our businesses on an ongoing basis for opportunities to fundamentally redesign and improve what we do. When we come across potentially important technological innovations, we should test and spread them quickly, taking risks and learning from our mistakes. After all, the nimble start-ups seeking to eat our lunch aren't just innovating incrementally—they're making quantum leaps, reimagining existing businesses from top to bottom. We can do the same, but only if we're willing to fire up our creativity with a new sense of urgency. Every day, we must rededicate ourselves to asking that simple but pivotal question: *What if?*

CULTIVATE THE TWO Cs

In general, finding specific innovations that will revolutionize our offerings comes down to two Cs: curiosity and creativity. We must stay curious about the world around us, constantly scanning the horizon. And we must also think creatively about what we encounter and how we might use it to transform our offerings.

I first met Keller at the Sun Valley Conference, an annual, invitation-only gathering of iconic leaders in technology, media, and sports and one of the most amazing places on the planet to meet smart people. I felt highly privileged to be at the conference that year and excited to learn about new technologies and business concepts. I wasn't disappointed! Recognizing that we don't have a monopoly on great ideas, my team and I regularly scour the business media and hold conversations with innovators in our industry and beyond. We stay alert in our personal lives, looking for innovations in other areas that we might bring to healthcare. I especially seek out ideas from unrelated industries and distant geographies, urging others to do so as well. I once even sent a team to India to understand how to develop higher quality care at much lower cost.

We're not afraid to borrow ideas from others, and of course, to credit them generously. In 2021, we began offering an educational benefit to our 42,000 employees, partnering with a company called InStride to offer tuition support to attend college and obtain degrees. I didn't come up with that idea myself. Rather, I observed the education initiatives rolled out at companies like Starbucks and Walmart and realized that such programs could make sense at Intermountain, too. Likewise, as we were designing our MyHealth+ digital portal for patients (launched in July 2020), we talked to Delta Airlines about their consumer portal.[4] Admiring what they'd done, we wondered which elements of it we could bring to Intermountain.

My own habit of staying alert to trends and new ideas the world over is not new. I first awoke to digital's potential during the early 2010s while traveling in Africa. I'll never forget going for a run with Masai tribesmen wearing traditional garb and watching as they pulled out their phones to check Facebook. Later, when I became CEO, I conducted a formal study of megatrends and industries being transformed by technologies, seeking to understand how technologies, including digital, might contribute to healthcare's future.

I also came to envision more specific applications of digital while noticing how companies I encountered in my personal life were enabling consumers to book haircuts or order products on their phones. Why, I thought, couldn't we create a platform that would allow our patients to proactively manage their own care, booking appointments, checking their symptoms, paying their bills, and so on? Doing so would help patients stay well, as it would empower them to better manage their own preventive care. That in turn would reduce the number of urgent care and emergency room visits, lowering costs for our system. Consulting closely with patients and caregivers, we've continued to add new functions to MyHealth+ (more on this later) to make care even easier to access.

I try to pay special attention to new startups in our space, especially those whose innovations might facilitate our move toward value-based care and population health. Early in my tenure as Intermountain's CEO, we spotted a couple of startups working to allow patients to access care in their own homes instead of in the hospital. That made enormous sense to me. Years ago, when I was Cleveland Clinic's chief medical operations officer, my team performed a study of patients admitted to the Clinic's excellent and very expensive main campus to see what percentage of them truly needed treatment there. Our stunning finding: less than 20 percent needed treatment on our campus, and we could have cared for the rest in less expensive settings that, in most cases, were located closer to patients' homes.

When you think of how much unnecessary expense the nation's healthcare system is taking on, it's unfathomable. Research also suggests that people like to heal at home, where they feel less anxiety and experience better outcomes.[5] And yet, most health systems don't aggressively embrace the idea of Hospital at Home. That's because they get paid based on how many people they get to come to the hospital. These outdated financial incentives simply don't serve patients well, but they still work for generating revenue for health systems. As a result, it's way too easy to make money doing the wrong thing.

What if you could make money doing the *right* thing? What if you realigned incentives to keep people well *and* allow the business to thrive? It turns out, you can. Our population health model pays us *more* if we keep patients well and care for them efficiently and appropriately when they're sick. Hospital at Home fits right in with that.

Patients achieve great outcomes because our hospital-based caregivers monitor them remotely and our specially trained nurses visit them at home. Meanwhile, it costs us much less to provide this kind of care, so our financial performance improves. The incentives work for everyone.

You might presume that only a few patients suffering from relatively minor ailments would be able to receive care at home. Not so. As of 2021, our Hospital at Home program was operating out of a dozen hospitals in Utah, serving patients suffering from ailments like congestive heart failure, pneumonia, infections, and cancer.[6] We're moving quickly to expand the program and keep even more people out of the hospital. Between December 29, 2019, and January 2, 2022, we saved close to 5,000 hospital days for patients by treating them at home. In this instance, we stayed alert to what small innovators in our industry were doing and ran with it ourselves.

I'm not suggesting that all powerful innovations originate outside a company's four walls. Our current pursuit of digital innovation builds on a foundation of innovation that my predecessors and their teams pursued for decades. And any number of specific innovations my team and I have pursued also predate me. We had been working on telemedicine offerings, for instance, since the early 2010s, developing programs in areas such as critical care or stroke care. My team and I consolidated and expanded these services, opening a virtual hospital called Connect Care Pro comprised of 35 programs and more than 500 caregivers.[7] Connect Care Pro provides telemedicine at our own network of hospitals and sells services to other hospitals as well, furthering our mission of expanding access to quality care, especially in underserved rural areas.

Another important innovation we're deploying called behavioral health integration also grew up within Intermountain. Imagine going to the doctor for a checkup, and in addition to having your blood pressure taken or your abdomen palpitated, you receive a screening for depression. Imagine as well that you interact with a primary care team of not just doctors and nurses but also a range of mental health providers. That doesn't usually happen—but it should.

We've been studying and experimenting with folding behavioral health into primary care since the early 2000s, led by a national expert in the field, Dr. Brenda Reiss-Brennan.[8] As our research has shown, we can keep people healthier by adopting this approach, reducing emergency room visits and hospital admissions. It's not hard to understand why: by attending to people's mental health needs, we can often prevent them from abusing drugs or alcohol, and we can empower them to take better care of themselves. It's an investment for our system to hire more behavioral health personnel and integrate them with primary care providers, but for every dollar we spend, we save over five dollars.[9]

We still have much more to do to fully integrate behavioral health and primary care. It's a challenge to hire enough social workers, psychologists, and psychiatrists, so we're also investigating how we might use digital tools to increase access for patients. We're pushing ahead because we see behavioral health as an important part of our ongoing efforts to make care better by keeping people well. In this case, we didn't have to scour the world asking, "What if?" Our own people were already doing it.

FORGE RADICAL COLLABORATIONS

Let's say you're an Intermountain patient, and you suffer from a significant health condition like diabetes or heart disease. Despite our use of digital technology, chances are still good that the vast majority of your care today will take place offline. The data we collect from our patients remains limited, and it doesn't flow freely between our caregivers and other companies that could provide you with important healthcare-related services. As a result, we aren't able to track your health very closely in real time and intervene proactively.

What if we could? One day soon, we might manage a wide range of specific illnesses on a daily basis through smartphone apps, using other digital devices to obtain health-related data that then become part of your medical record. Although many digital health applications exist, imagine if these apps were connected with one another and with any healthcare provider you might consult in a comprehensive way, allowing a team of caregivers to monitor your condition and to intervene quickly and proactively. Imagine, further, if advanced algorithms were analyzing your data, helping doctors spot developing problems and suggesting preemptive action. Our ability to keep you healthy and out of the hospital would improve dramatically, making healthcare much more affordable for society.

If you had diabetes, for instance, an app helping you manage your condition might automatically share data with your care team at Intermountain. When you come in for your annual checkup, your care team could review in detail your interactions related to that app for the preceding year. Algorithms looking at the data could alert your doctor to specific problems they might not have spotted, allowing them to adjust your care.

The algorithms might spot biomarkers suggesting a risk of a certain condition developing, prompting them to test you for it. Or they might notice changes in your behavior—for instance, that your diet has worsened in recent weeks. That might prompt a call from your healthcare team. If it turns out, say, that you've been depressed, your health team could send over a behavioral therapist to help you get out of your funk. Instead of your diabetes spiraling out of control or other health issues emerging, we'd be able to catch problems early and address them, keeping you well.

Such close, real-time attention to your wellness would represent a revolution in how we deliver healthcare. Bringing it to fruition isn't simply a matter of engineering a single digital innovation. Rather, we must put in place a whole *network* of devices, applications, algorithms, and flows of data paired with caregiver teams. This network would be enormously complex, incorporating numerous innovations. The technical challenges would be more than any one health system could surmount on its own.

As we've learned, truly big industry-shaking changes in offerings usually require powerful *collaborations*. We're working with two big players in the tech industry—Microsoft and the venture capital firm General Catalyst, an early investor in companies like Airbnb and Snap—to create a next-generation platform.[10] Our goal is to incorporate our existing MyHealth+ app into something much bigger: a true physical and digital health system. This system won't just revolutionize how Intermountain organizes and delivers care. It could do so for the entire industry.

Do you know how you can go to an app store and download thousands of apps onto your phone? Our platform will have something similar for healthcare systems. We want to create a new marketplace in which tech startups can create and market powerful apps to help health systems manage specific illnesses and run their own operations digitally. This platform will use common technical standards so that health systems everywhere can use them and so that data can flow between these applications. Right now, innovative startups can't create and market applications because health systems use different software platforms and data is fragmented. Consumers also can't easily move their data between health systems. By creating a common platform, we hope to unleash a torrent of digital innovation, revolutionize care, and make life much easier for consumers. Rather than having to design their own digital health systems from scratch, as they currently do, care providers like Intermountain will be able to build them quickly on a plug-and-play basis, choosing from among a huge library of applications.

This foundational platform we're building is immensely complicated—my description of it just scratches the surface. To pull it off, we need a merger of different kinds of expertise. Certainly, we must mobilize our own intimate knowledge of what it takes to care for patients. But we also need the technical ability to design and build platforms that General Catalyst and its suite of companies have. We need Microsoft's unrivaled ability to build software for large enterprises like ours. And we need the vision and expertise of hundreds or thousands of tech companies to design the specific digital applications for diseases like cancer, diabetes, and heart disease that health systems like ours can download and incorporate.

As managing partner of General Catalyst Hemant Taneja has created billions of dollars of value across industries like fintech, healthcare, and software. As he notes, it's not realistic to think that technology companies can come in and disrupt an industry as complex as healthcare. You need the participation of healthcare systems as well, not to mention another big player, pharmaceutical companies. A "radical collaboration between technology, healthcare, and pharma" must occur if we are to use digital to fundamentally reimagine healthcare. Further, he notes, "healthcare is too big for any one technology company. You need to embrace an *ecosystem* of companies that are focused on solving the various parts or components that go into transformative customer experiences."[11]

A company called Livongo Health, which Taneja cofounded with Glen Tullman, uses digital tools to empower people suffering from diabetes, high blood pressure, and other problems to manage their health. Another startup backed by General Catalyst, Plume, offers transgender people specialized healthcare, including gender-affirming hormone treatments, via an online portal.[12] Pointing to similar examples in women's health and elder care, Taneja says that healthcare's digital transformation will require a whole slew of companies "with teams that have empathy for the different stakeholders and segments of consumers, creating organized care on the Internet for them." In the years ahead, he believes that healthcare's wide-ranging digital transformation will lead to the creation of hundreds of billion-dollar companies partnering with traditional health systems like Intermountain.

Think of it this way: Major airlines don't build their own airplanes. They don't design and build their own airports. They don't build their own digital apps for their customers to use. They don't make their own meals to serve customers on board. They work with a range of partners to help them deliver their offerings. To revolutionize how we care for patients, we in healthcare are doing the same. Large, established companies everywhere can take a collaborative approach, seeking out and building exciting new partnerships in their industries and beyond.

A WORKFORCE OF INNOVATORS

During the early 2010s, when Intermountain oncologist Dr. Derrick Haslem first heard about our telemedicine initiatives, he was slow to get on board. Like many doctors, Haslem believed he could only deliver high quality care if he built a very close, in-person relationship with patients and caregivers. Treating patients entailed "lots of handholding and arms around shoulders and that sort of thing. I thought we'd never be able to replicate that through telemedicine."[13]

Haslem's perspective changed in 2014, when his uncle was diagnosed with incurable stomach cancer. This uncle lived in Haslem's hometown of Vernal, in Utah's rural northeastern corner. Since the care his uncle needed wasn't available in Vernal, his uncle had to make a three-hour drive to Provo to obtain it.

During the last six months of his life, his uncle drove round-trip to Provo an estimated 36 times. He would pack a bag because each time he left home he wasn't certain if his care would require him to stay overnight or if he'd feel well enough to drive back. All of this driving struck Haslem as both sad and tragic. "When someone is in the end stage of cancer," he says, "and that's what their life consists of, they're really missing out on the chance to be at home around the people they love, connecting with them."[14]

Moved by his uncle's struggles, Haslem decided to give tele-oncology a try. In 2015, he and his team began to set up tele-oncology services in local areas. One of the first towns in their footprint was Richfield, Utah, about two hours outside of Provo. Haslem remained skeptical, so when he went to pay an initial visit to the hospital in Richfield that would host videoconferences with physicians, he specified that his team would first see each patient in person to get to know them. To his surprise, not a single patient wanted to make that initial visit in person.

After the first few teleconferences with patients, Haslem realized that they were every bit as powerful as regular office visits. When these patients expressed gratitude that they could dash over to their local hospital and receive treatment for their disease, he was completely won over. "It just dawned on me that people do want the highest level of cancer care, but shortly after that, they want convenience, and they want to be around the people they know and trust. They want to be in their hometown. They want to run down to their local hospital and get their treatment. Then they want to go back to their lives, as normal as they can possibly be."

Since then, Haslem has played a key role in helping to establish telemedicine oncology clinics, not just within our system but at hospitals outside it as well. Telemedicine, he says, is "much more rewarding than you can possibly imagine. The patient satisfaction scores we get from these patients . . . is just off the charts. It's a real service that you don't really get to capture unless you try it."[15] Haslem is helping to spread the word about tele-oncology's benefits nationally and has become an evangelist for a more customer-centric approach to healthcare.[16] As he says, "We just have to get past this idea that it's bricks and mortar and everybody comes to us. We have the ability nowadays to really go out to people and improve that access and take care of them."[17]

When leaders focus on reimagining an organization's offerings, they unleash others within the workforce to effectuate change as well, even those who initially resist change. As we at Intermountain have learned, it's important not only to give growth opportunities to people like Dr. Haslem but to engage people throughout the organization around innovation.

An important way that we do that is through Intermountain Ventures, a separate company we founded in 2019 that is dedicated to finding and investing in startups that promise to benefit patients. As managing director Nickolas Mark notes, Intermountain Ventures is "the innovation portal for Intermountain Healthcare." "What if?" might as well be their motto.[18] Other health systems have venture groups, but because ours is a separate entity, it can move quickly to analyze and pursue prospective business ideas. Our main priorities, among others, include expanding value-based care, reducing total costs of care, providing world-class patient experiences, and achieving health equity objectives.[19]

In launching new ventures, we often start by engaging on a regular basis with our clinicians and business leaders across Intermountain, encouraging them to ask the same question: What if? What problems would *they* like to see solved for the benefit of patients? Our ventures team also engages externally to identify high quality innovation transforming health and wellness and maintain deep relationships with a range of experts in the technology space, including entrepreneurs, academics, nonprofits, investment banks, venture capital firms, and others. During these sourcing efforts, we explore exciting new innovations that we might potentially apply and learn from across Intermountain.

When we pilot new innovations, we rely on our clinicians to provide feedback. Dozens of physicians across our system help us evaluate and implement new innovations, serving as champions of these new technical solutions. As George Hamilton, former managing director of Intermountain Ventures, explains, "The most important component of the pilot work we do is having a clinical champion. We need someone inside the clinical organization to be excited enough about the opportunity to pound the table for it and represent it."[20]

The ability to test innovations in clinical settings is vital. Nickolas Mark notes that, "We have this active, living laboratory that allows us to engage and say, yes, this really works in a community-based care organization."[21] Our venture arm doesn't just help us by funding promising startups with the potential to transform healthcare. It also empowers people across Intermountain to stay alert to new ideas and helps us celebrate our collective success.

We also have an internal process in place that helps our clinicians and others within Intermountain to turn their own good ideas into workable businesses. This process—we call it our Foundry program—enables our people to gain financially from their innovations and for Intermountain to benefit as well. The Foundry allows employees to participate in a boot camp experience in which they refine their ideas. We then vet those ideas via a competition that resembles the television show *Shark Tank*.[22] Thanks to this process, a number of promising ventures have emerged from our frontline clinicians. Remember Dr. Brenda Reiss-Brennan, who championed the integration of behavioral health with primary care? Our ventures group started a new company called Alluceo that helps other health systems in our industry bring integration to life.[23]

THE VIRTUES OF "FAITH-BASED INVESTMENTS"

We've discussed several big innovations: telemedicine, deliveries by drone, revolutionary digital platforms. But what if you simply want to consult with your doctor without the usual hassle of having to arrive early to fill out bureaucratic forms?

Some months after introducing our MyHealth+ app, we added a new service to it that allows patients visiting practitioners at our internal medicine group to check in online prior to their visit. By entering health and insurance information digitally on their smartphones, customers can cut down the time it takes them to check in by 25 percent. If applicable, the app offers them a chance to consult with their doctor virtually, saving them a trip entirely. On our side, the system simplifies work for our administrative assistants, saving our teams time and money. In our initial test of the system, patients loved it, with 94 percent of them expressing satisfaction.[24]

Streamlining patient check-ins is just one of dozens of ways we're using MyHealth+ to improve how we deliver care to patients. Our patients can now pay their bills online, receive reminders to obtain lab tests and perform other preventive care, manage appointments for their kids, access their health records, check their symptoms to see what kind of care they might need, manage their prescriptions, and even estimate how much their healthcare will cost.[25] Collectively, these online tools make obtaining care much easier and more convenient. Our patients love it, as evidenced by the speed with which they've adopted MyHealth+. Within just six months, we counted over 350,000 registered users.

In bringing healthcare into the digital age, we're looking at every aspect of the patient experience, even the seemingly less significant ones. Staying ahead of disruption requires nothing less—a lesson that applies to leaders regardless of our industry. To outrun disruption and deliver for our stakeholders, we can't give ourselves and our organizations a pass on imagination and creativity. We must seek out novel solutions far and wide, as well as close to home. We must lead progress in our industries by building new ecosystems of partners. And we must take steps to engage our workforces in innovation as well.

Leaders at established firms sometimes balk at making these investments, fearing that updating their offerings will disrupt their existing business models. They worry that redesigned products and services might lower demand for their traditional, higher-cost products and services, causing drops in revenue. As we in healthcare know quite well, economic incentives can often discourage otherwise well-intentioned firms from innovating. In the short term, at least, these firms find that they'll generate more revenue offering products and services that cost customers more and please them less. Taking a short-term financial hit to implement an innovation for the sake of some uncertain future gains seems too risky.

We believe these are risks well worth taking. It's true that as a not-for-profit health system, Intermountain doesn't face the intense, quarterly market pressure that leaders of publicly traded firms feel. But we, too, must operate as a healthy, sustainable business over the long term. In this regard, our efforts in pursuit of the innovations I've described are, as our CFO Bert Zimmerli likes to say, "faith-based investments." He's not talking about religious faith. What he means is that we're making these investments because we know they're good for our patients, and we have faith that over time they'll be good for Intermountain, too.

Rather than pursuing innovation for its own sake, we should do it in ways that serve an organization's mission and are financially sustainable over the long term. Some might feel tempted to chase innovation simply because it's "cool," but we at Intermountain do it with a relentless focus on patients and their families. For each innovation, we ask hard questions about whether our investments will have an important impact on access, quality, cost, and so on. If we don't like the answers, we drop the innovation in question and move on.

In considering "What if?," leaders should also ask if potential innovations we're considering support a viable business model. Intermountain could undertake the innovations I've described because over the long term they'll help us run a healthy business *and* care for patients better, given our movement toward population health. Transferring patients out of the hospital more quickly and caring for them at home means that in the short term our hospitals lose revenues from procedures, tests, and other services. Implementing the MyHealth+ portal likewise keeps people healthier, cutting into revenues our physicians and hospitals might have earned. But since under population health, we increasingly earn revenues by keeping people well, innovations such as these will ultimately increase our systemwide revenues *and* are the right thing to do. We just need to sit tight and have faith.

In truth, we must do more than sit tight. Over the short term, we must also ensure that our organization is as well positioned as possible financially to make bets on the future. The process improvements and organizational shifts described earlier in this book are so important because they enable us to run our existing business as efficiently as possible, allowing for more financial stability and in turn more resources to invest in innovation. Stable businesses also allow us to weather short-term declines in revenue while we're waiting for innovations to bear fruit.

In most industries, leaders are aware of the big customer trends and technological developments. What's hard is actually engineering and delivering the winning customer offerings of tomorrow. We must constantly strive to redesign how we deliver value to make it more appealing to customers and more aligned with our ultimate mission. We must give it our full focus, attention, and passion, and we must devote sufficient resources. We must move quickly, testing ideas and spreading them as quickly as we can. We must even skip the pilot phase when we know with a fair degree of certainty that a proposed innovation is desirable, necessary, and practicable. We did without a formal pilot, for example, when we decided to reduce opioid prescriptions. We just knew that it was the right thing to do, and it would work, so we began phasing it in across the organization. We were not disappointed.

Our organizations and our stakeholders have so much to gain if we fire up our imaginations and relentlessly redesign what they do. Don't look fearfully at impending disruption and ask, "Why now?" Mustering both humility and curiosity, look around at new technologies and business ideas and ask, "What if?"

QUESTIONS FOR REFLECTION

1. How energetically are you and your teams pursuing innovation? Are you looking for opportunities across your business model to deliver value in new ways?

2. Are you constantly asking, "What if?" as you venture beyond your organization and your industry?

3. Do any innovative ideas exist inside your organization that you might develop more fully?

4. When it comes to innovation, do you feel your company has to do everything itself, or are you entertaining collaborations with outside players? How might you transform your industry by convening an ecosystem of partners?

5. Does your firm energetically solicit novel business ideas from your workforce? Do you approach your frontline teams as laboratories for testing and piloting?

6. How might you better position your organization financially to make long-term bets on promising innovations?

7. Are you moving fast enough to develop innovations?

7

MAKE "FRENEMIES"

Collaborate with competitors to solve industrywide problems.
Find excellent partners and forge relationships with them.

Some of us have radical, industry-shaking ideas when we're in the shower or just waking up. For Dan Liljenquist, an Intermountain executive who at the time was leading our population health initiatives, it happened while he was huffing and puffing on a treadmill. A former Utah state senator who had focused on Medicaid reform, Liljenquist was upset about the skyrocketing prices that hospital systems like ours and the patients we serve were paying for generic drugs. Companies were snapping up the FDA licenses to these lifesaving medications, establishing monopolies for themselves, jacking up prices to unconscionable heights, and causing rampant drug shortages.[1]

Bear in mind, society already paid for the development of these drugs when they were patent protected. Now those patents had expired, and society was *still* paying. Perhaps the most notorious instance of this practice occurred in 2015, when Turing Pharmaceuticals under disgraced "Pharma Bro" CEO Martin Shkreli bought Daraprim, a drug used to fight a terrible disease that strikes people with compromised immune systems, and promptly raised its price from $13.50 to $750 a pill.[2] It was simply outrageous, and it earned Shkreli a reputation as "the most hated man in America."[3]

How could bad actors like Shkreli hijack markets so effectively? I'll give you the Cliffs Notes version. For many generic drugs, just one or two producers claimed virtually all of the market. They slowed production to create supply shortages, forcing customers like Intermountain to pay higher prices. We had no choice—we needed those drugs, or our patients would die. It's no fun trying to buy what you need when someone has a monopoly.

If a new producer came in seeking to compete, these dominant producers could sustain their monopolies by lowering the price for a time so that everyone lost money. They'd made so much money already by pumping up the price of their drugs that they could afford to lose a little for a spell. The competitor would flee, and the established producers would then hike the price back up. Understanding these dynamics, few companies were willing to come in to challenge the primary producers of drugs like Daraprim.[4] These producers had the market all to themselves. They could continue to squeeze health systems all they wanted, to the detriment of patients and society.

You might argue that dysfunctional markets like these are ripe for government intervention. Whether or not that's true, a set of political realities made government action unlikely in this case. Thankfully, Liljenquist arrived at an entirely different answer. What if big health systems like ours came together to form our own generic drug company? This company could manufacture the lifesaving drugs we need and sell them at reasonable prices pegged to the cost of production, allowing us to circumvent market manipulators like Turing Pharmaceuticals. This generic drug company would act like your local power company does, keeping prices low for the public good.

By establishing this drug company as a nonprofit, we could ensure that it would never chase the dollar and instead further the public good in perpetuity.

Liljenquist's idea was brilliant, an utterly new way of dealing with corrupted markets. As he fleshed it out, he gained the support of some of healthcare's greatest minds, including the late Harvard professor Clayton Christensen and former secretary of health and human services Mike Leavitt. When Liljenquist came to me and requested a $10 million investment to help launch this generic drug company, I couldn't wait to write the check. Shortages of vital generic drugs had become a serious issue for us. At any given time, we were struggling to secure supplies of up to 200 different medications. These drugs should have been abundant, but our pharmacy personnel were spending a great deal of time chasing them down. Liljenquist's idea just seemed intuitively right. For an organization of our size, $10 million was a relatively small bet to make, especially on a venture like this that, if successful, could transform our industry.

In 2018, we announced the founding of a new generic drug company, Civica Rx, in conjunction with six other member health systems—including some of our notable competitors—and three major philanthropies.[5] This radical approach sent shock waves through our industry and beyond. Within a few weeks, some 2,000 news articles about it had appeared worldwide, and we received a whopping 12.4 billion media impressions.[6] People contacted us, saying that they couldn't afford their medication and asking if we'd produce it. "It was just amazing," Liljenquist says, "In fact, we had to stop talking to the press after three weeks because we had work to do."[7]

So far, Civica Rx's impact has been astonishing. We administered our first drug to patients in September 2019. We had hoped to bring 20 vital drugs to market within five years, but in the first three years we had already marketed more than 50. As of mid-2022, we had produced over 85 million doses of our drugs used by some 36 million patients, including 11 medications to treat Covid-19 patients. Fifty-five health systems had partnered with us, representing an astonishing one-third of all hospital beds in the United States. Thanks to Civica, member hospitals achieved a more reliable supply at an aggregate price point that was about 30 percent lower than previous levels.

In 2021, the federal government awarded us a $100 million grant to build a manufacturing facility in Virginia, allowing us to repatriate drug manufacturing, most of which had gone overseas.[8] That same year, we announced the formation of a sister company called CivicaScript, which will dramatically reduce the out-of-pocket drug costs for outpatient medications.[9] And in early 2022, Civica Rx announced plans to produce insulin, cutting prices by up to 90 percent. Let that sink in. This move will make an enormous difference for tens of millions of people in this country who have diabetes, many of whom are currently forced to ration insulin, a lifesaving medication, given its high cost. Civica Rx's lower price also will help change healthcare economics, singlehandedly saving America billions of dollars.

For many successful leaders, running a business is about taking on the competition and *winning*. But we can and must aim higher. We can aim for our industries and society at large to win, not just our organizations. Recognizing that so many challenges facing societies today require broad, collective action on the part of businesses, we can partner widely—including with competitors—to drive large-scale progress.

Collaboration with competitors is hardly novel. Companies in a number of industries have done it, and academics have published articles on the concept of "coopetition." The World Economic Forum has touted coopetition as a strategy for helping societies reach the United Nation's goals for sustainable development.[10] But as we've seen in healthcare and as is true in other industries, collaboration between competitors doesn't happen nearly as often or effectively as it might. A lack of imagination and foresight on the part of leaders often precludes it. Other times, leaders resist growing closer to those they've long regarded as their foes, either because of ego or because they fear sacrificing their business advantage.

The existential challenges facing humanity today should inspire all of us to venture beyond these traditional prejudices and make more "frenemies" among our competitors. As examples like Civica Rx suggest, we can succeed in the marketplace *and* partner with competitors to advance the greater good. Let's push coopetition more aggressively than we currently do, looking for opportunities to drive meaningful change together. Competition need not be a narrow, zero-sum game. It can become a more nuanced, productive relationship where enlightened self-interest and our common humanity intersect. If we learn to compete where we must and cooperate where we can, we'll do a whole lot of good while also catapulting our businesses to new heights.

YOUR BIGGEST COMPETITOR OF ALL

Companies can cooperate in innovative ways to help markets function better, but leaders can also drive smaller-scale progress in their industries by collaborating with competitors and others. When I was at Cleveland Clinic, I worried that trauma care in our local area wasn't nearly as good as it could be. A number of competing facilities were providing such care but in an uncoordinated way. We needed to share best practices better and collate data about trauma services regionally so that we could track trends and monitor for improvement.[11] During the late 2000s, I worked to set up a consortium of local hospitals called the Northern Ohio Trauma System (NOTS) with a mission of improving the quality of trauma care in our region, coordinating how we used our resources, and collaborating to educate caregivers.

The consortium brought together Cleveland Clinic and its direct competitors in trauma care. As I recall, our initial conversations were sometimes awkward. One health system that had built a solid helicopter transport program inappropriately asked us to do away with ours. I pushed back, noting that our transport program (which I helped found) was important to our patients, and that we couldn't make progress if our conversations amounted to an occasion to secure anticompetitive concessions from one another. To collaborate well, we had to abandon the zero-sum logic of traditional competition and instead focus on what we could all do to serve our common purpose—improving trauma care.

Cleveland Clinic did wind up downgrading one of its trauma programs that was obtaining suboptimal results—a lifesaving act of humility. It coordinated with other health systems to deliver the best possible care across our local area, especially in vulnerable, underserved areas. To date, NOTS members have adopted standard processes for delivering care, taken steps to improve quality, and "collectively worked to improve trauma patient outcomes."[12]

I saw another opportunity to affect change collaboratively a few years later while leading Cleveland Clinic Abu Dhabi. The United Arab Emirates, a country of about 9 million people, was struggling with public health issues such as obesity and diabetes. Given my orientation toward keeping people well instead of just treating them once they had become ill, I wondered if there might be a way to encourage the population to develop healthier habits around exercise. As an avid cyclist, I liked to ride my bike at Abu Dhabi's Formula 1 racing track on Tuesday evenings, when the track was open to cyclists. The roads in the area were dangerous, and this was a great opportunity to get a workout in.

It occurred to me: What if Cleveland Clinic Abu Dhabi bought hundreds of bikes and encouraged local residents to use them free of charge at the Formula 1 track and other venues? We wound up doing just that, creating a wellness brand called "Cycle for Health UAE."[13] The initiative took off, especially after Abu Dhabi's crown prince came out and rode one of our bikes. Today, cycling has become a popular sport in the country, contributing to better health. We couldn't have undertaken this initiative on our own—due to the state of the country's roads, we needed to partner with the Formula 1 venue. We also worked with DAMAN, the country's national health insurance company, to hold half-marathons, triathlons, and other events.

This initiative didn't involve our direct competitors per se, but a number of more recent efforts we've pursued at Intermountain have. In 2017, Intermountain funded a five-year, $25 million gift to support cancer research and clinical care at the Huntsman Cancer Institute, which is part of a local competitor, University of Utah Health. Part of the grant focused on helping adolescents and young adults diagnosed with cancer navigate some of the financial, career, and life challenges they face, a neglected aspect of their care.[14] We also established an initiative called the Utah Grand Challenges that sought to spur research collaboration between our two organizations by funding specific cancer-related projects.

In keeping with our population health model, we hoped this research would help us keep more residents of Utah cancer free and lead to better outcomes among those who did get sick. We also wanted our community and its leaders to see that we were working together to tackle the problem of cancer for the community's benefit. To date, projects pursued under the program have included studies on the early detection of melanoma skin cancer, the use of alternative medicine in cancer treatments, and the impact of genetic testing on cancer prevention.[15]

An important lesson of this collaboration is that we need not let entrenched habits of competition impede potentially valuable partnerships that might benefit our mission. The announcement of our collaboration with the Huntsman Center prompted some grumbling among our cancer doctors. Relations with their peers at the University of Utah hadn't always been warm and fuzzy, and some of our doctors quite understandably felt a degree of mistrust. These feelings subsided, though, as research projects got underway. Our clinical leaders were talking to their peers at the University of Utah on a regular basis and building stronger relationships. Members of the University of Utah's leadership team and I have also forged warm, productive relationships. We realize that we'll continue to compete strenuously in many areas, and that's appropriate. But in areas where we might be able to help one another for the benefit of the wider community, we'll happily do that, too.

This more nuanced relationship continued to deepen during the Covid-19 pandemic, paying great dividends to our local community. Intermountain's laboratories collaborated with those at the University of Utah to provide Covid testing.[16] Our two organizations worked together to establish clinical protocols and common patient visitation policies. When we saw spikes in Covid, we held Zoom calls with the University and other health organizations to coordinate our response.[17] We also partnered with the University and other organizations in our area to help address racial disparities that the pandemic revealed (Black people and Hispanics in our community experienced higher rates of Covid infection than other groups did).[18]

Building on our relationship with the University of Utah, we've found exciting new ways to enhance our commitment to population health. In 2021, Intermountain announced a $50 million investment in a partnership with the University to develop a first-of-its-kind program to train medical students in population health. Currently, medical students receive little training in how they might keep people healthy instead of just intervening once they become ill. Intermountain can't remedy that on its own; we don't have a medical school. But the University of Utah does. Together, we'll generate a new stream of talented doctors who are well prepared to practice under this model. Our community will benefit, because participants in the program commit to returning to work at Intermountain or other local healthcare organizations upon completing their education.[19]

None of these collaborations would have happened had we allowed our egos or our traditional notions of competition to get in the way. Setting aside our parochial perspectives, we found common ground in our commitment to better the community. This is not to say we don't continue to compete—we do. By putting clear, healthy boundaries on competition, we at Intermountain find that we can make even more progress in our pursuit of our mission.

My lifelong athletic pursuits have influenced how I see competitive relationships in business. Although I thrive on competition with others, I've learned over the years that my biggest competitor isn't another athlete. It's me. Today, when I show up for a triathlon, I can't control if a former Olympian will show up and beat the stuffing out of me. What I can do is push as intensely as I can to beat my own internal goals.

I like to think we've incorporated at least some of this ethic at Intermountain. To be sure, we compare ourselves to other health organizations as a way of gauging our performance and spotting opportunities for improvement. But ultimately, we aren't focused on "beating" the competition, winning prizes, or establishing ourselves as number one in some national ranking or another. It's our vision of serving as a model health system and our mission of helping people live the healthiest lives possible that counts. We're internally driven to deliver on it, so much so that we'll happily partner with others, including our competitors, to make progress.

TACKLING SOCIETY'S BIGGEST PROBLEMS

Partnering with competitors does good at the industry level, but just how much of a broader societal impact can it really have? As it turns out, quite a large one. Lately, some of the world's biggest companies have turned to coopetition to make significant progress on one of society's most entrenched and insidious problems, inequality and structural racism.

One of the visionary leaders who convened these companies, former IBM CEO Ginni Rometty, tells the story of a young Black man who worked for years at a Starbucks in one of IBM's locations.[20] Tony had been "kind of directionless" after high school, as he recalls, and didn't attend college.[21] Impressed by his work ethic, some IBM employees whom he served urged him to go back to school. Tony listened, taking technology-related classes at a community college and learning informally in his spare time with one of the employees.

An IBM employee who mentored Tony encouraged him to apply for a position in a newly created apprenticeship program at the company. Tony couldn't afford to take time off to learn full time, but he didn't need to: as an apprentice, he could generate income while gaining valuable training in coding and other skills. You've heard of blue-collar and white-collar employees. IBM's apprenticeship program was designed to produce nontraditional, "new-collar" employees so as to foster equity and render its workforce more inclusive.[22]

Tony isn't serving up lattes any longer. Today, he works full-time as a software engineer at IBM, a job with a starting salary in the $70,000 range. If you had told him at the outset that he could make such a significant career transition, he would have thought you were crazy. But with the support of others around him and IBM's apprenticeship program, he realized his dreams.

Prior to her retirement in 2020, Rometty spent a decade creating opportunities for people like Tony. For her, issues of inclusivity and equity are deeply personal. When she was 16, her father moved away, leaving her mother to raise four kids on her own. Her mother had nothing—no college degree, career, or money—and Rometty's family had to depend on government assistance to get by. And yet, in Rometty's words, her mother was "determined that this would not be the end of the story."[23] She attended community college at night and worked toward an associate's degree, eventually finding work running the administration of a sleep clinic at a large hospital.

Aided by neighbors and others in the local community, Rometty and her siblings all went on to earn college degrees and build successful careers. Rometty credits her mother's resilience and hard work, an example that shapes her own deepest values. "It taught me that your zip code shouldn't determine your capabilities. Not in this country at least."[24] So long as people are willing to learn and work hard, it's important that they have an ability to succeed, regardless of their background. And it's up to companies to ensure that access to the American dream remains intact.

Although IBM's workforce has traditionally been highly educated, Rometty pushed hard to hire people without the usual academic credentials, hoping to advance equity and inclusion. This shift made sense from a business standpoint. During the 2010s, as IBM transformed into a cloud and data–focused company, the company struggled to find enough talent with in-demand technological skills. By finding ways for the company to seek out and hire more people without traditional degrees, Rometty could help to remedy its looming skills deficit.

But Rometty's vision and efforts were hardly limited to IBM. Seeing the lack of access to higher education and, in turn, family-sustaining jobs as a systemic problem, she sought to launch "a movement in the country of a skills-first hiring approach, meaning please hire people for skills before you look at just their degree."[25] Economic opportunities, she notes, serve as a great equalizer within society. If IBM banded together with many other, like-minded organizations, including some of its own competitors, it could advance the cause of social justice, creating new pathways toward the American dream for millions of underserved people.

In 2011, IBM launched Pathways in Technology Early College High Schools (P-TECH), an educational model designed to facilitate the entry of underserved young people into STEM-related jobs. P-TECH partnered companies with local schools and community colleges, allowing young people to gain work experience as they attended high school. Upon graduation, they received an associate's degree in a STEM-related field and also had potential job opportunities open to them at their school's corporate partners. They could launch careers in technology without the expense of a four-year college degree. As of this writing, some 600 companies in 28 countries have joined this initiative, giving thousands of kids from underserved backgrounds a route into the middle class.[26]

More recently, in the wake of the murder of George Floyd, IBM joined with 37 other large companies, including Intermountain as well as direct competitors such as HP and Accenture, in a coalition called OneTen dedicated to helping Black people find pathways into the middle class. Recognizing that almost all professional jobs in corporate America require a college degree and that about 75 percent of Black Americans lack one, OneTen companies resolved to review job requirements, revamp hiring practices, and implement retraining programs, creating new opportunities for individuals lacking these degrees.[27] In particular, the coalition sought "to hire, promote, and advance one million Black individuals who do not have a four-year degree into family-sustaining careers over the next 10 years."[28]

Rometty regards it as both necessary and natural for companies like IBM to collaborate with its competitors. Individual companies could act on their own, but the effects would only be incremental. For a big systemic problem like racism, meaningful progress can come only if a coalition of companies takes concerted action. With OneTen, coalition members were collaborating to address the numerous practical barriers that prevent underserved people from getting professional jobs, and they were sharing what worked with one another. These companies could collaborate well because they all shared an economic interest in seeing that progress take place. "I believe everyone feels the same way," Rometty says, "that if we don't address this issue of social inequality, that it is bad for everyone's business."

You might presume you'd struggle to convince your competitors to participate in big public-spirited endeavors like OneTen or Civica Rx, but that's not necessarily the case. When we set up Civica Rx, some health systems that we approached declined to participate, fearing that Civica Rx would benefit some of their competitors or feeling uncertain about getting behind an idea they hadn't generated. But as Liljenquist relates, it was much easier to get competing health systems to participate than he'd anticipated. These players knew they had problems with generic drugs, but they had presumed there was nothing they could do—they were waiting for the government to step in and fix it. Once Liljenquist explained the logic of Civica Rx's model, it made sense to them. Together, they could take this problem into their own hands and do something about it.

One of Liljenquist's first conversations was with HCA Healthcare, a fierce competitor of ours in Utah. After he explained the concept of Civica Rx to Bill Rutherford, HCA's CFO, and walked him through the details, Rutherford was quick to express interest. HCA subsequently joined as a founding member, helping us refine Civica Rx's business model, while Rutherford joined Civica Rx's board. "The real innovation of Civica," Liljenquist says, "is not making drugs. It's creating a mechanism of collective cooperation that health systems felt they could buy into."

The Civica Rx model actually affords many potential applications—it isn't just about generic drugs. Remember the new platform I described in Chapter 6 that we're developing to boost digital innovation across the healthcare industry? The vehicle for it is Graphite Health, a new venture we launched in partnership with two other healthcare systems.[29] Organized as a nonprofit, Graphite aims to create a new platform that will standardize healthcare data and allow it to flow more readily between healthcare systems and other partners. Graphite Health will set up this platform in ways that serve the public interest, adopting a "digital Hippocratic Oath" that protects patients' privacy, gives them control over their data, and eschews the commercialization of data. Graphite Health will also foster innovation by hosting the app marketplace for healthcare systems described in Chapter 6.

Whereas Civica Rx sought to reform an existing market, Graphite Health will help to create an entirely new market for digital healthcare services, one that is designed from the outset to avoid the excesses and social ills visible in other technology markets. Once again, we're not waiting for government to do this work for us. As industry players with a public service–oriented mission, we're stepping up to organize the market in ways that will foster healthy competition that benefits patients and society. Graphite Health promises to dramatically accelerate the digitization of healthcare, in the process lowering the cost of care, increasing access, empowering patients, and giving healthcare systems like ours powerful tools to keep people well and out of the hospital.

I'd like to say that Graphite Health was our idea, but in fact the chief innovation officer at Presbyterian Healthcare Services, Dr. M. Ries Robinson, brought it to us. He'd been following our progress with Civica Rx and thought a similar model would help solve the problem of the fragmentation of data in healthcare. When he first told us about it, Dan Liljenquist thought it was a crazy idea. But after hearing Robinson out, he came away convinced that an entity like Graphite could make an even bigger impact on the industry than Civica Rx did. There's a lesson in this: the best ideas for fruitful collaborations won't always originate with you. It's important to stay humble and open-minded. Rather than always inviting competitors to come aboard your ship, so to speak, it's important to show a willingness to come aboard theirs as well. A good idea is a good idea—period.

It's easy to become fatalistic when confronted by big challenges. We presume that since these challenges are too big for any one organization to handle, we must rely on government to get the job done. That's a convenient line to take, as it absolves us leaders of responsibility. It's enough, we think, to focus on the narrow matter of our own organization's performance. But it isn't enough. While government in my view has important roles to play, we must take responsibility as well for tackling big problems. Thanks to Graphite Health's nonprofit structure, industry can organize the digitization of healthcare in ways that foster innovation while protecting the interests of patients and society. Think of what we might accomplish in other industries if we worked together in innovative ways to solve problems rather than took a fatalistic attitude. When competitors become "frenemies" rather than enemies, everyone really can benefit.

INVITE CUSTOMERS ON YOUR TEAM

Larry Gabriel is a cancer survivor, but he almost didn't make it. Since his diagnosis, he has undergone virtually every treatment known to medical science, including multiple surgeries, at some of the best healthcare centers in the world. None of them worked. His doctor told him that there was a 99 percent chance he would die within the year. On the verge of giving up hope, Gabriel underwent an evaluation at Intermountain's precision genomics group. Performing a genetic analysis of his tumor, doctors found it might be particularly susceptible to treatment with a specific chemotherapy drug (the group also offers patients personalized treatments designed to remedy specific genetic causes of disease). The medication Gabriel received knocked his cancer out entirely. Today, he is disease-free and enjoying life.[30]

In the future, we'll be able to offer many more lifesaving personalized treatments to patients like Gabriel not just because we have the very best medical experts on our team but because we have patients on our team as well—hundreds of thousands of them. In 2019, we launched HerediGene, a massive study designed to explore the complex connections between DNA and disease. Partnering with deCODE genetics, a global leader in population genomics based in Iceland, we're obtaining data from 500,000 people in our patient population in what is the world's biggest genomics study. Participants receive genetic counseling if our research turns up anything worrisome in their genetic makeup. Analysis of this vast database will not only revolutionize our understanding of many diseases and assist in the development of personalized treatments; it will also help us to prevent diseases by allowing us to identify previously unknown genetic, behavioral, and population risk factors in patients so that they and their doctors can take preemptive action.

Our efforts with HerediGene grew out of earlier work we did in the field of precision medicine. Mapping the DNA of cancer patients' tumors, we created tailored treatments that improved patient outcomes. We extended this work beyond oncology, mapping the genes of people with depression and anxiety and determining what drugs were most likely to help them. We also mapped the genes of premature babies in our neonatal ICUs and identified underlying genetic disorders. One of our doctors involved in this work, Dr. Lincoln Nadauld, joked with me and other leaders that perhaps we should map *everyone's* genomes to understand genetic predispositions to disease across an entire population.

As our push into population health deepened, we started taking this idea much more seriously. Traditionally, doctors haven't known much about patients' genetic predispositions—that is, until they wound up in the emergency room with a massive heart attack, stroke, or some other clinical event. By mapping patients' genes and understanding their underlying risk of particular diseases, we could take preventive actions, like providing extra cancer screenings or administering medications to lower cholesterol.

In late 2017, we approached deCODE genetics, a potential competitor in this space, about partnering with us on a genetic study of a large-scale population. It turned out that leaders at deCODE had noticed our efforts at precision medicine and were interested in a collaboration. It took almost a year, but we came to an agreement to launch HerediGene. In addition to the direct benefits participants gain by learning about their own genetic risks, the data we collect through a routine blood sample will allow us to discover new connections between specific genes and diseases.

Under Dr. Nadauld's leadership, HerediGene had enrolled 125,000 participants as of July 2022. We protect patients' privacy by anonymizing the genetic material we extract. We've already made our first important discovery, identifying a series of genes linked to vertigo or dizziness, one of the leading complaints of patients who come to our emergency rooms. Armed with this knowledge, we'll soon be able to warn vulnerable patients about vertigo symptoms and what to do if they occur. When patients do present with vertigo, we'll be able in many cases to avoid the costly medical workup that patients with dizziness go through to determine a cause. We'll know that their genetic makeup likely has caused them to experience these symptoms.[31]

We're also drawing on HerediGene to prevent disease and cut costs. We're finding that about 5 percent of participants in the study have genetic mutations that immediately impact their health. In the case of cancer, we can in many cases prevent the onset of serious disease by performing simple screenings and procedures to remove affected parts of the body. Not only are we saving our patients and their families untold pain and suffering; when you consider that annual chemotherapy regimens for cancer often run into the hundreds of thousands of dollars, we're cutting considerable cost from the system. We can then use these funds to improve our care or lower costs to patients and others who pay for healthcare. By alerting families to genetically based health risks, we're also enabling them to inform children and grandchildren about future risks they might face, giving them a head start on living a longer and healthier life.

This chapter has focused on engaging with "frenemies" to serve the public good, but as our experience with HerediGene suggests, we shouldn't neglect another important constituency: customers (in our case, patients). Many companies already work with customers to develop new opportunities and innovations—what some have termed "showcase projects."[32] Some companies partner with customers to deliver social benefits in line with the organization's mission. TOMS Shoes, for instance, gives away one-third of its profits to "grassroots good," which it defines as "deep partnerships with organizations and leaders addressing issues in a community."[33] We might consider that model a de facto partnership, customers and a company working together to do good.

Businesses can become far more creative in designing these collaborations, just as they can orient themselves more fully to engaging with competitors, suppliers, and other partners. Through HerediGene, we're inviting our patients to not only live healthier lives but to contribute in a small way to the advancement of human health generally. They get to be involved in something bigger than themselves. Many leaders might find that they can enlist customers in research that might yield benefits for the wider community. They also might be able to convene customers to cocreate solutions with them that enable progress in public health, sustainability, diversity and inclusion, combating inequality, and more.

Engaging with outside partners to have a social impact generally entails taking on a bit of risk. You're putting money on the line as well as your time and attention. As we've found, it's worth listening to people who approach you with new ideas, even if they sound crazy at first. Many of these ideas won't amount to much, but some will. When an idea does seem promising, go for it.

When I worked in the ICU, our mantra in caring for patients was "Do as little as possible, inspire confidence, remain calm. And if you have to intervene, go big or go home." A similar principle holds here. Be choosy about which ideas for collaboration you pursue, but when you select one, invest the financial resources and talent you need to succeed. When investing in Graphite, we moved some of our best IT talent over to this new venture. Notably, Ryan Smith, our chief information officer and one of the best in the country, became Graphite's chief operating officer. We believe in Graphite's ability to transform healthcare, so we're not hesitating. We're going big.

When collaborating on projects with social benefit, try to build strong, two-way partnerships. As we've found, that entails showing a bit of humility and soliciting expertise from outside our organization. With Civica Rx, philanthropists we consulted helped us design a governance model ensuring that the venture remained purely non-profit. Our competitor HCA Healthcare, a for-profit company, used its expertise in business planning to help us ensure that Civica Rx would be financially sustainable while still pursuing its mission. In these and other cases, Civica Rx allowed us to learn and build new expertise, and it allowed our collaborators to feel valued and to have more of a stake in the venture's success.

Perhaps the most important advice I can offer when it comes to engaging with frenemies and others is to stay sharply focused on social good. Think hard about how you might best mobilize your organization to solve real, tangible problems in the world. Stay away from superficial measures that might make you and your organization look good but that deliver little real impact. As ideas percolate, consider how you might partner with others in ways that will benefit your organization or at least not hurt it. Don't hesitate to reach out to competitors and suggest initiatives nobody has executed before. It can feel strange at first to have these conversations, and they don't always amount to anything. But when they do, it's exhilarating for everyone involved. And it makes a massive difference.

QUESTIONS FOR REFLECTION

1. You probably think about your competitors a lot. But are you collaborating with them to solve bigger social problems consistent with your mission?

2. Think about the time you spend contemplating your business and its strategic initiatives. How much time do you devote to pondering potential collaborations with frenemies large and small?

3. Are you oriented toward competition with others, or are you internally driven to compete primarily with yourself?

4. Think of your biggest competitor. What areas of common ground can you identify that might be ripe for collaboration in the public interest?

5. Would some in your organization resist coopetition? If so, how might you overcome that opposition?

6. If dysfunctions exist in your market, how might you collaborate with other players to solve them? If a monopoly situation exists, would it make sense to aggregate demand in the market, as we're doing with Civica Rx?

7. Are you taking a fatalistic approach, waiting for government to solve big problems? If so, how might you engineer real, enduring solutions?

8. How might you collaborate with customers in innovative ways for the public good?

8

WHAT IS GROWTH?
AND IS IT ALWAYS GOOD?

To unleash your organization, forge a growth strategy
that helps you become better, not just bigger.

Most administrative assistants don't go on to become CEO of Fortune 500 companies, but my trailblazing friend Beth Mooney did. After talking her way into a management training program in 1979, she began a meteoric rise in the banking industry, taking on leadership roles at a number of American financial institutions. In 2006, she joined Cleveland, Ohio–based KeyCorp, the country's fifteenth largest bank, and was tasked with overseeing the bank's 1,000 local branches.[1] She succeeded yet again, and in 2011 the institution named her its chairman and CEO, making her the first woman to lead a top 20 American bank.[2]

But Mooney was just getting started. KeyCorp and the banking industry were then still recovering from the Great Recession. Mooney's job was to stabilize KeyCorp and lay the foundation for future growth. She spent her first couple of years regaining the confidence of investors, building trust with regulators, and restoring its base of capital.[3] She also refocused KeyCorp's culture on its purpose and values. In her view, the financial crisis had taken hold because the banking industry had abandoned its social purpose, with leaders making risky and ultimately disastrous investments. "People lost sight of the fundamentals," Mooney says, which included a service orientation, building strong relationships with clients, and investing in ways that would enhance communities. KeyCorp had to go back to basics and pursue what Mooney described as "sound, profitable growth."

By the mid-2010s, as the bank began to acquire other firms, Mooney remained focused on achieving the *right kind* of growth. Corporate decisions to merge typically reflect hard-boiled strategic considerations. A firm might have a business line that an acquiring company wants, or resources that will allow an acquiring company to enhance its own offerings. It might have a set of loyal customers that an acquiring company can claim as its own. Mooney and her team considered such factors, but they also asked another set of questions: Is there a culture match? Does a firm they're thinking of acquiring do business in the elevated, mission-focused way to which KeyCorp aspired? If so, KeyCorp would consider doing a deal. If not, it would pass. Decisions to buy other companies had to contribute to "sound, profitable growth" just like decisions the firm might make to expand its existing businesses.

By 2020, the year of Mooney's retirement, KeyCorp had made a number of acquisitions, most notably its 2015 purchase of First Niagara, a Buffalo, New York–based bank with $39 billion in assets.[4] At the time, the deal was the largest acquisition in the banking industry since the Great Recession.[5] All told, KeyCorp's assets under management nearly doubled during Mooney's tenure, rising from $89 billion to $170 billion.[6] Shareholders did well: the bank's stock price nearly doubled during that period.[7] KeyCorp also made massive investments in the community, lending and investing more than $18 billion over a four-year period to increase economic opportunity among low- or middle-income customers (via small business loans, financing for affordable housing projects, and so on). In addition, the company committed $4 billion in financing for renewable energy projects. Had Mooney found a path to sound, profitable growth? I think so.

Almost every business wants to grow. But too many leaders focus on profits, not purpose; on financial success, not service. Most healthcare organizations that decide they want to enter a new market opt to simply buy an existing hospital, hire specialists to work in that hospital, compete head-to-head with other local hospitals, and try to get as many patients in their hospital beds as possible to drive revenue. That's great for the healthcare system, not so great for patients and communities. The more specialists exist in a local area, the more likely it is people will be referred for the services of these specialists. Beyond a point, the mere presence of specialists can mean that people receive expensive treatment they may not need. Further, you're only treating people once they're sick, not preventing them from getting sick in the first place.

Drawing inspiration from leaders like Mooney, we can take a more deliberate and creative approach. Keeping our missions foremost in our minds, we can craft deals that over the long term benefit patients, caregivers, communities, and society—what Harvard Business School's Michael Porter has termed "creating shared value."[8] To drive progress, we must aim for such "good growth" and reject out of hand opportunities that don't advance our organization's mission, even if they might prove financially lucrative. Expanding businesses at all costs might create financial opportunities for investors, but only good, mission-focused growth can galvanize organizations, transforming them and their people into powerful engines of progress.

A MIDDLE PATH LESS TRAVELED

In March 2019, I took my family to Colorado for a quick and much-needed ski getaway. I was on the top of the mountain preparing for a run when my phone started buzzing. I ignored it, but it buzzed again. And then again. Seeing that it was our chief strategy officer Dan Liljenquist, I picked up, a bit annoyed that he would call me on a rare day off. "Hey Marc," he said, "do we want to buy HealthCare Partners Nevada?"

All of a sudden, I wasn't annoyed anymore. I was thrilled. Healthcare Partners Nevada was a sizable group of 340 physicians and other caregivers that, although operating as part of a for-profit company, had adopted a population health model to keep people well. They offered exceptionally high-quality care and were especially adept at serving seniors, keeping them well through a network of nearly two dozen local clinics.[9] They were also a well-managed and financially solid organization, generating $1 billion in revenue each year, and their Las Vegas–area market was growing fast. About a year earlier, we had entered into negotiations to buy them, but the purchase price had been too high, so we reluctantly walked away.

For a variety of reasons, we now had a chance to buy them at a much more favorable price. In the weeks that followed, Dan and other members of our team worked hard to get a deal done quickly. They succeeded, and in June 2019 we announced our acquisition of HealthCare Partners Nevada.[10] Although members of my team were elated, others in our organization harbored their doubts. It wasn't that people didn't like or respect HealthCare Partners Nevada or that they second-guessed the specifics of our deal. It was that they were leery of the very idea of growing into new markets.

Early in its history, Intermountain had grown aggressively in accordance with its charge to be a model health system and its vision to provide better health services to more people. During the 1970s, 1980s, and 1990s, we expanded beyond our original hospital footprint in Utah, Idaho, and Wyoming, adding smaller health ventures in several other states. We entered into an entirely new line of business by starting a health insurance plan and also built out a medical group.

During the 2000s and 2010s, however, we turned away from growth outside of Utah and Idaho. Although some inside our organization did want to expand, others worried about losing what they proudly thought of as "the old Intermountain." They loved what we'd accomplished as an organization and didn't want to risk diluting our culture of quality and service by acquiring other organizations. Instead of growing, they thought it would be better to focus on continuing to improve our quality. Let's perfect our own ways of delivering care, they said. Then we can grow.

Such fears about growth had a certain logic to them. As some have noted, pursuing growth poses potential pitfalls. It can damage the brand of a business, leading to a coarsening of its culture and what formerly made a company successful.[11] I see it differently, and during my first few years at Intermountain, I challenged those with an antigrowth sentiment. If companies weren't striving to grow, I argued, they were decaying. I challenged people to name a single great organization in the history of business that shrunk its way to success. Moreover, it was becoming increasingly difficult for midsized players in our industry to compete. The largest health systems were growing more quickly than midsized ones, and as they continued to grow, their size would afford them all kinds of competitive advantages. Right now, we weren't feeling the impact of this dynamic, but we couldn't afford to wait around and let the big guys bully us with their size. We had to act preemptively by growing.

As we soon found, the threat of being pushed around by bigger players wasn't theoretical. In 2020, the second largest health insurance company in Utah, United Healthcare, called us with some bad news. Although we had been the exclusive provider to their customers in the state, they had just inked a national deal with a much bigger healthcare system with facilities in Utah and would no longer work exclusively with us. Clearly, we didn't have the pull we used to—bigger players with a larger geographic reach were overshadowing us. "This was a real wake-up call," our chief operating officer Rob Allen says. "It brought home the idea that our influence level will diminish if we don't grow."[12] It wasn't just a question of economic or geographic heft, but also policy influence. We have long enjoyed a seat at the table in national debates about healthcare. If we didn't continue to grow, we risked losing the ability to exercise meaningful industry influence.

Competitive considerations were one thing, but I also felt that we had a moral imperative to grow. If we really believed in our mission and in our emphasis on keeping people well—if we really thought that this approach allowed us to provide better quality and safety and more access at lower cost—didn't we have a duty to operate in more communities and spread our model to serve as many patients as possible? Likewise, if the largest healthcare systems were gobbling up the industry, didn't we have an obligation to ensure that *we* were the ones doing the gobbling rather than another company without our strong mission focus? Weren't we obliged to promote our ideas about healthcare and be a force on the national stage? We were already moving fast to transform healthcare. But if force equals mass times acceleration, it was high time Intermountain picked up some mass.

We had another reason to grow: to return more value to the community. As a nonprofit system dedicated to increasing access to healthcare, we pride ourselves on taking care of people regardless of their ability to pay. But doing that costs money, and strong growth would provide us with the financial resources we needed to subsidize it. Growth also would allow us to maintain our large, traditional hospitals even as we managed to keep more people well. As an example, if our existing patients would need 25 percent fewer heart procedures because we're keeping them healthier, our high-quality, hospital-based cardiac programs might soon become unsustainable. But expanding our telehealth services to more non-Intermountain hospitals would help us to build trusting relationships in those local communities by supporting local care for patients when possible. If people there did need to come to a major hospital for a heart procedure, they'd more likely come to us, offsetting the loss and keeping our cardiac programs economically viable.

We didn't want to try to grow at all costs, including in ways that didn't benefit patients and the wider community. That's the kind of growth that could get us in trouble. But staying at our present size wouldn't serve our mission either. What I was arguing for—and what I continue to champion today—was meaningful, mission-focused growth. We would expand in a way that allowed us to continue to improve safety, quality, patient experience, equity, access to care, and stewardship to the communities we serve. We would expand in a way that allowed us to enhance our commitment to population health and value-based care and that wasn't focused on simply boosting revenues.

Over time, our organization came to welcome growth, especially as we began acquiring companies and showing that we could succeed. Each acquisition or merger we've completed—there have been four major ones, with a number in the pipeline—has served our mission of helping people live the healthiest lives possible by enhancing our ability to deliver on population health.

Take Healthcare Partners Nevada. As I've suggested, most health systems buy or merge with other players to acquire hospitals or profitable services and then fill their beds and technologies with patients. The very presence of these facilities encourages people to seek more treatments once they get sick rather than stay well. It would have been easy for us to go to Las Vegas, build a hospital, and compete with existing players for patients. We'd make money, but we'd only be exacerbating the problems of a health system built around sick-care.

We took a different approach, making an acquisition that *wasn't* focused on brick-and-mortar assets. We saw an opportunity to join forces with a like-minded organization and expand the population of people we were keeping well. Although Healthcare Partners Nevada was a sizable business, they couldn't expand as quickly as they might have liked because they couldn't afford big investments in areas like digital innovation, marketing, and communications. Given our larger size, we could provide these resources and help them care for more patients in their market.

Although our integration of Healthcare Partners Nevada is ongoing, the deal so far has been a success. In 2020, our operations in Nevada grew 10 percent year over year, achieving the highest patient experience scores ever in the history of Healthcare Partners Nevada, with strong caregiver engagement.[13] Patients and the local community are benefiting because we're keeping people healthier by preventing illness rather than only treating them when they are sick, an approach that in turn lowers costs. We're also proving that we can keep people well and lower costs not just in places like Utah, which has a relatively healthy population overall, but in places like Nevada, which historically has had relatively poor health outcomes.

If you've been pondering whether and how to expand your organization, don't listen to those who say you must grow at any cost. Ignore, too, those who want to avoid growth altogether. Aim for a middle path. Growth doesn't just have to be a cold, calculated business strategy. It can also be a higher calling. You're not growing for its own sake, solely to line investors' pockets or for the ego boost of being number one in your industry. You're doing it to allow the maximum number of people to benefit from the good work your organization does.

SUBSTANCE, NOT JUST SIZE

Not long ago, a frail woman in her eighties—I'll call her Irene—came to one of our primary care facilities in Utah complaining of shortness of breath and feeling unwell. We asked if she wanted to go to the emergency room, and she said she preferred to come into the clinic because she was familiar with it and trusted the caregivers there. When our team examined her, they found her quite sick. The oxygen levels in her blood were low, and she was struggling to breathe. Other signs indicated that one of her preexisting conditions—congestive heart failure—had worsened.

If a patient in Irene's condition arrived at one of our emergency departments, we would have admitted her to the hospital and probably to the intensive care unit (ICU). But that's not what our clinic did. They provided oxygen to Irene and consulted with her cardiologist remotely via telemedicine. They gave her some medication to help her body release fluid from her system (a consequence of congestive heart failure), which helped her feel better. A couple of hours later, our clinic sent her home, but continued to monitor her closely. Irene recuperated and was able to resume her normal activities without ever being admitted to the hospital.

This episode might sound mundane, but it's actually quite remarkable. Caring for patients in ICUs costs a lot—we're talking thousands of dollars per day. Caring for Irene at a local clinic might cost only about 5 percent of that, representing a massive savings. And the outcome for patients is *better*. Because we were well prepared to manage the care of a patient like Irene, we could send her home knowing that we could quickly intervene if her condition deteriorated.

Meanwhile, Irene never had to subject herself to any of the risks associated with hospitals. For elderly people, a hospital stay can feel scary, even traumatic. Deprived of their usual setting and caregivers, they can become disoriented and delirious. They can fall and sustain serious injuries because they're staying in an unfamiliar room and don't know how to get to the bathroom. Irene avoided all of this because we had become much more adept at the complex challenge of caring for people like her outside of the hospital.

How had we gained that know-how? Part of it we'd developed on our own, thanks to our yearslong effort to advance population health, but we'd also learned a great deal from Healthcare Partners Nevada. When we entered Nevada, we didn't simply impose our own ways of operating on our new employees, assuming that we knew everything and our new workforce in Nevada would now do things the Intermountain way. After all, growth is more than simply getting bigger; it's about listening and evolving. While we certainly sought to integrate Healthcare Partners Nevada into our system by sharing our processes and practices, we also paid close attention to what they could teach us.

HealthCare Partners Nevada had extensive experience keeping elderly people well and out of the hospital. They used an innovative, team-based approach to care similar to one we were already deploying at some of our primary care facilities in Utah and were seeking to scale up. They had great processes in place for collaborating to keep track of patients' conditions and determine which patients to see proactively, *before* their health worsened. They also had systems in place for compensating healthcare providers in ways that incented them to keep people well and also worked economically.[14] These elements sound simple, but the details get hairy pretty quickly. Our new

Nevada colleagues taught us some of their best practices, which we could quickly spread to our existing facilities to provide better, less costly care to patients like Irene.

Proponents of growth often emphasize the benefits that come by virtue of an organization's size. If you serve more customers, you can often operate more efficiently and profitably, for instance, by using your volume to negotiate lower prices from your suppliers. That in turn might allow you to sell your products and services more inexpensively, so that you can attract still more customers.

But good growth doesn't benefit companies by simply making them bigger. It should help them become *better* at what they do, improving their ability to compete and to deliver on their broader social mission. By allowing our missions to lead us, and by staying true to them when seeking out and evaluating potential opportunities, we can sustain and deepen the cultures that make us special and position our organizations to thrive in tough, competitive environments. We can also provide investors with a fair return or, in our case, use margin to lower the cost of healthcare, improve the value we provide, and return value to the community.

Other deals we've made have allowed us to improve our ability to keep people well instead of just caring for them when they're sick. In 2021, we announced that we were purchasing Classic Air Medical, an air transport system aimed at serving rural communities across the Intermountain West. Classic Air had a long history of providing extremely safe transport for patients at low cost and a service footprint that overlapped with Life Flight, our existing air transport service, but that also allowed us to reach new areas of the Intermountain West. With Classic Air, we'd be able to integrate rural areas more fully into our network. As we treat patients remotely via telemedicine, we'd now have a greater ability to move them from local areas into our major hospitals, should they need more significant care.

But that's not the only reason Classic Air would be a boon for Intermountain. Because Life Flight specializes in moving extremely sick patients over long distances, it is a relatively high-cost service. We use expensive helicopters and staff them with sophisticated crews providing world-class care that patients with specific conditions require. Classic Air has made its mark by providing basic transport service at a much lower cost. They fly less expensive helicopters, staff their crews with paramedics as opposed to highly trained medical specialists, and source their operations with lower-cost vendors. They really understand how to work with local fire and police departments to provide great care. By acquiring Classic Air, we are learning how to run a bread-and-butter transport service, using some of that knowledge as appropriate to improve Life Flight and other services at Intermountain.

In addition to operational knowledge, acquisitions enhance our ability to deliver on population health and value-based care by improving our base of talent. Our acquisitions so far have added many thousands of people to our workforce, including talented senior leaders whom we're able to either keep in place or elevate to other roles within Intermountain. Our mission-based acquisitions also allow us to become a magnet for top talent and to retain up-and-coming talent in our own ranks. Marti Lolli, a seasoned, growth-oriented executive with an impressive track record of success, came onboard in 2021 as CEO of our SelectHealth insurance plan. She never would have come if we hadn't put ourselves on a growth trajectory. With smart, ambitious leaders like her in our ranks, we're much better positioned to move forward as an organization and deliver on our strategy.

Acquisitions can also improve our ability to deliver on our mission by opening up new business relations, sometimes in unexpected ways. Classic Air, for instance, has longstanding relationships with many rural hospitals in our service area. Our deal to acquire them already has created opportunities for collaboration and potential acquisitions. These hospitals trust Classic Air, and now more of them feel they can trust Intermountain.

Ultimately, good growth helps organizations better deliver on their missions by rendering them more adaptive. Expansion into new businesses and geographic territories gives companies the capacities and talent they need to evolve, in addition to more financial heft and industry influence. Bert Zimmerli, our chief financial officer, tells young people that they should redo their résumés every year or two and see how many new items they're adding. If they have hardly anything new to add, they should be worried—they're not keeping up with a changing world. Something similar holds true for organizations. The world is changing fast. Good growth helps organizations to change with it.

SEEK THE GREATEST GOOD

Do you remember all those stimulating conferences I go to that expose me to new opportunities for innovation? A gathering of CEOs I attended in 2018 unfortunately wasn't one of them. Although I'd arrived eager to engage, the conversation seemed fixed on a single topic: money. Leaders were going on and on, complaining about the tremendous financial challenges they faced and discussing how best to remedy them. They weren't exploring deeper questions related to their social purpose, such as how to serve patients better and at lower cost.

There was one exception: Lydia Jumonville, the CEO of SCL Health, a Catholic nonprofit healthcare company operating in Montana, Colorado, and Kansas. She spoke not about money but about her organization's commitment to providing charity care to the vulnerable. I hadn't met Jumonville before, but her passion and enthusiasm made a big impression. Indulging the rebel in me, I spoke up and chastised our group for how intellectually uninteresting and self-serving our conversation had been. I didn't win many friends that day, as you can imagine, but I felt that I said what needed to be said.

One friend I did make was Jumonville. After the session, we got to know each other and learned that we shared a board member in common and that our organizations were culturally quite similar. Jumonville suggested that our leadership teams meet to discuss possible areas of collaboration, so they did. Over the next couple of years, we partnered on a number of projects; in one case, Intermountain provided telemedicine services to an SCL Health hospital in Colorado. In early 2021, after a high-profile merger we were pursuing fell apart, Jumonville called us and asked if we might be interested in merging with them instead. After months of analysis and negotiation, we were quite interested. In December 2021, Intermountain and SCL Health formally announced our decision to merge, creating an integrated healthcare organization operating in seven Western states.

SCL Health was economically strong and had a great deal of cash on hand. Other companies had approached SCL Health, seeking to acquire or merge with them, but Jumonville and her team refused. They sensed that these other firms didn't care much about their culture or mission but were only after their cash. My team approached the deal from a much different lens, one that aligned well with SCL Health's mission. We liked that SCL Health was strong organizationally, delivering excellent clinical quality. We also liked that SCL Health's geographic area was complementary to but distinct from ours, so a merger would increase our footprint. But what mattered most to us was the opportunity we saw to expand the number of people we were keeping well.

Although SCL Health provided its services largely on a fee-for-service basis, its leaders wanted to move toward keeping people well through value-based care, with all the important social and economic benefits that would provide. Here, then, was the chance to take a healthcare company that was already great at providing high-quality, low-cost care to people who were sick and help them shift toward keeping people well. As in Nevada, we wanted to prove to the world that keeping people well really is a better way of doing healthcare. If we could succeed with a population health approach in states like Montana, Colorado, and Kansas, then we would further disprove all those naysayers who thought we could only focus on wellness for populations in Utah that were generally healthy.

In addition, merging with SCL Health, a company with $3 billion in annual revenues, would form the nation's eleventh biggest nonprofit health system, with combined revenues of about $14 billion. That kind of size would allow us to make even bigger bets in digital technology and other innovations, further enhancing our ability to deliver on our mission of keeping people well.

With the SCL Health deal, we didn't merely allow our mission to inspire us. We used it as a tool for systematically vetting and analyzing the deal. As we've found, using the mission as a filter—and being transparent about that with our board—is vital for ensuring that the deals we pursue truly represent good growth. As our chief strategy officer Dan Liljenquist puts it, "We committed to our board that the value focus lens is the number one filter we go through" in vetting potential mergers and acquisitions. "If we can't see how a deal leads to better health outcomes and better value for the communities we might enter, then we don't have a good case for going forward."[15]

We're hardly the only organization that employs this kind of discipline around mergers and acquisitions. We've seen that KeyCorp applied a mission orientation as a filter when vetting potential deals. Another firm that does this is the pharmaceuticals giant Amgen. As CEO Bob Bradway explains, everyone in the company "can draw a direct line" between their daily work and the company's basic mission of saving patients' lives and restoring them to health. He himself joined Amgen in hopes of "making a difference in the lives of individuals who were suffering from challenging conditions, diseases, and disorders." Such mindfulness of the mission applies to the company's merger and acquisition activities as well. "When we look at acquisitions, the first question we have to ask ourselves is, How does it align with our mission? How is it embodied in our strategy? How is it embraced in the boundaries of our strategy?"[16]

To illustrate the use of mission as a filter when analyzing acquisitions, Bradway cites the company's 2021 deal to buy the biotech company Five Prime Therapeutics for $1.9 billion.[17] Five Prime had developed an exciting, first-of-its-kind treatment to help fight gastric cancer, one of the deadliest forms of the disease globally. Few treatments exist to help patients with late-stage illness, and Five Prime's new therapy performed well in early clinical trials. As the only treatment of its kind, Five Prime's technology clearly supported Amgen's mission. From there, Bradway and his team assessed whether Amgen's own resources and capacities in manufacturing and marketing would allow it to bring the technology to market better than its current owners, benefitting shareholders as well as patients. Only when they determined that Amgen could be a better steward of that technology did they consider acquiring it.

Using the mission as a filter becomes especially powerful as firms proceed in their growth journeys. As we've found, becoming more active in mergers and acquisitions has led to an increased number of potential deals coming our way, more than we could possibly undertake. Focusing on our mission allows us to dismiss a large number of these opportunities out of hand. "We turn down at least four deals for every one we really look at," Dan Liljenquist says, "and for the remaining deals, it's a coin toss if we do them. We try to be very selective." We aim, of course, to fix healthcare everywhere, but we have a limited amount of attention and energy. If we can apply that energy carefully to notch some great early successes, we'll establish that keeping patients well really is a better way of delivering healthcare. Others will join us, and together we'll change the entire industry.

To be more precise about how our mission-oriented filter actually works, we know that in any new locale we might enter, we must put three key components in place to truly keep people well. We need primary care doctors and other providers, hospitals for patients to use when they get sick, and a way to get paid that rewards us for keeping people well. No deal we make will allow us to put all three of these elements in place in a given location all at once—we know that. What we're looking to understand is whether we can see a way to put all three of those elements in place *eventually*, starting with the deal at hand.

As Liljenquist says, "We're looking for a pathway to value, understanding that the beachhead in each place might be a little different. We're asking: How might we take full clinical and financial accountability for people's health?"[18] With our Nevada deal and our 2020 acquisition of Idaho-based Saltzer Health, we started with the primary care provider piece. With SCL Health, we moved on to hospitals and primary care. And with Classic Aviation, we added an ancillary service that allowed our existing system to penetrate more completely into rural geographies.

Although using mission as a filter facilitates the task of selection, landing on the right opportunities is never perfectly straightforward. With limited resources, we often must decide between multiple opportunities that would each serve our mission, although to varying degrees. "You have to try to think through where the greatest good is," Amgen's Bob Bradway says, "where we can create the biggest return from a societal public health standpoint for our investment." As Bradway notes, leaders also must balance the interests of various stakeholders, recognizing that some deals will benefit them unevenly or benefit some while hurting others. "We don't often find ourselves in this position," Bradway says, "but what we try to do is keep patients as our North Star. We try to say, 'Gosh, let's try to make every decision with the patient in mind. What makes the most sense from that standpoint?'"[19]

Many leaders talk about serving the greatest good, only to see their priorities shift when it comes to mergers and acquisitions. Don't let this be you. Revenue matters. Being competitive matters. But social impact matters more. Maximizing that impact while also running a strong, sustainable business will lead, over time, to attractive returns. It has for us. Between 2016 and 2021 our revenue grew from $6.6 billion to $10.8 billion, fueled by our ongoing shift to the population health model. Meanwhile, our financial ratings from Moody's were the best in healthcare. And we were able to return over $1 billion during that period to the community via our charitable foundation.

I deeply believe that the best kind of growth originates from within, reflecting our abiding passion to make a difference in the world. This good growth arises when we seek not to steal someone else's market share but to realize our highest, most altruistic aspirations. I invite you to think more deeply about growth and commit to making a positive difference. The world's problems are dire. In many industries, including healthcare, progress is slow. We must move faster—and we can. Take the good you already do via your core commercial activities, and do more of it. Your stakeholders—all of them—will thank you.

QUESTIONS FOR REFLECTION

1. Do you pursue growth at all costs, or do you allow your organization's mission to guide your merger and acquisition decisions?

2. Do some in your organization resist growth, fearing that it will degrade the organization? How might you best counter those arguments?

3. How have your organization's previous mergers and acquisitions benefited your ability to deliver on your mission?

4. Do you actively deploy your mission as a filter when evaluating potential deals?

5. How willing are you to navigate trade-offs between stakeholders?

6. Are you pursuing growth as aggressively and deliberately as you should be?

9

GO UPSTREAM

To truly change the world, try to tackle the underlying problems
that cause people to need quality products and services.
Don't focus solely on production, delivery, and profits.

One night during the late 1990s, when I was working at a pediatric intensive care unit (ICU) in Syracuse, New York, ambu-
lances brought in four young victims of a house fire. As the ICU
physician on call, I ran down to the emergency room to help. I arrived
to find an absolutely horrific scene, one that haunts me to this day.
Four young girls—all sisters—lay on gurneys in the trauma room,
badly burned and either dead or dying. Members of our team tended
to them, doing everything possible to save them.

For the next 30 or 40 minutes, I worked frantically to save those
girls. It was futile. None of them survived. An entire family of siblings—gone. As you can imagine, the parents were devastated. I'll
never forget the sound of their wailing as they learned of their daugh-
ters' deaths, nor will I forget the distant, dazed looks in their eyes or
the smell of smoke, which suffused everything in the room. I regularly encountered death and dying as a doctor, but this episode hit me

especially hard. My own family was everything to me (my wife, Mary Carole, calls me "Dr. What's Next," but she knows that our family always comes first). I had two young kids at home, my sons Alex and Martin, and my wife was pregnant with our third, my daughter Settie. I saw myself in those parents. Their kids easily could have been mine.

In one respect, though, I knew they couldn't have. Like many patients in this hospital, this family was low-income, while mine was privileged to be middle class. I wondered whether these four girls had fire alarms installed in their home—so many of our patients' families didn't. If the girls did have fire alarms, I wondered whether their parents had the $10 or $20 it might have cost to replace old batteries in those alarms so that they worked. I wondered whether these girls lived in adequate housing, with electrical wiring that was up to code. I wondered whether they could afford heat, or whether their parents were forced to use their oven to keep warm. I wondered whether their neighborhood was safe, or whether someone in the building had been abusing drugs or alcohol and perhaps had gotten careless with a lit cigarette.

Many presume that genes play the greatest role in determining whether we'll live to a ripe old age and enjoy good health. Others think patients' ability to access quality care is decisive. In truth, our zip codes—whether we live in an area that is relatively prosperous, stable, and environmentally safe—influence our health even more powerfully. As research shows, social and environmental factors like access to healthy food, adequate housing, education, good jobs, safety, and a supportive family coupled with our health behaviors (whether we smoke, exercise, eat well, and so on) account for up to 60 percent of our health outcomes.[1]

For caregivers like myself, the health challenges faced by people low on the socioeconomic ladder are glaring. Earlier, I recounted my shock at discovering the adversity that caused one of my patients, a single mom with inadequate housing, to arrive late at our clinic. During the years that followed, I encountered many tragedies in which life circumstances—what we in healthcare call the "social determinants of health"—played an important role. There was the teenage girl who, after being shamed and punished for being gay, took a fatal overdose of aspirin. The desperately sick kid in the emergency room whose asthma owed to chronic exposure to dust mites in his house. The child who was fatally injured while playing in his parents' restaurant, probably because they couldn't afford good childcare.

You might wonder why we don't do something about these horrible socioeconomic disparities. More health systems today are talking about it, but only a few have taken meaningful action. It's not that most caregivers don't care—of course they do. But medical schools don't focus on teaching young doctors about social circumstances and the complex ways they affect health. They don't train them to screen for social needs and help patients address them. More fundamentally, if you get paid to care for people once they're already sick, as most caregivers do, you're not going to spend much time thinking about the environmental factors that cause patients to become sick in the first place, and you won't proactively address those factors. You'll be less curious about patients and their complex lives, and you won't see it as your role to make their lives less complex. You'll do your best to fix what's wrong and leave it at that, resigning yourself to seeing disadvantaged patients back in your emergency room again and again.

In recent years, we at Intermountain have made addressing the whole person—including social and environmental factors that influence health—one of our top organizational priorities. We appointed a senior leader—our chief community health officer Mikelle Moore—to oversee efforts in this area and adopted enterprise-level goals related to addressing social needs. We pumped hundreds of millions of dollars back into communities to make progress on social issues impacting health, engaging in an array of innovative programs and partnerships. We redesigned how our caregivers engage with patients, empowering them to address patients' social, emotional, and economic needs in the course of treating them. We embedded an ethic of treating the whole patient into our culture, encouraging caregivers to take the initiative to redress social and economic disparities that affect health.

As we've discovered, leaders can push themselves to grow their core businesses in ways that benefit society. But they can also do much more. Thinking more broadly about their mission, they can "go upstream," as we call it, addressing the root causes of social problems, including those whose downstream effects their own goods and services help to remedy. Some companies are moving in this direction, but most aren't. Leaders often don't see the business advantages to doing so. Somewhat perversely, they might fear that they'd ultimately be reducing demand for their goods and services if they helped to solve customers' problems at the root.

These fears are unfounded, assuming you deploy the right business model: one that rewards you for doing good. At Intermountain, basic morality inspires us to address social and economic disparities, since we can keep patients healthier and out of our hospitals. But it's also good for our business. Remember, under the value-based care/population health model, we get paid for keeping people well. That means anything we can do to keep people out of our clinics and hospitals allows us to cut costs, improve our financial position, and channel more value back to improving health and services for people in our communities, since they are our only shareholders. Tackling social and economic disparities is a powerful approach for keeping people well that complements others we've discussed, like telemedicine or digital innovation. Applied across American health systems, it could greatly improve health and reduce the burden of healthcare on society.

Imagine how much impact *your* company could have if you thought more broadly about your company's mission, looking upstream instead of construing your customers' needs more narrowly. Imagine how energized your workforce would be, knowing that they're not just helping customers in superficial ways but fundamentally transforming their lives. You might think you can't make headway on the deeper, systemic problems, but by applying some curiosity, an experimental mindset, a bit of elbow grease, and the right business model, you absolutely can.

GO BEYOND CHARITY WORK

Not long after becoming Intermountain's CEO, I traveled to Chicago to attend a conference of American healthcare leaders. While waiting at the baggage claim at O'Hare airport, I happened to spot former Utah governor and secretary of health and human services Mike Leavitt, who planned to attend the conference as well. I had met Governor Leavitt before and admired his work, but I didn't know him well. Striking up a conversation, I asked if he would like to share my car into the city.

We piled into our ride and began to chat. After getting acquainted, I took the liberty of explaining my hopes for Intermountain, and specifically, my desire to demonstrate that keeping people healthy rather than caring for them once they're sick was a better model not just for Utah but for American healthcare. Intermountain had begun focusing on population health back in 2011, and I wanted to build on that foundation and scale it up. I put a question to the governor, who I knew was not only smart and politically astute but also had decades of experience in healthcare. If he were in my shoes, what would he do? How would he mobilize Intermountain's resources to do the greatest social good?

Thinking for a moment, Governor Leavitt replied that he was interested in how social and economic circumstances shape both a person's life span and health. He was chagrined at the disparities that afflict marginalized groups, not merely in inner cities but also in rural areas, and he wondered what innovative steps we might take to address them. His response led to some brainstorming that I now regard as among the most important, exciting, and meaningful of my career.

By the end of our trip, which was prolonged thanks to heavy traffic, we had mapped out an idea for a novel project that would explore what happens in a local community when we care for the *whole* patient, addressing the many elements of their life circumstances that affect health. We would pick one or more specific places in our footprint whose populations were low on the socioeconomic ladder. Rather than attempt to address just one or two pressing needs that were impacting the health of people in these communities, we would bring to bear a wide range of resources alongside the medical care we were providing, tracking changes in people's health.

Our goal was twofold. We wanted to demonstrate the positive impact of addressing the entirety of patients' needs. If we did that, we thought we'd be able to spur change in healthcare nationally. We also wanted to uncover specific practices we could spread to help our health system and others around the country address underlying social and economic disparities in ways that affected health.

Let me say more about this second goal. When companies think about social responsibility, they often approach it as charity work. They find a social need—often one that relates to their mission—and write a check in hopes of doing some good. That's fantastic and worth celebrating. But what many companies *don't* do is attempt to reengineer their core business to have social impact. In launching this demonstration project, that was exactly our goal. We didn't simply want to change life in one or more of our local areas. We wanted to change *ourselves*, so that over the long term we could make more of a difference in all the communities we served.

After my return from Chicago, we formed an organization called the Utah Alliance for the Determinants of Health, providing it with $12 million from Intermountain. We launched pilot programs in Utah's Weber and Washington Counties, two zip codes where Intermountain already cared for patients and whose populations faced social and economic challenges. In each of these places, we took a 360-degree approach, helping people to access the full range of resources—housing, food, prenatal care, and more—they would need to stay healthy. We chose these two counties because their populations varied considerably. Weber County was more urban. People who lived there tended to be younger and were more liberal politically. Washington County was more rural, older, and more conservative. Confident that our comprehensive efforts to address social needs would work, we wanted to anticipate skeptics who would say, "Oh, that approach only works with a specific population—it won't work elsewhere." We hoped to show that caring for the whole person and taking into account their life circumstance is *always* a good idea.

In these two communities, the problem wasn't so much that resources for low-income patients didn't exist. It was that patients often couldn't access resources they needed because providers weren't working systematically to spot these needs and help patients fill them. To remedy that problem, we convened a large network of local partners that provided services—homeless shelters, local educators, food pantries, low-income health clinics, mental health providers, and the like. We provided questionnaires that frontline staff at these organizations and at our own hospitals and clinics could use to screen people they encountered for the full range of social needs. Had they gone without food in the past 30 days? Had they had trouble paying rent? Were they having issues getting rides to their medical appointments?

When people in these communities had only one or two unmet needs impacting their health, frontline providers could connect them with resources provided by organizations in our network. Quite often, though, patients had multiple, intersecting needs that were both profound and complicated to address. To help in these situations, we hired a corps of community health workers in each zip code who would work with patients over time to obtain the help they needed to get back on their feet.

Critically, these workers would interact with patients in their native language, which was often Spanish. We also provided these workers with a budget to cover small, incidental costs that prevent people in need from obtaining help. A person eligible for government housing assistance might not be able to obtain it because they don't have $15 to cover the application fee. Someone else applying for a job as a construction worker might not have money for steel-toed boots, which were required. Such gaps might seem small, but to people in need, they are enormous and often insurmountable. With funds at their disposal, community health workers could help patients bridge these gaps and get people what they needed. That, in turn, would help keep them healthy and out of the hospital.

As this work got underway, the profound impact it was having on individuals and their health soon became evident. Consider the story of "Randy," a 52-year-old resident of Washington County. For years, he'd suffered from a slew of chronic ailments, including heart disease and rheumatoid arthritis. Unemployed and struggling with substance abuse and violent behavior, he had a hard time taking care of his health and made numerous trips to our emergency rooms to treat his chronic conditions.

Community health workers and providers in our network assigned to Randy's case arranged for him to receive temporary housing at a homeless shelter. They got him a cell phone and a primary care provider, helped him to apply for disability insurance, and arranged for him to meet with mental health counselors to help with his substance abuse. Over time, Randy was able to afford a car of his own, which allowed him to get to his medical appointments, and he moved into a home of his own. Randy had setbacks, but he continues the process of getting back on his feet. Since he can access the preventive care he needs, he can better manage his chronic conditions without frequent emergency room visits, removing cost from our system while lowering his out-of-pocket expenses.

Happily, stories like Randy's abound. By the end of the Alliance's three-year pilot project, a total of 320 organizations had joined our network of providers in Weber and Washington counties, serving over 1,800 people. Frontline providers began to rigorously screen people they encountered for social needs—our data showed they did it 96 percent of the time. Although it will be years before we'll be able to gauge the full health impact of providing for people's social needs in these two communities, early signs suggest that this impact is profound. During the pilot, we tracked how often people were going to an emergency room to handle chronic health needs rather than true health emergencies. If we saw fewer people using the ER in this way, it would mean that they were better able to navigate the healthcare system and were likely also staying healthier. We had hoped to see 8 percent fewer ER visits that weren't true emergencies. Instead, these visits dropped *by over 34 percent.* Weber and Washington counties are continuing the Alliance's work, and we're expanding the program to other counties in our service area.[2]

After the project's first year, Intermountain took what we learned and began using it to change how we deliver care. Remember those questionnaires we developed that allow frontline providers to screen for social needs? We've incorporated such screening across our emergency rooms and are rolling it out to primary care facilities in our system. When was the last time you went to the doctor and someone bothered to ask you whether you had appropriate housing or enough to eat? When was the last time someone bothered to ask you whether you were feeling depressed or anxious or whether you were abusing alcohol or drugs? At Intermountain, we increasingly do, and we can also connect you with services to provide for the specific needs you might have.

To help with more complex cases, our primary care teams include caregivers who function like community health workers, helping patients to navigate social services and address many needs at once. We're also rolling out screening procedures among our medical specialists. Obstetricians, for instance, are asking patients whether they can take care of their basic needs during their pregnancies and whether they have access to services that might help with postpartum depression. Our kidney care specialists are asking patients whether they have access to the nutrition, medications, and transportation to and from medical appointments they need to manage their conditions and to avoid costly, painful, and debilitating dialysis treatment.[3]

Changing our own ways of working with patients hasn't been easy. Our caregivers already do a lot, and now we're asking them to change familiar work patterns and do even more. But after some initial resistance, most caregivers and administrators in our system are welcoming the changes. Rather than complaining about having to screen patients, they're now pushing for even more resources to provide to patients facing social and economic disparities. Our caregivers understand how important it is to keep people healthy. Many of them have seen firsthand how devastating social and economic disparities can be to patients' health. For them, it's exhilarating to finally address the basic problems that cause people to become sick rather than see them in the emergency room again and again.

Think about the customers you serve and the underlying needs that prompt them to use your goods and services. Are there innovative ways you might address these needs in the course of operating your business? If your business model doesn't incentivize you to do this, how might you change that to render your efforts to go upstream financially sustainable?

In addressing underlying social issues, we at Intermountain regard it not as a charitable contribution, but as a core part of how we operate. Consider another patient—I'll call him Greg—who lived in one of the two geographic areas served by the Alliance. For years, Greg's battles with diabetes and opioid addiction sent him repeatedly to our emergency room. As part of the Alliance's work, a case worker met with him and discovered that because of his diabetes, his feet no longer fit properly into his shoes, and he suffered severe pain that made it impossible for him to hold down a job. The caseworker arranged for him to receive a modestly priced pair of shoes, which led to a reduction in his pain. He also agreed to receive counseling to help with his drug addiction. As his physical condition improved, his caseworker arranged for him to see a primary care physician, who could help keep track of his health and take preemptive steps to prevent it from worsening.

Thanks to these measures, Greg has held onto a steady job, and his visits to the emergency room have declined. Greg wins because he enjoys better health and can attend to his financial needs. Society wins because of the cost savings that accrue, thanks to the reduction in emergency room visits and because we're helping social service agencies to better collaborate and integrate their services. But

Intermountain also wins because it costs us much less to care for Greg over a period of time. In addition, we earn a small return on the care we do provide for him, and our efforts to drive improvements in community health enhance our reputation locally. All these gains became possible because we challenged ourselves to address the wider needs our customers have, and because we've transformed how we get paid to incentivize us to go upstream.

Customers today don't reward companies that simply donate to good causes. They reward transformative organizations that engineer new ways of doing well even as they do good. Investors increasingly value these organizations, as do employees. If your business model penalizes you for addressing underlying social problems, it's time to disrupt yourself. Keep an eye out for innovative ways of doing business that allow for both profit-making *and* long-term benefits to other stakeholders. With the right business model in place, you could be making real progress on fundamental issues plaguing society and inspiring others in your industry to do the same.

BUILD UP LOCAL COMMUNITIES

Nick Fritz isn't the kind of person health systems have traditionally hired. Originally from Ohio, he studied engineering in college and served as an officer in the Marine Corps. Becoming interested in business, he earned an MBA from the University of Utah and then went to work in impact investing, an approach that aims not just to generate financial returns but to help society or the environment in some way. Most money managers seek to obtain the greatest possible returns for investors. Impact investors want to make money, but they also want to support projects that will do significant good.

In July 2019, we brought Fritz over to Intermountain to start an impact investing practice for us. In our efforts to go upstream, we were thinking big. We didn't simply want to help individual patients in specific communities, as important as that is. We wanted to enhance the resources available across our entire geographic footprint to remedy health disparities, mobilizing every tool available to us. Fritz's assignment was to find investment opportunities in our service area that would improve life for underserved populations while generating a small return for Intermountain.

During his first six months on the job, Fritz drove around Utah, talking to community and business leaders about how Intermountain could best make an impact. Two themes kept popping up. First, communities needed more affordable housing for low-income folks. Second, they needed more economic opportunity. So far, most of Fritz's work has focused on the first area. Research has shown that when people can access safe, stable, reliable housing, they stay healthier. If your home is poorly ventilated and moldy, you're at higher risk of asthma. If you suffer a foreclosure and have to move, you might be more likely to suffer from a range of mental health conditions. If your cost of housing eats up too much of your monthly budget, you might lack money to buy healthful food or visit the doctor when you need to.[4] Again, your health might suffer.

Aware of these important connections between housing and health, Fritz in 2020 led investment in a new flagship project called the Utah Housing Preservation Fund. Every year, governments pump money into building affordable housing, but after a period of time, the owners of those properties are allowed to sell them on the open market. When they do, developers buy these homes and kick out the low-income people who are renting them. The developers either knock down the existing homes and build new ones or invest to improve these properties. They then sell them off as high-end properties. Thanks to this dynamic, a certain amount of affordable housing vanishes each year, exacerbating shortages in communities and leaving more families homeless.

The fund we created works as an affordable housing stabilizer. Instead of leaving developers free to buy the properties, the fund buys them at the market rate, upgrades them, and maintains them as affordable homes in perpetuity, charging rents that low-income folks can afford. The fund doesn't lose money on these deals, but the returns it earns are below the market rate—a small price to pay for families to access the housing they need to stay healthy. "The whole purpose of the fund is to keep people stable in their housing," Fritz says.[5] Instead of being evicted and suffering dislocation and perhaps even homelessness, low-income renters in this property can stay and continue to pay affordable rents. Coordinating with social service agencies, the fund also helps to provide people who are currently homeless with affordable units as they become available.

The Utah Housing Preservation Fund is just one of several impact investing projects we've helped fund to date. Others include a program that helps those suffering from addiction get jobs and secure housing and programs that assist low- and middle-range income workers with their down payments so they can afford homes.[6] All told, we've committed about $50 million to our impact investing efforts and hope to deploy $180 million within a few years. So far, our projects have led to the construction and preservation of more than 1,000 units of affordable housing.

It's important to approach going upstream from multiple angles and not just through impact investing. To help remedy economic disparities, we have adjusted how we purchase goods and services from others to prioritize local suppliers. Our goal here is to support the creation of good jobs in our communities, which in turn will help keep these communities healthier. We also mobilize our hiring strategy to benefit local communities, increasing diversity and hiring more workers in rural areas to bring opportunities to underserved segments of the population. We conduct a number of efforts in the area of food security, providing food and connecting patients, caregivers, members of our insurance plan, and members of the community with resources.[7]

At times, going upstream forces us to acknowledge that we, too, can contribute to community health problems. When I became CEO, Utah had one of the worst rates of opioid overdoses in the country. We had partnered on efforts to raise public awareness about the opioid epidemic and to educate our own caregivers about it, with limited effect. To tackle this problem, we couldn't simply focus on the behavior of users but also on that of suppliers of opioids—in other words, our own doctors. As we found, physicians in Utah were prescribing these medications at among the highest rates in the country.

We pushed physicians to adopt a goal of reducing opioid prescriptions by 40 percent.[8] As Mikelle Moore, Intermountain's chief community health officer, remembers, "That took a ton of work, figuring out an education program for every provider, giving physicians real-time data about what they were prescribing relative to their colleagues, surveying patients about how many pills they actually needed or were taking, and sending that feedback to physicians so that they didn't feel like they were leaving their patients in pain by prescribing less."[9]

These efforts paid off. As of 2021, we reduced the number of opioids our providers prescribed by 11 million pills, and between 2015 and 2020 Utah saw a decline in opioid deaths of about 3 deaths per 100,000 people in our population.[10] We took other measures to reduce overdoses, such as distributing medication that reverses the effects of opioid overdoses, but in Moore's view, "probably the most impactful thing is the way our prescribers are behaving differently."

Tackling underlying social problems at the community level requires humility, and it also requires persistence and determination. This isn't the kind of work we as leaders can simply do once and then check off our list. We must stick with it, applying constant intellectual curiosity. As Moore observes, "we often make the mistake of patching a program with a charitable contribution or putting work into something at the surface. Before you figure out what to address, you really need to have the rigor in place to ask, 'Why is this true,' and, 'Why is that true,' and, 'Why is that true?'"

A long-term view is important, too. When addressing social issues at the community level, investments might require years, even decades to show results. It's a different way of approaching business, one that's admittedly easier to sustain if you're a nonprofit like we are and free from the tyranny of the quarterly earnings report. But I contend that it's a viable strategy for public companies, too. After all, when entire communities are better educated, better housed, more financially stable, safer, and healthier, the people who reside in them are able to consume more products and services. Going upstream is not only the right thing to do; it helps ensure the long-term health and prosperity of everyone in a community, including business.

EMPOWER PEOPLE TO GO UPSTREAM

In 2021, Shannon Clegg, a neonatal intensive care nurse and member of our strategy team at Intermountain, received a call from her church, asking if she'd help on a volunteer project. The Utah State Correctional System wanted to open a new prison nursery in about a year's time for incarcerated women who were pregnant or had newborns. The space for the nursery was built, but the program hadn't yet been organized. Officials were way behind schedule and needed someone who understood maternal care and healthcare management to help them get the program up and running. Among other tasks, they needed this person to staff the nursery with the right people and put policies and procedures in place that would ensure that mothers and babies were well cared for.

Clegg didn't hesitate. Like many who work in healthcare, she had dedicated her life to public service. She had participated in volunteer missions around the world, teaching neonatal resuscitation in developing countries. "Anything where I feel like I can have a direct impact in improving the life of a human being brings great meaning to my life," she says.[11]

Working on her own time, Clegg reached out to Intermountain and the wider community, assembling a team of specialists who agreed to help on a volunteer basis. An Intermountain neonatologist agreed to serve as the nursery's medical director. Child development specialists at one of our children's hospitals helped map out policies specifying how long infants should stay with their mothers in the nursery after they were born and ensuring that the nursery space was developmentally appropriate. Educators from the University of Utah, Intermountain, and several community agencies worked together to oversee the nursery's offering of parenting classes to new moms. A team of lactation consultants from Intermountain and the local community convened to create protocols for helping new moms breastfeed. Clegg helped identify community partners and governmental agencies that are collaborating to provide supportive care to ensure success as these mothers and babies transition back to society. With the help of Clegg's church, a volunteer program was designed to augment prison resources in the provision of mentorship and childcare both while moms are in the prison and upon their release.

As Clegg relates, a prison nursery like this is a prime example of an initiative that goes upstream to solve underlying problems. By keeping the mother and infant together, the program enhances bonding between them. It offers babies the opportunity for healthy brain development and secure attachment with their mothers, which improves long-term outcomes and reduces the likelihood of intergenerational incarceration. By teaching new moms to breastfeed successfully, the program improves their health and that of their newborns, helping them to avoid future illnesses. Extensive research has shown that children who receive breastmilk enjoy a lower risk of many health conditions, including infections, obesity, diabetes, and cancer. They are also healthier later in childhood. Meanwhile, mothers who breastfeed have lower risks of conditions like heart disease, cancer, diabetes, and postpartum depression.

But that's just the beginning. Research shows that pregnant women cared for in prison nurseries don't commit new crimes as often as those who don't receive such care. Since these women receive mentorship and training in parenting and job skills, they often can establish more stable family lives after they leave prison, gaining custody of other children they might have. Once launched, the program will also help women transition back into society upon their release, connecting them with resources for healthcare, food assistance, housing, and the like.

In all these ways, the new nursery keeps moms and children healthier, lowering the burden on society. We could certainly opt to do nothing for these moms and newborns and then take care of them after they became ill. We could wait for these new moms to struggle with parenthood, lose their children, commit more crimes, and then just put them back in prison. Going upstream to solve social problems at their root is a much smarter and more humane move, one that benefits us all.

As Clegg's story suggests, companies need not do all the work of going upstream. If organizations orient themselves toward tackling social problems at their root, altruistic employees will also connect the dots and find their own ways of helping. Clegg notes that not a single person at Intermountain turned her down when she asked for help with the prison project. Some of this response owes to the cultures of Utah and the healthcare industry, both of which emphasize public service. But when organizations move decisively to address root causes, as we have, it also unleashes new energies among the workforce. It's up to us as leaders to celebrate employees like Clegg who volunteer their time and to support them by making our own resources available.

Great employees like Clegg take the initiative. They do more. They make it personal. Great leaders do the same thing. They make it their business to go home each night, knowing that they and their organizations have helped make the world a better place. It can feel overwhelming at times, but that's not a reason not to engage. Rather, it's a reason to push your hardest and then push some more. At Intermountain, we know we always could be doing more, so we're constantly looking for new ways to buttress our communities. Most recently, we committed $250 million to create an endowment to fund innovation in education across the state of Utah. Does this money directly improve the health of our patients? No. Will it do so indirectly? Absolutely. A more educated population will be more socially and economically stable and will be healthier over time.

It's true that we as an organization can't single-handedly solve for every problem people in our footprint have. That's frustrating for us. But we'll continue to make progress, working in tandem with partners in our community. I invite you to deepen your own efforts to solve bigger social problems, changing your core business if necessary to make these endeavors sustainable. Take the basic social problem that your company solves as part of its mission, and then think about what you can do to address not just that problem but its root causes.

Humanity is at a crossroads, and so is our country. As is patently obvious, many aspects of how we live and work are unsustainable. With government unable to drive change on its own, leaders and organizations can and must help meet the challenge. Opening your gaze wider allows you to see the greater good, and along with it, a whole new array of business opportunities.

QUESTIONS FOR REFLECTION

1. Think about your company's existing corporate social responsibility efforts. Do you currently go upstream, attempting to remedy deeper social problems that affect your customers?

2. If you do attempt to go upstream, how deep do your current efforts go? Have you adapted your core operations to solve for underlying problems?

3. Does your current business model incentivize you to go upstream, or does it penalize such efforts? If the latter, what new business models might you adopt that allow you to do more good and also continue to do well financially?

4. How might you make a business case to your board and other stakeholders for going upstream?

5. Do you currently employ impact investing as a way to go upstream? What other innovative practices might you try?

6. Do you encourage and celebrate employees who go upstream on their own initiative? What else might you do to establish a culture of addressing deeper social issues?

10

STAND UP FOR WHAT'S RIGHT

Leading isn't a popularity contest, especially when it comes to your organization's core mission and aspirational values.

Newly arrived leaders can shake up organizations in any number of ways. They can announce major cost-cutting measures, make significant personnel moves, introduce new strategies, advance new operational structures. As it turns out, they can also march in parades.

In early 2019, members of our recently formed LGBTQ+ caregiver resource group asked if Intermountain could sponsor Utah's annual Pride Festival. At many health systems, this request might have been no big deal, but Intermountain had never aligned itself with the LGBTQ+ community in such a public way. Believing it important for people to feel comfortable and accepted at work, I agreed to the sponsorship. In June 2019, Intermountain hosted a booth at the festival, and I proudly marched in a parade alongside hundreds of our caregivers. Intermountain further affirmed its support internally with messages on screensavers, in social media posts, in employee trainings, and in other corporate communications.

I knew supporting Pride would stir emotions, but I hadn't anticipated how much. One caregiver approached me at the parade with her 13-year-old daughter and told me, "This is the first time I've ever been able to acknowledge that my daughter is gay and the first time that she's ever been able to do something associated with Intermountain that acknowledges that." The phlebotomist at the laboratory I go to told me, "Marc, I've worked here for 35 years. I've been an openly gay woman the entire time, and I finally feel like I can bring my whole self to work." Dozens of caregivers registered their excitement on our internal social media site and in our caregiver surveys. "I never thought I'd see this day," one wrote. "I now know we're welcomed and celebrated here," said another.[1]

Some caregivers with more traditional beliefs reacted differently. They expressed anger and frustration, arguing that we were ramming a progressive agenda down caregivers' throats. "We are a hospital, not an engine for social change," one caregiver wrote.[2] Some religiously observant caregivers felt we were condoning or promoting a lifestyle with which they disagreed. We were being too "trendy" or politically correct, they said, and it was damaging the organization. A few senior leaders and board members approached me, wondering if we had gone too far on this issue and were disrespecting our heritage.

Although I empathized with these critics and appreciated that they wanted the best for Intermountain, I respectfully disagreed with them, particularly the notion that taking a stand on behalf of inclusivity somehow marked a departure from our mission. As I saw it, the opposite was true. To help people live the healthiest lives possible, we needed to take the lead in defining health in society, including healthy social relationships. Internally, we couldn't foster health unless we had an inclusive workforce where everybody could feel respected and accepted for who they are, nor could we deliver on our strategy of building a tightly integrated system if we allowed divisions based on race, ethnicity, gender, sexuality, and so on to remain intact. Diversity is so important that it stands as one of our organization's stated values: "We embrace diversity and treat one another with dignity and empathy."

In the wake of the festival, I continued to affirm our support for the LGBTQ+ community and for inclusivity, explaining its connection to our mission. I had come to this organization to drive progress. If we were to remain a model health system and deliver more fully on our mission, we needed to have uncomfortable but frank conversations clarifying our standards for how we treat people. I wanted to make us more welcoming not merely in relation to LGBTQ+ people but to any individual who might feel marginalized. The goal was to open our minds even wider and advance the core aspirations that had long guided us. Rather than simply publishing a statement on what we stood for, I wanted us to take action, doing something meaningful and visible in the community. Words are nice, but actions are so much more powerful. As leaders, we must practice what we preach.

Many leaders shrink from taking controversial positions related to the organization's mission, thinking it too risky. But remaining silent is risky, too. It can alienate people, including younger employees and customers, who increasingly expect organizations to speak out about diversity, equity, and inclusion (DEI) and other pressing social issues. Leaders these days are often damned if they do *and* if they don't, but I'd respectfully suggest they are more damned if they don't. Speaking out carries important benefits, regardless of whether it also causes offense to some. By clarifying and affirming what the company really believes in, we can more sharply define the culture and galvanize stakeholders to adopt the mantle of change. Over time, strong, mission-oriented leadership sharpens an organization's sense of self, focusing it to drive progress on behalf of its ideals.

The Pride Festival and the conversations it sparked didn't change our culture overnight, but they did send a clear message about our mission and values that resonates to this day. As you might imagine, members of the LGBTQ+ community came away inspired. As Katy Welkie, CEO of Intermountain Primary Children's Hospital and member of the LGBTQ+ community, puts it, "When you know that your organization accepts you as an individual fully and is going to be there for you, your family, and your culture, it makes you lean in and want to do more. You have a loyalty you didn't have before."[3]

If you're not speaking out in a principled way, I hope you'll start. Making trouble for its own sake is distracting and unproductive. But unless you're reliably standing up for your organization's mission or social purpose, you're not much of a leader. There's bad conflict and good conflict. Making waves to reinforce the organization's social purpose and its underlying values is the good kind. As scary and unpleasant as conflict is in today's polarized environment, we can't let the prospect of it scare us. We owe it to our employees, customers, and communities to brave the turbulence of public discourse and lead them to stand up for what's right.

ADVOCATE STRATEGICALLY

As you've probably surmised, speaking out isn't just another leadership tactic for me. It's a longstanding habit, a way I have of seeing and engaging with the world. Back in high school, I wrote a history paper exploring how Black slaves resisted white hegemony through music and humor. In college, I became fascinated by the movement to oppose apartheid by divesting from South Africa. When the AIDS crisis struck, I spoke up against the persecution of gay people, affixing a bumper sticker to my truck that read, "Fight AIDS, not people with

AIDS." I got some interesting looks from other drivers, but I didn't care. As a second-year medical school student, when I first donned a white coat, I rounded out my look by attaching a pin that informed others that healthcare was a right, not a privilege. I believed in that concept then and still do.

Later, as an idealistic young doctor, I challenged the organizations for whom I worked to take responsibility for remedying injustices. At Cleveland Clinic, I spoke out against our policy of rejecting low-income patients covered by Medicaid. Our main campus abutted some of the poorest communities in the United States. We would care for residents when they needed help from medical specialists—the government reimbursed us well for that. But we didn't accept these patients in our primary care clinics, where reimbursements weren't so lucrative. Our policy forced these patients to venture outside their communities in search of care, making it harder for them to stay healthy and adding to the disadvantages they faced. As someone who had become a pediatrician because he wanted to serve and give a voice to underprivileged or marginalized children, I thought that was a travesty, and I let the powers that be know about it. Unfortunately, our policy didn't change.

I also lobbied the Clinic to provide benefits to partners of LGBTQ+ employees. To me, providing these benefits only to heterosexual, cisgender employees was morally wrong. But I made a business case to my colleagues as well. We had tried to recruit a top doctor to serve as chairperson of one of our clinical departments, and she refused to come because her wife couldn't receive benefits. As I argued, our policies were preventing us from accessing the portion of available talent that was LGBTQ+. How was that a smart move? We wound up changing our policy. A couple of years later, we were able to recruit this very same doctor.

At Cleveland Clinic, my focus first as a clinician and then as a leader was to push an organization committed to providing exceptional clinical care to adopt elements of a social mission. When I came to Intermountain, the context for my advocacy shifted. I was attracted to this organization in the first place because we had a long and storied history of dedication to a social purpose. Remember, Intermountain was charged at its founding with operating as a model healthcare system. We cared for people regardless of their ability to pay and channeled revenues back to local communities via healthcare financial assistance, community resources for the underserved, and improved health services and facilities. What I wanted was to prod people in the organization to lean further into this historic commitment, so that we could do even more good for patients, local communities, and society. Although our people remained deeply devoted to service, I felt it was time to take it to a new level. By advocating energetically on behalf of our mission and values, I hoped to shake up our culture and unleash new levels of vitality, focus, and mission-oriented innovation.

What I didn't quite realize was how much *I'd* learn about advocacy. Here as in other areas, my tendency was to push forcefully—too much so, on some occasions. I learned the hard way that wise leaders pursue advocacy empathetically, strategically, and collaboratively. They take care not to cause undue offense or mire the organization in endless, unproductive conflict.

It's important, of course, to advocate forcefully—we can't just take a stand once and think we're done. During my first couple of years at Intermountain, I spoke up on numerous occasions for a more diverse, inclusive, and equitable culture. In addition to personally marching in the Pride parade, I wrote letters to our local newspaper in support of transgender people; diversified our senior leadership team, which had been largely white and male; asked a senior leader to bring her wife to one of our board retreats (a step she had feared taking); oversaw the creation of our LGBTQ+ resource group;

spoke out on behalf of undocumented immigrants who were working for Intermountain under the Deferred Action for Childhood Arrivals (DACA) program; and introduced the celebration of Martin Luther King Jr. Day.

In taking these actions, I sought to get people's attention and shake them up a bit. I certainly succeeded, but with some negative effects I hadn't anticipated. Although many caregivers supported my new statements and policies, others chastised me for disrupting the organization, calling me a "cultural wrecking ball" or worse. Some said I was a poor fit for Intermountain, even a bad person.

Public stands I took on other issues cost me support as well. Ask caregivers, and you'll find many traditionally haven't had the best diets on the job. Soda, chips, donuts, candy bars—we love that stuff and snack on them all the time. Unfortunately, a significant percentage of people in our local communities and in our workforce have paid the price for that behavior, suffering from high levels of diabetes and other chronic conditions. When I arrived at Intermountain, I wanted to broadcast the message that we're not just here to treat patients when they get sick. We're here to help prevent them from getting sick in the first place, and more broadly, to promote a healthier society. To make my point, I made one of my first actions as CEO taking all sugared soda and candy out of our vending machines, cafeterias, and gift shops.[4]

Many in the workforce went ballistic. *What? He's taking away our Twix bars?* Many caregivers accused me of being heavy-handed and authoritarian. Even those who might have agreed with the dietary advice enshrined in my policy disliked their organization telling them what to do. "We are adults," one caregiver wrote. "I would really like to be able to have the right to choose what I drink and eat!"[5] To them, it seemed that I didn't understand the experience of frontline caregivers very well. Taking care of sick patients was a stressful job. Couldn't

I appreciate the need for caregivers to reach for a sweet treat once in a while? And was it my place to make these decisions for them?

Discontent with the junk food ban took on a life of its own, becoming a rallying cry for some who didn't like my other policies and felt I misunderstood the culture. Caregivers brought in bottles of sugared sodas and drank them openly in the break room as an act of rebellion. Patients and visitors also voiced their displeasure, noting that they, too, were adults who could make decisions for themselves. Many shared that being in the hospital was a stressful time, and they wanted comfort food like candy and soda. "If I want a damn Coke," one wrote, "get me a DAMN COKE."

My well-intentioned advocacy fell short, and I wished I could have a do-over. I was trying at this time to rally our organization to embrace other internal changes, such as controversial restructuring. With so much change happening at once, many of our caregivers understandably felt unsettled—they were used to a relatively stable, predictable organization.

It has taken a few years, but my team and I have managed to rebuild much of the trust that my early rush of advocacy eroded. Reversing our soda ban in 2020 certainly helped (more on this later), as did other efforts we made to support our caregivers during the pandemic. As regards diversity, equity, and inclusion (DEI), we gained more internal support for our policies in the wake of the 2020 murder of George Floyd. Not only did we hold dialogues across the organization, we adopted equity as one of our fundamentals of care, alerting people to the massive disparities in health outcomes that exist in our society along racial lines—disparities that the pandemic was laying bare as never before. Further, we identified specific areas of equity that mattered to us, adopted measurable goals, and launched dozens of clinical projects to render our care more equitable.

This new focus on equity and its implications for patients recast DEI for our caregivers, allowing us to make a far clearer link between it and our mission. That in turn normalized DEI in caregivers' minds, removing it from politics and putting it firmly in the realm of healthcare. Our caregivers care about serving patients, and they care about mobilizing data to improve clinical care. As many of them came to recognize, DEI wasn't about some East Coast guy imposing a liberal agenda and taking jobs away from longtime employees. It was about our traditional mission of making *all* people healthier, regardless of who they were or their station in life. At a time when healthcare systems like ours were struggling to hire enough people, it also was about taking steps to compete better for the talent we needed to serve patients.

Our chief people officer Heather Brace notes that focusing on equity and linking it to the mission made it easier to have difficult conversations about identity.[6] Mikelle Moore, our chief community health officer, agrees, observing that our clinical teams are really excited about grassroots equity projects "even though there might be some critics on the margins."[7] Filtering out the food fight on cable news and social media around this topic wasn't easy. We had to get people focused on DEI around healthcare specifically, not politics. Doing so empowered us all to row in the same direction, steering our entire community toward better and more equitable health outcomes.

I don't regret my early advocacy on behalf of our mission. I remain convinced that my public stands were correct. But if I had been a bit humbler and more culturally sensitive, I would have gone more slowly and achieved similar results with less stress on the organization. As leaders, we should pick our battles carefully. Some public stands are so important that we might be willing to suffer potentially serious consequences. Others, not so much. It's vital to know the difference. Did I *need* to ban junk food in 2017? Maybe not. Would taking time to build up more trust first and allow people to get to know me have been a good idea? Perhaps. We can't simply charge in as leaders and interpret the mission in new ways all at once. We stand to gain much more if we first take a measure of the organization, understand the degree of change people can manage, at what pace, and work with them.

STICK TO THE FACTS

On August 31, 2021, at a monthly Covid-19 briefing convened by Utah governor Spencer Cox, I did something that for me was quite unusual. With the highly contagious Delta variant of Covid raging, I stood up in a crowded room and took off my own mask to address the public. As I explained to the officials and reporters present, many of whom were unmasked, I made a practice at the time of avoiding large gatherings. My immune system was highly compromised, as I'd recently had cancer and undergone treatments, including a bone marrow transplant. If I contracted Covid, chances were much higher that I'd have a serious or even fatal case. But I was taking the risk for an important reason: to voice the challenges faced by our 42,000 caregivers and to implore members of the public on their behalf to take simple actions like vaccination and masking to prevent infection.

By this point in the pandemic, Utah's public health situation was dire. Mask mandates and vaccines had become political lightning rods for many. Misinformation circulated online, discouraging people from taking these preventive steps and questioning the motives and integrity of caregivers. Meanwhile, the Delta surge was straining our system to the breaking point. Caregivers were turning away patients with other serious ailments or transporting them to other facilities—in the process, negatively impacting their care—since we just didn't have the beds. Caregiver morale was plummeting to new lows. It's hard enough to watch sick patients decline and die, but our caregivers were seeing deaths in young, previously healthy patients that proper masking and vaccination could have prevented.

At the briefing that day, I made a highly emotional appeal to the public to mask up, get vaccinated, and express appreciation to our caregivers. I did it in a very deliberate way. I didn't harangue those who stubbornly ignored the science that supported masking and vaccination. I didn't try to score political points by arguing for or against mask mandates or other government policies. I didn't share my own political views or even my dismay that people refused to wear masks. Instead, I kept my remarks focused firmly on the facts. I relayed data about how full our intensive care units were and how many of those seriously ill patients had been vaccinated (almost none of them). I relayed data about how our caregivers felt and the messages *they* wanted to communicate. And I relayed data about my own situation, telling my audience: "I hope that all of you who aren't wearing masks aren't carrying the Delta variant, because if you are, you could kill me."[8]

In advocating on behalf of their organizations' mission, leaders often fail to achieve their desired impact because they stray from portraying objective reality. By talking about themselves and what they think, they can come off seeming overbearing and self-absorbed. By attempting to make political arguments, they can spawn unproductive, bad conflict, further polarizing their audience. The perils of straying from the facts became readily apparent to us at Intermountain during the pandemic. By sometimes taking political positions, our peers at other healthcare systems found themselves embroiled unnecessarily in controversies that inflamed tensions and made collaborative efforts on the part of their local communities less likely.

To be fair, neither we nor our peers had ever led organizations through a global pandemic before. And given the highly politicized nature of the public health discourse around Covid, which in the United States at least first appeared during a highly contentious election year, it was impossible for any health system to avoid controversy entirely. Despite our best efforts, we at Intermountain found ourselves pulled repeatedly into the political fray on issues ranging from stay-at-home orders to testing to masking to vaccines. Still, because we tried consistently to stay out of politics to the extent we could and focus on facts, we were a bit more successful than many other health systems in retaining broad credibility within our local community. We could focus a bit more on adapting to the shifting pandemic in partnership with political leaders, competitors, and others in our community, and a bit less on fighting unproductive political battles.

My remarks at the Covid-19 briefing were a good example. In our state, it was risky to deliver a strong pro-mask message consistent with our mission. If I had attacked people, I could have subjected Intermountain to massive attacks from those opposed to masking. Because I stuck to the facts, I managed to avoid further antagonizing audience members and perhaps even win a few over. People seemed to appreciate that a healthcare leader and a physician had spoken to them in a way that wasn't patronizing or driven by a political agenda. Even our governor, whose personal reluctance toward wearing masks was well known, expressed his intention "to try to wear a mask more often—especially when I'm around unvaccinated people and immunocompromised people. I'm going to try a little bit harder, so that I can protect people like Dr. Harrison and others who are immunocompromised or struggling, and even those who have chosen to not get the vaccine."[9] The governor is a good man with a huge heart, and he would never intentionally put others at risk. I've always appreciated his ability to have a healthy discourse with me on all healthcare matters.

To my surprise, my remarks also helped to shore up our caregivers, who desperately needed an emotional lift. A couple of days after the briefing, when I was rounding at one of our facilities, a couple of them came up to me in tears, thanking me for my remarks. They had asked me to speak on their behalf, and I had done it in a way that I hoped would be constructive.

It's necessary at times to take risks and wade into politically charged debates. But we can mitigate those risks not only by picking our battles carefully but by setting our egos aside and opting not to take the political bait that others might dangle. Let's forget about trying to prove ourselves right and others wrong. Let's forget about buttressing our own personal sense of self-righteousness. We stand the best chance of influencing others if we craft a strong, nonpartisan, factual case in support of our organization's mission. And if we meet people where they are.

FOSTER A LOYAL OPPOSITION

In 2021, my leadership team and I announced we were closing over two dozen of our community pharmacies located in or near our clinics.[10] The decision was ultimately an economic one: demand had dropped, and these pharmacies were no longer viable. We had made valiant efforts to salvage them, cutting costs and then seeing if we could find another company to run them for us. Nothing worked. Chalk it up to the internet. When we had started these businesses, the vast majority of consumers bought their prescriptions in person at local retailers. Now, they went online in increasing numbers and got their medications shipped to them. Pharmacies like ours were anachronistic and increasingly going the way of the dodo.

We reassured our workforce that the 250 caregivers who worked at these locations wouldn't lose their jobs—we'd find options for them elsewhere in our organization or at other companies.[11] Nevertheless, many caregivers and others in our communities found the closures upsetting. Some accused us of being greedy and focusing on profits over a public mission. They feared we'd be making life more difficult for patients, many of whom have trouble obtaining medications and complying with their treatment regimens.

These were legitimate concerns, and we took them seriously. To ensure that patients experienced a smooth transition, we arranged for the seamless transfer of their prescriptions to local CVS pharmacy locations. Many other high-quality, community pharmacies also stepped up to make filling prescriptions convenient for patients. As we pointed out, closing our pharmacies didn't represent a departure from our mission—it was actually a way of supporting it. We were losing about $11 million each year running these businesses. Wasn't it better to take that $11 million and channel it back into cutting costs for patients or improving our ability to keep people well?

No leader likes discontent in the ranks. But on this occasion, I felt encouraged and even grateful that so many caregivers spoke up to voice their concerns. As I've learned, it's important not just for leaders to take stands on behalf of what is right but for frontline people to do so as well. Employees with a license to dissent tend to be more engaged and committed to drive progress. They also tend to generate ideas and perspectives that leaders need to hear, even if they don't agree, allowing organizations to pursue their missions more forcefully and comprehensively.

We can't fully unleash our workforces' potential unless we nurture a loyal opposition willing to dissent on behalf of mission and values. But how exactly might we do that? For starters, we can applaud people who have the guts to speak up instead of punishing them. That includes when these individuals go beyond words and take action on their own initiative to serve the mission.

During the late 1990s, when I worked in a pediatric ICU in Syracuse, New York, an adolescent came in who was near death from an infection. His kidneys had stopped working, and if we were to save him, he needed a special treatment to help reduce fluids in his body so his kidneys could hopefully get back online. The other doctors didn't know about this treatment, but I did. Although I knew I was violating protocol, I borrowed a piece of equipment from the adult floor, set it up in the pediatric ICU, performed the procedure, and saved the boy's life. As I saw it, our mission was to serve patients, and our policies in this particular instance prevented me from delivering on it. I couldn't wait around to ask permission. I did what was required, creating a positive outcome for this patient.

Rather than reward me for taking the initiative, the organization punished me. The chairman of my department called me in and tore into me for violating protocol. He threatened to fire me but eventually relented. Do you suppose employees who receive such treatment, or who see others receiving it, will be more likely in the future to play the role of loyal opposition? Of course not. Employees who can't help but make good trouble will eventually leave on their own accord or be fired. Others will just soldier on. They'll keep their mouths shut, silently resenting the hypocrisy of an organization that talks about mission but punishes well-intentioned employees for taking the initiative and acting on it.

Remembering what it was like to be a member of the loyal opposition, I do my best these days to applaud dissent when I encounter it. I also actively encourage it, including while onboarding new members of my team. When conversing with Tiffany Capeles, our new chief equity officer, I specifically urged her to make people uncomfortable as part of her role. As I explained, I wanted her to ask really tough questions of people, taking care, of course, to choose her words carefully so as not to cause unnecessary offense. Our organization's baseline tendency was to be too comfortable, and we needed to fight that. As I made clear, I wanted her to be bold and direct when she had to be.

Perhaps the most important step we can take to nurture a loyal opposition is simply to *listen*. When individuals raise concerns, as our LGBTQ+ caregivers did when requesting that we sponsor the Pride Festival, we can take those ideas seriously and address them. If we disagree with specific proposals, we can explain our positions and rationales as best we can. We can also maintain an open mind, entertaining the possibility that our people might be right. If indeed they are, we must be willing to muster our own humility and change our minds.

When caregivers objected to our pharmacy closures, I didn't relent. We had performed extensive research and analysis and knew what we needed to do. But I have relented in other situations, most notably as regards our junk food ban. Two members of our leadership team—chief people officer Heather Brace and chief nursing executive Sue Robel—played the role of loyal opposition here, relaying to me the dip in morale we were experiencing because of our policy. I didn't act on their advice at first, but to their credit, they persisted, arguing passionately that I was making a mistake by keeping the ban in place. They were making good trouble. With the pandemic hitting hard and some in our community vilifying healthcare, our caregivers were feeling diminished and unheard. They needed to know that their leader cared about what they were going through and was responding to their concerns.

In 2021, we announced that we were reversing course and would bring back junk food for sale in our facilities. Did I think my initial decision to implement a ban was misguided from a medical stand-point? Not at all. But is there value in giving people the freedom to choose what to eat and drink rather than dictate their choices to them? I now think there is. Our caregivers continue to think so as well. The reversal of our policy was warmly received and appreciated. In the dark days of the pandemic, it seemed to ease the burden, if only just a little.

Advocacy is a complicated proposition for leaders. We might find ourselves questioning the status quo in the course of advocating for our organization's mission, but because we occupy power in our organizations, we also define the status quo for our followers. To lead effectively, we must project authority and decisiveness while also allowing space for dissent. Empathizing with the loyal opposition, we must harbor strong beliefs without allowing those beliefs to become too rigid. We must stand up for what is right and also, at times, admit when we could have done better.

SAY WHAT YOU *REALLY* THINK

Have you ever attended an industry event and wished that once—just once—a speaker would stand up, cut through the bullshit, and speak the truth? In 2018, I decided to take that risk. The occasion was a leadership forum for the healthcare industry sponsored by *U.S. News & World Report.* At my session, toward the end of a question-and-answer period, the moderator posed a provocative question: What would I do differently going forward to make *U.S. News & World Report* more relevant? I couldn't help but articulate what I really thought. Each year, the magazine released its much-anticipated rankings of hospitals in the United States. These rankings, I argued, weren't relevant anymore because they inadvertently drove up costs in healthcare, encouraging our national healthcare system to become even more burdened than it needed to be.

As I explained, the rankings mattered a great deal to systems like mine. Get a high ranking, and you can boost your reputation and entice more patients to choose you for their healthcare needs, increasing your revenues. Unfortunately, the drive for good rankings led to perverse behavior. Because the ranking methodology favored systems that offered advanced technology, leaders felt compelled to invest heavily in those technologies, even if having them didn't impact patient outcomes all that much. An entire industry was wasting billions buying bells and whistles that didn't really benefit patients, all so leaders could put banners in front of their hospitals reporting that *U.S. News & World Report* said they're number one. Meanwhile, many patients were struggling to afford the care they needed.

It's not every day that a participant in a conference calls out the conference's sponsor so openly, albeit also respectfully and politely. Hearing my response, the magazine's executive editor was nonplussed. "Well, Marc," he said, "I guess we asked, and you certainly told us."

I presumed I would be persona non grata at the magazine, but to their credit, organizers invited me back the following year (regrettably, I couldn't attend, but we sent another member of my team). They also took what I said seriously, modifying their ranking methodology in ways that reward systems better for improving the value and affordability of their services. In this instance at least, a small dash of "principled insubordination," as one academic expert calls it, appears to have had a positive impact, all because *U.S. News & World Report* kept an open mind and acted on it.[12]

Principled insubordination can help drive progress inside organizations, too, if we deploy it deftly. We can't inspire our people to embrace progress if they don't understand what it really means to realize the organization's mission and values. And they won't develop that understanding if leaders lack the courage to step up publicly when it counts, accurately interpreting the mission and defining and affirming what's right. Can you take public advocacy too far? Absolutely. Companies aren't political organizations. To avoid sparking unhealthy conflict, we should stay focused on our purpose and the service we render to the community, and we should stick to the facts. Let everyone know how committed we are, while avoiding partisan politics as best we can.

As I hope you agree, it's not enough to run a great, high-performance organization. All of us also should try to make the world a better place and help our organization attain its highest aspirations. Once we've determined our organization's purpose or North Star, we should stand up for it, even if we upset a few people, and even if we suffer a bit of blowback ourselves. Leadership isn't a popularity contest. It's a unique opportunity to make a difference, now and for posterity. If we stand up for what's right and embolden our people to do the same, we just might succeed.

QUESTIONS FOR REFLECTION

1. What have you done lately to shake up your organization and reinvigorate its pursuit of the mission?

2. Do you make a habit of advocating for mission and values? If not, what's holding you back?

3. If you have already made a practice of standing up for what's right, are you calibrating your advocacy to what the organization can reasonably tolerate? Conversely, are you speaking out loudly or often enough?

4. Do you take care to stick to the facts and refrain from political partisanship?

5. What issues or values are you willing to advocate for, even at significant personal or professional cost?

6. How strong is the loyal opposition inside your organization?

7. Do you and other leaders tend to punish or reward people in your organization who speak truth to power?

11

COLOR OUTSIDE
THE RED AND BLUE LINES

*Despite political polarization, individuals of different beliefs
can still work together to solve common problems.
Leaders must point the way and inspire by example.*

I vy League–trained experts who harbor strong, progressive beliefs
and hail from the Northeast generally don't befriend conservative
pro-gun activists in the Intermountain West. They certainly don't
visit gun ranges and learn to shoot automatic weapons. But that's
precisely what Morissa Henn, former community health director at
Intermountain, did during the summer of 2017.

As a graduate student in public health at Harvard, Henn wanted
to do something about the plague of suicides afflicting the United
States. Visiting Intermountain on an academic fellowship, she
learned that youth suicide was an especially urgent problem in Utah
and that guns figured prominently in these deaths, much more so
than in states with low gun ownership rates.

Guns are part of the fabric of life in Utah. Almost half the population owns them, even more in some rural areas.[1] Many in our state are avid hunters and outdoorsmen, and with relatively nonrestrictive gun laws on the books, many also keep guns for self-defense, target sports, or to exercise their Second Amendment rights. I have deep respect for Utah's gun culture and its emphasis on responsible gun ownership. But as gun advocates themselves acknowledge, the presence of so many guns makes it easier for people to accidentally or intentionally injure or kill themselves. More than other common means of self-harm, guns are lethal, and their effects on the body are often irreversible. When people experience a bad breakup, when they get fired from a job, or when they suffer some other setbacks, access to guns can turn what might otherwise be a passing moment of extreme distress into a catastrophe.

Mindful of these facts, Henn had an idea. Instead of approaching suicide solely as a mental health issue, as healthcare systems typically do, what if our efforts at prevention went further and specifically addressed the role played by firearms? Rather than simply hire more counselors and psychiatrists, we could engage with gun owners to help prevent distressed people from accessing weapons to harm themselves. Henn recognized that gun enthusiasts opposed laws that restricted gun access or that increased government's role in their lives. But she envisioned many potential interventions that gun enthusiasts might accept and even embrace, ranging from better training of clinicians working with families to the distribution of gun locks and safes to new messaging in suicide prevention awareness campaigns.

When Henn brought her ideas to leaders at Intermountain, we greeted them enthusiastically. Not only was she focusing on prevention—she was looking farther upstream than health systems traditionally had. We also liked that Henn took a deeper, humanistic approach to this work. In her view, collaboration on new programs would yield better results if it were grounded in real, human relationships. She felt it vital to build bridges between healthcare and gun enthusiasts, two worlds that often didn't mingle. By reaching out to gun enthusiasts and getting to know them, she thought she could build mutual trust and respect. As she says, "It's really hard, if not impossible, to convince people who do not trust you to change their behavior."[2]

Henn reached out to Clark Aposhian, Utah's most prominent gun-rights advocate and chairman of the Utah Shooting Sports Council (USSC). The two became acquainted and began to discuss a collaboration. As Henn and Aposhian both realized, this was an unusual move, to say the least. Henn had never fired a gun and was utterly unfamiliar with the culture that surrounded these weapons. She had never personally known someone harboring Aposhian's strong pro-gun beliefs. Still, she had learned that Aposhian, although opposed to restrictions on Second Amendment rights, was deeply concerned about the problem of gun-related suicides. If little else, she and Aposhian had this in common.

In their early conversations, the two openly discussed their motivations, values, and beliefs while also respecting their differences. "I asked as many silly questions as I could," Henn said. "He was willing to walk me through in a way that didn't assume I would subscribe to his politics or his beliefs."[3] Each sought to go beyond stereotypes and political talking points to understand what made the other tick. "Here's a guy who thinks about guns all the time," Henn recalls. "It's his job, his mission, his identity. And I'm like the alien from outer space who has never had any connection to that. I think he was super curious about what I thought. And I was super curious about what he thought."[4]

Such curiosity led Henn to make a surprising request: would Aposhian be willing to take her to a gun range and introduce her to shooting? Aposhian looked at her in disbelief—he couldn't believe this doctoral student from Harvard really wanted to go shooting. But indeed she did. As she saw it, learning to handle and shoot firearms would help her to understand and relate with gun-rights activists like Aposhian. She would become a better advocate for gun safety and suicide prevention if she had at least some firsthand knowledge about firearms and gun culture.

One summer morning, the two met up at a shooting range outside Salt Lake City. "This was very outside my comfort zone," Henn recalls. "This is beyond showing up in a country where you don't speak the language, beyond eating at a restaurant where you've never eaten the cuisine. I literally didn't even know what to wear." Aposhian had brought a number of weapons from his own collection for her to try out, including a Glock pistol, a fully automatic machine gun, and an AR-15 rifle.[5] For the next hour, Henn fired them off, with Aposhian providing expert instruction. Afterward, the two debriefed over lunch at a nearby restaurant.

As Henn recalls, shooting a gun took some getting used to. She was surprised at how loud it was; as she fired she "physically jumped an inch off the ground every single time for the first several minutes."[6] Although she wasn't instantly transformed into a gun lover, she did find the experience agreeable enough, acknowledging that, "There was a fun, exhilarating aspect to it."[7] More broadly, her efforts to enter Aposhian's world, and his willingness to serve as her guide, confirmed that it was possible to engage in a more meaningful way with people on the other side of issues. "I think what we seemed to see was that we don't have to focus on our differences, that there's a way of engaging that's based more on shared human values, and that this can be our focus. We don't need to obsess over a sense of blame or a sense of what policy or regulation is necessary. We can look for common ground and start from there."[8]

In the months and years that followed, Henn collaborated with Aposhian and other gun-rights activists as part of a suicide prevention coalition. She and gun-rights advocates developed training that healthcare practitioners could use to interact with patients at risk of using a gun against themselves,[9] a public health campaign that talked about guns and suicide, and a voluntary "no buy" law that allows people to give up their right to buy guns on a temporary basis if they feel they might face a future suicidal crisis.[10] Testifying before Congress, Henn described the effort this way: "By moving outside of our comfort zones we've been able to find a common denominator: We're all universally horrified there are so many gun deaths, and we all want our loved ones to be safe. We've found a level of trust with different groups, including gun owners, because neither side has a monopoly on grief from losing a loved one."[11] Although it's too early to gauge the full impact of Henn's collaboration with gun-rights advocates, they believe their efforts will eventually help to lower suicide rates in Utah.

The polarization that grips the United States and other countries today stymies us by locking us into the same old assumptions and limiting our understanding of potential solutions. But well-intentioned individuals of different beliefs can break free of this trap, working together to solve big important problems. By building relationships with our perceived opponents and exploring common ground, we can arrive at compromises that might not perfectly address a given issue, but that yield important progress. As we at Intermountain have found, leaders can unleash organizations to drive that progress by encouraging approaches like Henn's. Leaders can also set an example for others, entering their own discomfort zones and building personal relationships across political lines. This is some of the most difficult work leaders undertake, but it's also some of the most essential, meaningful, and rewarding. Fertile ground for collaboration and comity still exists. We just need to look for it.

ONCE YOU KNOW PEOPLE, IT'S HARD NOT TO LIKE THEM

In May 2021, I was saddened to learn that a favorite restaurant of mine in Salt Lake City, the Blue Plate Diner, was closing.[12] The diner was nothing fancy, and that's why I liked it. You could sit on stools at the counter and enjoy a cheap breakfast of bacon, eggs, and home fries. But what really made the place special was spending time there with former Utah governor and health and human services secretary Mike Leavitt. Before the pandemic, we would meet there every couple of weeks on weekend mornings to talk about our lives, healthcare, and the challenges of leadership. I would describe situations I was facing in my role as Intermountain's CEO, and Leavitt would offer the benefit of his wise counsel.

Leavitt and I continue to meet, and I count him as my good friend and valued mentor. By most measures, our friendship seems as unlikely as the one that emerged between Henn and Aposhian. Leavitt is a Republican who served in the administration of George W. Bush. I don't identify as a Republican and have voted for Democrats. Leavitt is a member of the Church of Jesus Christ of Latter-day Saints. My background is Jewish. Leavitt is a Utah native. I was born and raised in Pittsburgh. Leavitt had a successful business career before becoming a political leader. I worked as a frontline clinician.

Despite these differences, Leavitt and I have forged a strong personal connection and friendship. I first met him years ago when I was working at Cleveland Clinic and he came to visit with our executive team. Later, when I arrived at Intermountain, I sought him out, primarily because I admired his track record of success and wanted to see what I might learn from him. This is a longstanding practice of mine: whenever I encounter successful people in any domain, whether it's sports, the arts, politics, or business, I try to understand how they came to excel, and I apply their wisdom or tactics to my own work in healthcare. I don't worry too much about how different their backgrounds might be from mine. My curiosity and desire to learn win the day.

As Leavitt and I became acquainted, we discovered that we actually shared quite a bit in common. We might have played on different teams, but our political inclinations were both centrist. I can sum up my own politics as follows: I want a clean environment. I don't care who sleeps with whom, as long as they're adults. And I think the free market is very effective at solving many problems, so long as we regulate it properly. If you asked Leavitt, I believe a good deal of this would resonate with him. Do we agree on every specific policy issue? Not at all. But our general outlooks on the world and on politics are remarkably congruent.

Thanks to our conversations, I also realized that liberals and conservatives often have a strikingly similar commitment to healthcare. Liberals tend to talk about healthcare as a right, not a privilege. They sympathize with the underserved in society and feel obliged to help them. But Leavitt, too, speaks in very sincere and meaningful ways about caring for the frail and vulnerable in the community. A strong sense of social responsibility is core to his values and undergirds his belief that Intermountain should function as a model healthcare system and provide care for those who can't afford to pay. Other conservatives I've become friendly with, including several on Intermountain's board and leadership team, feel similarly. Again, we might not agree on specific policies, but we share a vision of a world in which people of all backgrounds suffer less and access the care that they need.

As it turns out, my common ground with Leavitt runs even deeper than this. Like me, he doesn't see himself as having reached some final state of intellectual maturity. He's not finished learning and retains an openness to hearing alternative interpretations or new facts that might change his approach to problems. To that end, he's always reading, thinking, and engaging with people across a wide range of backgrounds. More than anything else, it's his openness and desire to learn that makes it fun to spend time with him. Because I never know what new idea or perspective he'll share with me, he sparks me to question my own beliefs and push my thinking further.

I believe Morissa Henn has it right: in making forays across political lines, personal relationships really do matter. We can make the most progress if we take time to get to know people, opening up to them and inviting them to express their cherished beliefs and values. Personal relationships allow us to identify common ground that might otherwise go unnoticed in the context of partisan rancor. We come to see political adversaries in more nuanced ways, and we come to trust them. It's hard to hate people if you spend time with them and get to know them as human beings.

I've been privileged as well to form a strong friendship with Brad Wilson, Republican speaker of the Utah House of Representatives. I first met Wilson early in my tenure during a visit to the House floor, but we became better acquainted during the pandemic, dining together on multiple occasions with our wives. I found that I liked Wilson very much and that he shared my own values around family and service to the community. Although his politics are considerably to the right of mine, we've been able to build a great friendship that transcends those differences. Once again, far more connects us than divides us.

Our relationship in turn allows us to bring balance and perspective to others in our respective camps who might disparage their opponents. When I hear people complaining about "those crazy legislators," I assure them there are good folks in government who are working their hardest to make the world a better place. I suspect Wilson at times has gently deflected people on his side who have tried to vilify me. Wilson and I know and trust one another's deeper motivations. That allows us to lower the temperature in political debates and to collaborate effectively to solve problems. Of course, I intercede with critics directly as well to lower the political temperature. Even in situations of overt conflict, I've found that reaching out and attempting to make a personal connection can enable more productive interactions.

When I first arrived at Intermountain, I managed to alienate an influential political figure in the state. I'm not sure exactly what I said or did, but I heard that this individual, a very conservative Republican, had concluded that I was irredeemably "woke" and too radical for Utah, and that he wanted me gone. Before long, it became apparent that this person was indeed planning to take action that could hurt Intermountain.

I was mortified that I had hurt the organization by making a powerful opponent. I was also angry. Although I felt tempted to dig into my corner and fight back, I chose to do the opposite. With the help of an intermediary, I arranged a meeting with this person and offered up a genuine apology. He affirmed his mistrust, telling me to my face that he thought I was wrong for Utah. Maintaining a respectful tone, I made it clear that I would not allow him to run me out of town. I asked him to give me a chance and take some time to get to know me. I also conveyed the respect I had for him as a political leader.

My overtures didn't automatically repair our relationship, but they did at least help to stabilize the situation. About a year later, I invited this individual out to lunch, and we had quite a good time, coming away with more respect for one another. We've since seen one another socially on a number of occasions. Although we're not necessarily friends, we're always civil and cordial. With a bit of outreach across the political divide, we were able to avoid some of the acrimony that riles so many communities and that could have proven distracting or worse to Intermountain.

Many leaders talk about mutual respect, but how many of us practice it? More often, we surround ourselves with like-minded folks who reinforce our own points of view. We feel safe and protected in our certainty, and we might even feel superior to those who think differently. But feelings of superiority don't help us solve problems. They only make collaboration more difficult. What does help is rediscovering our shared humanity, whether by extending an outstretched hand to those who attack us or building friendships with those who think differently than we do. It really is hard to hate people—or even just dislike them—once you've gotten to know them. And it's a heck of a lot easier and more productive to work with them.

STAY PRAGMATIC

Although Morissa Henn made progress working with Clark Aposhian and other gun-rights advocates on measures to help reduce gun suicide, it wasn't long before she discovered the limits of their collaboration. Initially, she recalls, she harbored the somewhat naive belief that if she could convince gun-rights advocates to embrace nonregulatory measures like voluntarily using gun locks or undergoing training in gun safety, they could eventually find ways to collaborate on government regulations designed to help keep guns out of the hands of people at risk of suicide. In particular, Henn sought to obtain the support of Aposhian and others for "red flag" laws that would allow people to petition judges to remove guns from those who posed an imminent threat to themselves or others.

Collaboration on policy proved quite difficult. "I tried so hard to bring Clark and others together," she says, "not to convince them that it was the answer, but just to have a really robust dialogue around, 'What are the possibilities? What does the data tell us? How does that relate to what we're doing in Utah?'" As she came to realize, gun-rights advocates just couldn't go there—anything involving government regulation was a nonstarter for them. Having built a collegial relationship with Aposhian, Henn found it jarring to see him take what she regarded as hard-line positions on policy matters. "It did feel a little disorienting in that I was like, 'Well, this is the same person who's working with me on something productive,' but also refusing to be open-minded about what I thought were some policy areas we could explore together."

At one point, Aposhian's organization compared gun rules and gun control to Jim Crow segregation, a move that Henn found overtly racist and unacceptable. On another occasion, Henn attended a meeting with gun-rights advocates at the state capitol only to find them sharing information she regarded as factually incorrect about a particular policy issue. Such episodes taught Henn an important lesson about coloring outside the red and blue lines. As important as it is to pursue collaboration, political differences will remain that we cannot fully bridge—and that's OK. Even if we show flexibility when we're working across political lines, many of us still have core values from which we won't stray.

How do we sustain progress in the face of strong, persisting differences? The answer is to adopt a pragmatic posture, respecting boundaries, adopting realistic goals, and notching gains where we can. Henn describes her years of work with the gun-rights lobby as an ongoing process of "disagreeing on a lot of things until we found that alignedness." She tried repeatedly to engage Aposhian and other activists around policy issues, with little to show for it. But rather than throw up her hands, she accepted this boundary on their work and pushed ahead in the areas where they could make headway. It was important, Henn relates, "to just constantly return to the common goal. It really keeps people focused and keeps them realizing that they want to be part of the solution."

Gun violence prevention advocates criticized Henn, claiming that by continuing to engage with the gun-rights lobby, she was capitulating to gun owners and giving them political cover. Henn pushed back, arguing that addressing gun violence required "engaging on every different level, on so many different levels, to affect change." Working with gun-rights advocates was one path to progress, but it didn't mean that people with her beliefs couldn't pursue change in other ways, too. Instead of judging people as "good" or "bad," we could appreciate and accept their complexities and "really look for the nuggets of productive engagement we can tease out." Doing so could invite them to do the same. Such an approach is messy, and it might not satisfy our need for certainty and clarity. But over time, it allows us to make headway on otherwise intractable problems.

As we at Intermountain have repeatedly seen, leaning pragmatically into the complexity really does yield results. In Chapter 1, I described our decision to delay mandating Covid-19 vaccination for our workforce. We focused on encouraging voluntary vaccination by offering incentives and sharing information about vaccines' safety and health benefits. We implemented a mandate only in October 2021, when the Biden administration required it. In making this decision, we listened to the concerns of caregivers opposed to vaccines and recognized that the removal of personal choice via a mandate represented an important boundary. We knew that in general these caregivers could accept that we favored vaccines and encouraged their use, but the moment we made vaccination a requirement for employment, we would be crossing a line. Studying the experience of other health systems that implemented mandates, we anticipated that turmoil would erupt and a significant number of caregivers would quit, worsening a staffing shortage wrought by the Covid-19 pandemic. We also doubted a mandate would increase vaccination rates enough to warrant such a disruption to our organization.

In avoiding a mandate for as long as possible, we made strong progress vaccinating our workforce while retaining the staff required to care for a surge in Covid-related hospitalizations. Prior to our mandate, the vast majority of our caregivers—about 82 percent—were either fully or partially vaccinated.[13] We did anger some doctors who supported a mandate, but overall, our approach allowed us to ease tensions inside of our organization. When we did finally issue a mandate, we won over at least some vaccine opponents by tying our decision to our mission. Intermountain exists to keep people healthy, and that means actually providing healthcare. Since at least 40 percent of our business was funded by the government, failing to issue a mandate meant we wouldn't be able to care for all of those patients. Forget about the financial implications for us—we simply couldn't abandon millions of patients over a vaccine mandate.

At the same time, we assured our workforce that we were going to make a mandate as palatable as we possibly could. We would respect the Biden administration's regulations, but we also would do our best to ensure that our caregivers knew all of their options when it came to obtaining exemptions. Meanwhile, we would continue to be diligent about providing personal protective equipment (PPE) to caregivers and mandating its use, ensuring that any caregivers who remained unvaccinated wouldn't compromise the safety of our patients. (By the way, PPE really works: as of this writing in 2022, we aren't aware of a single case in which one of our caregivers has transmitted Covid-19 to a patient.)

As we implemented the mandate, we worked very closely with individual caregivers who were wary of vaccination. In some cases, after speaking with others and reviewing data, caregivers decided that vaccination was the right choice for them. One of our nurses had suffered a series of miscarriages and finally managed to get pregnant. Unfortunately, she had encountered information about vaccines online and believed that they would harm both her and her unborn child. She was quite frustrated that she would lose her job if she didn't get the vaccine. In truth, vaccines aren't harmful to pregnant women, but Covid-19 is—pregnant women have a much higher death rate from the virus than the general population. When one of our caregivers sat down and explained the evidence to her, she decided to get vaccinated.

In other cases, working through an individual's concerns led us to help them to apply for a religious or medical exemption if they met the relevant criteria. One nurse had been experiencing strange and unexplained neurological symptoms, including muscle weakness and cognitive deficits. These symptoms were impacting her life and causing her distress, and she worried that the vaccine might exacerbate them, given its effects on her immune system. Although strictly speaking, she didn't meet the criteria for a healthcare-related exemption, we explored other ways that she might qualify. This caregiver knew she was subjecting herself to some level of risk by forgoing vaccination and continuing to work for us, but she was willing to accept that. She had legitimate concerns and just couldn't bring herself to get vaccinated. Since her presence on the job wouldn't harm patients, we wanted to work with her as best we could to help her stay employed with us.

Life isn't perfect. We usually can't achieve all our goals and still hope to win the support of a diverse coalition. That's just reality. Over the long term, working pragmatically and collaboratively can allow us to have the greatest impact, but only if we're willing to respect boundaries, make accommodations, and at times sacrifice some of our ambitions while still remaining true to our core principles. In building relationships with our partners across the political aisle, we must accept that they will need to disagree with us and uphold core principles of their own. Rather than cut off the conversation, we should keep it going and collaborate when possible. It's easy to grandstand, much harder to actually make progress. I'll take progress over grandstanding any day.

BE A CONVENER OF STATURE

Like other states across the nation, Utah has a homelessness problem. It also has a homelessness *policy* problem. Between 2016 and 2020, state government spending to address homelessness skyrocketed by 600 percent. Despite all that money flowing into shelters and other service organizations, the number of homeless people in Utah rose by 12 percent, and the number of those who lacked shelter tripled.[14] As it turns out, those numbers reflected underlying political tensions. While leaders in recent years managed to build new facilities to help the homeless, they couldn't agree on ways to increase the homelessness system's overall capacity. Clark Ivory, a prominent philanthropist focused on the homelessness issue, observes that differences of opinion "led to dysfunction and impacted, in the end, what we could accomplish."[15]

As a successful homebuilder with a strong sense of civic responsibility, Ivory took pride in his local business community's pragmatic, nonpartisan approach to important issues like immigration and transportation. "We just want to get stuff done," he says. "We've been able to bring a lot of like-minded, solution-oriented business leaders together, and we haven't really cared about politics. We're able to do things that some people would maybe call progressive. I just call it common sense." In recent years, Ivory and other prominent business leaders sought to apply this pragmatic, nonpartisan approach to overcome divisiveness and spur progress on homelessness.

In 2020, Ivory and Intermountain board member Gail Miller funded a study to assess the state's approach to homelessness and recommend how better to organize it. As part of the data-gathering process, the researchers convened an array of groups and individuals with a stake in the homelessness issue, including businesses, philanthropists, elected officials, service providers, mental health practitioners, and law enforcement. Members of the group held diverse political views, but with the support of prominent philanthropists and the business community, they were able to put aside traditional disputes and hold productive conversations. In a final report issued to the Utah legislature, the group aligned behind a number of measures to improve the formulation and execution of homelessness-related policy. These included the creation of a Homeless Service Officer who would serve as the state's "chief policy officer and advisor for homelessness" and of a Utah Homeless Council composed of key public and private sector leaders to drive homelessness strategy.[16]

In 2021, the Utah legislature put these and other recommendations into law, resetting homelessness policymaking in the state and spurring new projects and strategies. Bringing diverse stakeholders to the table was critical, as was keeping the dialogue nonpartisan. "They're listening to people who are out there in the trenches," Ivory says, "and getting everyone engaged so that they understand the issues and are responding." Two projects have kicked off with a mixture of public and private support, one designed to help preserve affordable housing and the other to help homeless people with substance abuse issues. "But more importantly, the group is intact, they're collaborative, they're moving forward. That's something we hadn't seen happening on this issue."

Leaders can drive progress not just by forging relationships across political lines or enacting organizational policies with a nonpartisan lens but by creating opportunities for others to do so as well. My friend Mike Leavitt has thought deeply about how leaders can reverse political polarization and foster more comity and collaboration. The basis for engagement across political lines starts, he argues, with a common outcome that everyone can agree on, such as reduced homelessness or fewer people dying of gun-related suicide. Leaders of different political persuasions must then take time to understand one another's points of view—what their concern or "pain point" is and how we might address it.

But as noble and difficult as this shared understanding is, it isn't enough. Adversaries often require a gentle nudge to engage productively with one another. The people who can deliver those nudges are what Leavitt calls "conveners of stature," respected leaders who possess enough status and influence to "bring people together and get them to operate in good faith." In Leavitt's telling, George Washington was precisely one such convener. After defeating the British, the American colonists were struggling to self-govern under the Articles of Confederation. Washington was the only person with enough gravitas to bring representatives from the various factions together and encourage them to make the compromises necessary to adopt a new constitution.[17]

Leaders today must follow Washington's example, convening warring sides and establishing dialogue built on mutual respect. We can do it on a grand scale at the national or state levels, and we can also do it within our organizations. For over 15 years, our chief financial officer, Bert Zimmerli, has held meetings in local communities across Utah to gather input about financial needs related to healthcare and how our system can best mobilize its charity dollars to help the underserved. These meetings include a wide range of stakeholders—large and small business interests, government, community advocates—that collectively straddle the political divide. With their help, we can fine-tune our policies on financial assistance and foster healthy, productive discussions between those in our community who pay for healthcare and those advocating for healthcare consumers.[18]

Leaders also can convene others across political lines while managing their own teams. At Intermountain, our executive team includes leaders who harbor an array of views across the political spectrum. As convener, I've encouraged open debate and tried to help team members forge deeper, personal relationships with one another by arranging retreats, social events, group exercises, and the like. Although we tend to keep our individual political views in the background, they've crept in at times, prompting us to do the hard and messy work of muddling ahead toward common ground. Our challenge at these moments is to find a way to do what is right for the organization while also allowing each of us to walk away with our personal dignity intact.

During one episode of fairly intense conflict, I tried to rally our team by relaying an anecdote from when I was practicing medicine in the pediatric ICU. A sad but necessary part of our job was withdrawing life support from patients who had no hope of survival. One of our partners—I'll call him Rich—held religious beliefs that made it extremely difficult for him to take patients off life support. Another partner and I were willing to perform the necessary procedures because we knew we had to and because we also understood that we were giving these patients a gift by sparing them from horrible and constant pain and suffering. We wound up creating a protocol whereby we would take Rich's patients off life support ourselves when that was warranted, removing the burden from him. This arrangement allowed our team to serve patients and the organization as required while still leaving everyone's dignity intact. As I told our team at Intermountain, we, too, could arrive at solutions together, so long as we were willing to persevere and work through painful issues. So far, we've always managed to do that, and our team has emerged even stronger.

All leaders have it in them to serve as conveners of stature, and more generally, to color outside the red and blue lines. It takes strength and focus as well as a number of other traits we've referenced in this book: empathy, courage, openness, pragmatism, and a tolerance for complexity. Is it sometimes scary to reach out to perceived enemies or antagonists? Absolutely. But the more we do it, the more we discover that it won't kill us, it won't rob us of our sense of identity, and it won't erode the principles and values we hold dear.

Please don't let the divisiveness of our times discourage or distract you. Push aside either-or thinking when you encounter it. Forge new, nontraditional partnerships of your own and help others to do the same. Remember, people who share your beliefs don't have a monopoly on good ideas and noble intentions. Make it a priority to become friendly with those who disagree with you—to learn from them, to unleash their energies. We really can ease tensions and build a more harmonious, compassionate, and prosperous society. We can turn our organizations into agents of civility and comity, replacing extremism and dogmatism with a healthier pragmatism— all in the name of meaningful progress. But only if we're willing to step up, work together as leaders, and make some good trouble across red and blue lines.

QUESTIONS FOR REFLECTION

1. When was the last time you made yourself deeply uncomfortable for the sake of building a relationship with someone outside of your political bubble?

2. Does your organization currently pursue initiatives that break new ground by partnering with players across the red-blue divide?

3. Do you initiate new friendships with potential or perceived adversaries? If not, what's stopping you?

4. When a political opponent attacks you, can you find opportunities to reach out and make a human connection?

5. When conflicts arise between you and your partners, are you too quick to disengage on principle? How hard do you *really* try to find small areas of commonality where you might continue to engage?

6. What opportunities might exist for you to serve as a convener of stature, both in your community and organization?

UNLEASHING OURSELVES

In 1993, my wife, Mary Carole, and I moved to Bangor, Maine, to work at a small regional medical center. I had finished my residency, and before I started my fellowship training, we thought we'd slow down our careers for a year and take some time for ourselves. We each planned to work half-time, Mary Carole as a general pediatrician and I as head of the center's small pediatric ICU. I wound up working constantly that year and absolutely loved it. Although I had only two months of experience in an ICU previously, I now had the opportunity to run one myself and lead a team of caregivers.

It wasn't long before I felt the full weight and responsibility of leadership. One day, paramedics brought in a 16-year-old patient with meningitis who was gravely ill with septic shock. It's a bad sign when patients tell you that they think they're dying. But that's exactly what this patient muttered to us before losing consciousness. Our job was to stabilize him enough so that we could airlift him to Boston Children's Hospital for more specialized care.

We didn't normally get patients this sick in this ICU. My small team—composed of a respiratory therapist, a pharmacist, and a couple of nurses—was terrified. With very little hands-on ICU training, I was terrified, too. My pulse quickened as they wheeled the patient in—if we screwed this up, this child would die. Fortunately, I managed to stay calm and be there for my team. Standing at the head of this patient's bed with my team standing around me, I took a deep breath to center myself and gave a short pep talk. "Look," I said, "we're a really good team. We know how to do this. Let's take care of one another, and let's take care of this patient. If we do, I think it's going to go really well."

These words weren't especially profound or poetic, but they galvanized all of us to do our best. By acknowledging the fear that we all were feeling and by offering reassurance, I was able to provide emotional relief to my team at a critical moment. They were now reinforced in their belief that they were up to the challenge of saving this patient's life. In asking them to take care of one another, I was setting an important ground rule: we would surmount the obstacles in our path by pulling together and operating as a unified, cohesive team.

We quickly intubated this patient, inserted arterial and central venous lines on our first try, and started him on a medication to support his blood pressure. Thankfully, his condition stabilized. As it turned out, we couldn't fly him out right away—a storm had rolled in, and the weather was too rough. I wound up staying at his bedside for almost 72 hours until the helicopter finally arrived. The patient went on to make a full recovery. His family was so grateful that they sent me a signed poster to express their thanks. Today, it hangs in my home as one of my most treasured keepsakes.

I've described how my cancer diagnoses have lent urgency to my efforts to unleash others, but it was in Maine that I first came to regard the pursuit of progress as my life's purpose. Operating under extreme pressure, I galvanized a *team* to tackle a seemingly impossible challenge, and it left me feeling both humbled and exhilarated. I wanted to spend my career leading people through adverse circumstances, creating conditions that allowed them to question their own assumptions about their existing mental and physical limits and surpass them. I wanted to unleash people to make a difference in the world, whether it was saving a sick child's life, creating a new business, taking an accomplished organization to new heights, revolutionizing the reigning business models in healthcare, or even building a more equitable and compassionate society.

As I've argued in this book, all of us have it in us to drive progress. We can think *bigger*, adopting innovative business models that add more value for all stakeholders. Implementing those models aggressively and at scale, we can unleash our workforces to make the world better—more equitable, safer, more prosperous, more compassionate. We can take our established, successful organizations and improve on them, so that they not only endure but stand as models for others to emulate.

Unleashing possibility starts with embracing the foundational principles of empathy and openness to those in outsider positions. We can't achieve meaningful change unless we first learn to see the world with new eyes. Understanding viscerally the needs of those whom we serve can fire up our collective passion to drive change, while bringing outsider perspectives to bear can help us to dislodge parts of conventional thinking that might be holding us back.

We also must become more brutally honest with ourselves about how our organizations perform, putting structures and systems in place that foster introspection and enhance our organizations' capacity to transform themselves. Fine-tuning our strategies, we can unleash others by innovating our offerings, collaborating with competitors, pursuing "good" growth, and looking upstream to address the root causes of social and health problems. Finally, we can rally our workforces behind change by taking public stands on behalf of our purpose and values and by reaching pragmatically across political lines.

So much of this challenging work boils down to navigating a perennial tension between imagination and fear. On the one hand, leaders can unleash others by expanding their sense of what's possible. Questioning conventional wisdom, we can evoke a desirable future and empower others to take risks in pursuit of it. On the other hand, we must manage the fears that innovating and risk-taking naturally trigger. We must emphasize that it's OK at times to throw out established rules and guidelines to put our mission first. We must affirm that it's acceptable to make mistakes and that our failures fuel our growth. We must set an example by taking risks ourselves and occasionally falling on our faces. Ultimately, we must create contexts in which it becomes safe to take the initiative and try something new.

When we do the sustained and difficult work of unleashing others, we position established organizations to reach new heights of performance and social impact. Workforces become more engaged and inspired. Consumers (or in our case, patients) are better served. Ultimately, the organization creates more economic and social value. And as leaders, we walk away with the deep personal satisfaction that comes with having delivered positive change on a large scale.

The task of unleashing others might well feel daunting. In this regard, I have one final story to share. During the summer of 1987, I had just finished my first year of medical school and was taking it easy (in relative terms), working in a lab in Vermont and training like crazy for the Cape Cod Endurance Triathlon, my first full Ironman distance race. I had raced triathlons over the past five years, but this one was a whole different beast. To complete an Ironman, I'd have to swim 2.4 miles, bike 112 miles, and run 26.2 miles. I had never ridden a bike for more than 100 miles at a time, nor had I run more than 20 miles. I planned to run the race the following autumn in Cape Cod, and I knew it would be tough.

Each day that summer, I pushed myself as hard as I absolutely could. By the time autumn came and I was back in school, I thought I was ready. But when race day came around, I suddenly felt overcome by fear and doubt. Standing at the starting line, waiting for the gun to go off, I thought to myself, "What have I gotten myself into? Am I in too far? Will I fail? Why am I doing this?"

The gun went off, and guess what? I didn't turn around and go home. I pushed forward, shifting my thinking to remove some of the pressure. "You've done the work," I told myself, "now let's see what happens. If worse comes to worst, you'll fail. And if you do, you'll just try again." I kept going, one mile at a time, and let the momentum carry me. I wound up finishing and thoroughly enjoying the experience. I also found that I came out mentally stronger. Now that I had completed an Ironman, I wondered what other seemingly impossible challenges I might take on, both athletically and in my career.

Before we can unleash others to grasp possibility, we must first unleash ourselves. We must fire up our own imaginations and manage our own fears. In this instance, I had a dream of finishing a triathlon. More recently, I had a dream of transforming a storied healthcare system. What's your ambition as a leader? How might you best be of service to others?

After reflecting on such questions, you must bring yourself to take that difficult first step. Don't perseverate. Just do it. Let the momentum carry you. You might fail, but if so, don't worry. You can pick yourself up and try again. And the failure will teach you something.

Once you take a risk and do succeed, I suspect you'll feel both humbled and emboldened, as I did, to take on still more challenges. You'll believe that other people, too, can do incredible things and that you can help them get there. Over time, driving progress will become an indelible part of who you are. You'll still feel fearful, but you'll realize that sticking with the status quo just isn't good enough, and that with enough diligence you really do have it in you to do more. You'll experience setbacks, as I did with my cancer diagnoses, but you'll keep pushing forward, working harder than ever and enjoying every minute. In the end, you'll make meaningful change happen—for your community, your people, and yourself.

I wish all this for you—and good health, too.

ACKNOWLEDGMENTS

'd like to begin by recognizing my talented and dogged book team. Casey Ebro, executive editor at McGraw Hill, greatly improved this book with her keen eye and smart advice. To my agent, Jim Levine, thank you for believing in this book and helping me navigate the process of finding a publisher. Seth Schulman, Brian McKenna, Debbie Ostrander, Katherina Holzhauser, and Rachel Gledhill: you are all strategic, brilliant, persistent, and fun, prime examples of the good and talented humans whom I want around me. I wish to thank as well the dozens of phenomenal, self-reflective leaders who agreed to be interviewed for this book. I feel inspired by your examples and deeply appreciate your stories and insights.

I'm fortunate to have received a vast amount of guidance, coaching, and friendship over the course of my career. Thank you to Joe Hahn and Toby Cosgrove for seeing a glimmer of capability in me and allowing me to run hard—and for forgiving my mistakes. I'm grateful to have worked under the guidance of spectacular board chairs, including Waleed al Muhairi al Moukarab, Scott Anderson, Gail Miller, and Mike Leavitt.

Over the years, I've led some truly phenomenal teams—low drama, high speed, low drag, marked by an obsession over mission and an unparalleled ability to execute. Thank you to my PICU colleagues, Medical Operations executive team, CCAD leaders, and Intermountain's Executive Leadership Team. To my ELT, we've been through reorganization, growth, stumbles, sickness, health, pandemic, social unrest, economic headwinds, social polarization. I've learned that this team can do literally anything. You are the best of the best. My feelings for you and your families run deep and true.

I take great pleasure in hearing stories of the skill, spontaneity, and compassion that Intermountain's 60,000 caregivers (post-merger with SCL Health) bring to bear on behalf of our neighbors. People are the heart and soul of any business, and all of you prove that every day. Thank you for your dedication and hard work. Please know that leading this organization has been the privilege of a lifetime.

When you become the CEO of a big organization, you have lots of new "friends." Here's to old friends: Owen Young, Kirk Miller, Marci Price-Miller, Jonathan Kaye, Lesley Kaye, Morris Wheeler, Joanne Cohen, Lou Bonelli, Josette Beran, Steve Davis, Denise Davis, Abdulla al Shamsi, Babbie Lester, and Lessing Stern.

My mom and dad, Rosanne and Tony Harrison, raised three kids in a home that valued family, education, and service. My brother and sister, Ed and Janet, are fine human beings and wonderful siblings. I'm grateful for everything that our family taught me, and I try to live my life in ways that pay homage to the spirit of our upbringing.

Finally, I'd like to acknowledge my wife, Mary Carole, and our children, Alex, Martin, and Settie. Over a cocktail one night, MC and I were talking about this book. I told her that I doubt that my (considerable) drive would have been as productively channeled in the absence of our family. Our journey started in New Hampshire in 1989. I was a fourth-year medical student delivering babies, and MC was a freshly minted pediatric intern resuscitating them. I thought she was smart, sassy, and filled out her scrubs nicely. She thought I looked like a baby. We've been married for 32 years. Her sense of fun, talents, and open heart have enriched my life. Our three remarkable kids have grown into strong, talented adults who are determined to make our world more tolerant and just. My love for these four is infinite. The way they live their lives inspires me every day to be the best person I can be.

NOTES

Introduction

1. I've often spoken publicly of my illness and its impact on me. See Erin Goff, "New Intermountain Healthcare CEO Talks About How He Stays Healthy," KSL, May 18, 2017, https://www.ksl.com/article/44295268/new -intermountain-healthcare-ceo-talks-about-how-he-stays-healthy; "Building the 'Tesla' of Health Systems: Where Marc Harrison Plans to Take Intermountain Next," Advisory Board, June 6, 2017, https://www.advisory .com/blog/2017/06/marc-harrison-intermountain.

2. "Dr. A. Marc Harrison Named Upcoming CEO of Intermountain Healthcare," Business Wire, May 20, 2016, https://www.businesswire.com/ news/home/20160520005866/en/Dr.-A.-Marc-Harrison-Named-Upcoming -CEO-of-Intermountain-Healthcare.

3. "Q&A: Dr. Marc Harrison's Transition from Abu Dhabi to Intermountain," Modern Healthcare, October 29, 2016, https://www.modernhealthcare. com/article/20161029/MAGAZINE/310299957/q-a-dr-marc-harrison-s -transition-from-abu-dhabi-to-intermountain; "White House Recognizes Intermountain Healthcare and Syapse for Their Commitment to Precision Medicine," press release, February 2016, syapse.com, https://syapse.com/ news/press-releases/white-house-recognizes-intermountain-healthcare-and -syapse-for-their-commitment-to-precision-medicine.

4. Please see the "About Us" section of our website, intermountainhealthcare.org/ about/.

5. "FDA Approves BCMA-Targeted CAR T-Cell Therapy for Multiple Myeloma," Cancer.gov, April 14, 2021, https://www.cancer.gov/news-events/ cancer-currents-blog/2021/fda-ide-cel-car-t-multiple-myeloma.

Chapter 1

1. Brené Brown, *Dare to Lead: Brave Work. Tough Conversations. Whole Hearts.* (New York: Random House, 2018), 142.

2. John H. Noseworthy (former CEO of Mayo Clinic), interview with the author's research team, October 13, 2021.

3. Courtney Tanner, "In Separate Rallies, Utahns Protest Mask Mandate and Demand In-Person Classes," *Salt Lake City Tribune*, July 15, 2020, https://www.sltrib.com/news/education/2020/07/15/packed-meeting-utah/; Katie Karalis, "'No More Masks': Hundreds Attend Anti-mask Mandate Rally in St. George," *ABC4*, updated September 14, 2020, https://www.abc4.com/news/top-stories/no-more-masks-hundreds-attend-anti-mask-mandate-rally-in-st-george/.

4. Tanner, "In Separate Rallies, Utahns Protest Mask Mandate and Demand In-Person Classes."

5. "Utah Protest Says Mask Mandates Curtail Civil Liberties," AP, August 6, 2020, https://apnews.com/article/virus-outbreak-utah-provo-ammon-bundy-infectious-diseases-4653e5ed676d1d5fffe38037c00d833a; Ivan Pereira, "Utah Public Hearing on Schools Dismissed After Angry Parents Pack Room Without Masks," *ABC News*, July 16, 2020, https://abcnews.go.com/US/utah-public-hearing-schools-dismissed-angry-parents-pack/story?id=71825487.

6. Joshua Bote and K. Sophie Will, "Hundreds Turned out for Anti-mask Protest in Utah, Which Is Being Mocked as 'A Straight Parody' on Social Media," *USA Today*, updated September 15, 2020, https://www.usatoday.com/story/news/nation/2020/09/14/st-george-utah-anti-mask-protest-social-media/5799567002/; Claire Lampen, "This Anti-Mask Rally Is Beyond Parody," *CUT*, September 14, 2020, https://www.thecut.com/2020/09/viral-utah-anti-mask-rally-clip-feels-like-a-parody.html.

7. Bob Kerrey (former Nebraska governor and senator), interview with author, October 5, 2021.

8. Seraphine Kapsandoy (chief clinical information officer at Intermountain), interview with the author's research team, October 20, 2021.

9. Please see the about section on our website: intermountainhealthcare.org.

10. For Utah, please see "Vaccinations in Utah," https://coronavirus-dashboard.utah.gov/vaccines.html.

Chapter 2

1. "From Disney to Doctors: The Uncommon Path of a Patient Experience Leader," *Qualtrics*, September 8, 2021, https://www.qualtrics.com/blog/patient-experience-path/.

2. I'm proud to say that in May 2022, Sue Robel became the president of our Canyons (Utah and Idaho) region.

3. David Epstein, *Range: Why Generalists Triumph in a Specialized World* (New York: Riverhead, 2019).

4. KLAS Research, "Kevan Mabbutt, Bringing the Disney Experience to Healthcare," YouTube video, 32.20, November 3, 2021, https://www.youtube.com/watch?v=tGZ2COP125U.

5. "From Rep. John Lewis, Quotes in a Long Life of Activism," *Washington Post*, July 18, 2020, https://www.washingtonpost.com/national/from-rep-john -lewis-quotes-in-a-long-life-of-activism/2020/07/18/7ee684d8-c8b0-11ea -a825-8722004e4150_story.html.

6. Orit Gadiesh (chairman of Bain & Company), interview with the author's research team, November 29, 2021.

7. Gail Miller (chair of the Larry H. Miller Group of Companies and former owner of the Utah Jazz basketball team), interview with the author's research team, November 8, 2021.

8. Denitza P. Blagev, et al., "On the Journey Toward Health Equity: Data, Culture Change, and the First Step," *NEJM Catalyst,* 2, No.7 (July 2021), DOI: https://doi.org/10.1056/CAT.21.0118.

9. Kathleen E. McKee (assistant professor of neurology at Intermountain Healthcare and associate medical director, Intermountain Neurosciences Patient Experience & Research), interview with the author's research team, October 6, 2021.

10. "Intermountain Healthcare Reaches Agreement to Acquire HealthCare Partners Nevada," *State of Reform*, June 21, 2019, https://stateofreform.com/ news/utah/2019/06/intermountain-healthcare-reaches-agreement-to-acquire -healthcare-partners-nevada/.

11. Dr. Paul Krakovitz, MD (region president of Intermountain Healthcare in Nevada), interview with the author's research team, November 15, 2021.

Chapter 3

1. These datapoints all appear in "Intermountain 2017—Marc Harrison, MD Message to the Community," YouTube video, 54.28, April 7, 2017, https:// www.youtube.com/watch?v=EjufyYBO8KE; "Patient Safety Movement Ranks Intermountain in Top 3 for Eliminating Preventable Deaths," *St. George News*, August 9, 2015, https://www.stgeorgeutah.com/news/archive/ 2015/08/09/patient-safety-movement-ranks-intermountain-in-top-3 -eliminating-preventable-deaths/#.Ya7LUvHMKXg.

2. These datapoints all appear in "Intermountain 2017—Marc Harrison, MD Message to the Community"; "Patient Safety Movement Ranks Intermountain in Top 3 for Eliminating Preventable Deaths."

3. These datapoints all appear in "Intermountain 2017—Marc Harrison, MD Message to the Community"; "Patient Safety Movement Ranks Intermountain in Top 3 for Eliminating Preventable Deaths."

4. Dr. Shannon Phillips (chief medical officer for community-based care at Intermountain and president of Intermountain Medical Group), interview with the author's research team, October 12, 2021.

5. Rob Allen (senior vice president and chief operating officer at Intermountain), interview with the author's research team, October 5, 2021.

6. See, for instance, Brent C. James and Lucy A. Savitz, "How Intermountain Trimmed Health Care Costs Through Robust Quality Improvement Efforts," *Health Affairs* 30, no. 6 (June 2011), doi: 10.1377/hlthaff.2011.0358. For a description of the general approach, please see "Lean Healthcare: 6 Methodologies for Improvement from Dr. Brent James," *Health Catalyst* (executive report), accessed May 16, 2022, https://www.healthcatalyst.com/wp-content/uploads/2021/05/Lean-Healthcare-6-Methodologies-for-Improvement-from-Dr.-Brent-James.pdf.

7. A. Scott Anderson (chair emeritus of the board at Intermountain and president and CEO of Zions First National Bank), interview with the author's research team, November 9, 2021.

8. Dr. Shannon Phillips (chief medical officer for community-based care at Intermountain and president of Intermountain Medical Group), interview with the author's research team, October 12, 2021.

9. Dr. Mike Woodruff (emergency room physician and senior medical director for the Office of Patient Experience at Intermountain), interview with the author's research team, December 2, 2021.

10. Dr. Mike Woodruff (emergency room physician and senior medical director for the Office of Patient Experience at Intermountain), interview with the author's research team, December 2, 2021.

11. Data compiled by Intermountain from third-party healthcare data collection firms.

Chapter 4

1. Cara Camiolo Reddy, MD (associate chief medical officer, clinical shared services at Intermountain Healthcare), interview with the author's research team, December 21, 2021.

2. Rob Allen (senior vice president and chief operating officer at Intermountain), interview with the author's research team, October 5, 2021.

3. "Intermountain Restructuring: Overview of Forces Shaping Healthcare," *Intermountain Healthcare*, accessed May 17, 2022, https://intermountain healthcare.org/about/who-we-are/trustee-resource-center/newsletter/newsletter-archive/intermountain-restructuring-overview-of-forces-shaping-healthcare/.

4. "Intermountain Healthcare Announces New Clinical Structure," *Intermountain Healthcare*, accessed May 17, 2022, https://intermountainhealth care.org/about/who-we-are/trustee-resource-center/newsletter/newsletter-archive/intermountain-healthcare-announces-new-clinical-structure/.

5. I put it similarly in "Intermountain Restructuring: Overview of Forces Shaping Healthcare."

6. Stephen Heidari-Robinson and Suzanne Heywood, "Getting Reorgs Right," *Harvard Business Review*, November 2016, https://hbr.org/2016/11/getting-reorgs-right: "According to a McKinsey survey we conducted, more than 80% fail to deliver the hoped-for value in the time planned, and 10% cause

real damage to the company. More important, they can be damned miserable experiences for employees. Research suggests that reorgs—and the uncertainty they provoke about the future—can cause greater stress and anxiety than layoffs, leading in about 60% of cases to noticeably reduced productivity."

7. This paragraph incorporates language from an internal Intermountain presentation entitled "Intermountain Operating Model."

8. General Stanley A. McChrystal (former commander of the Joint Special Operations Command), interview with the author's research team, December 13, 2021. Also see Stanley A. McChrystal et al., *Team of Teams: New Rules of Engagement for a Complex World* (New York: Portfolio, 2015).

9. "Intermountain Restructuring: Overview of Forces Shaping Healthcare."

10. "Intermountain Restructuring: Overview of Forces Shaping Healthcare."

11. Rob Allen (senior vice president and chief operating officer at Intermountain), interview with the author's research team, October 5, 2021.

12. Employee review of "Intermountain Healthcare," posted on July 2, 2018: https://www.glassdoor.com/Reviews/Employee-Review-Intermountain-Healthcare-RVW21302586.htm.

13. Ben Lockhart, "Intermountain says it eliminated 396 positions in overhaul, but added 107 new jobs," *Deseret News*, August 27, 2018, https://www.deseret.com/2018/8/27/20652124/intermountain-says-it-eliminated-396-positions-in-overhaul-but-added-107-new-jobs.

14. Matthew Piper, "Intermountain Healthcare Employees Brace for More Job Cuts as Utah's Largest Employer Readies to 'Adapt or Die,'" *Deseret News*, March 19, 2018, https://www.deseret.com/2018/3/19/20641954/intermountain-healthcare-employees-brace-for-more-job-cuts-as-utah-s-largest-employer-readies-to-ada#intermountain-medical-center-in-murray-is-pictured-on-thursday-march-15-2018.

15. John Commins, "Intermountain Healthcare to Cut 250 Admin Positions to Lower Care Costs for Patients," *Healthleaders*, October 14, 2020, https://www.healthleadersmedia.com/strategy/intermountain-healthcare-cut-250-admin-positions-lower-care-costs-patients; "Intermountain Healthcare Emerges with a Stronger and Focused Brand," *HR Healthcare*, accessed May 17, 2022, https://hrhealthcare.wbresearch.com/blog/intermountain-healthcare-emerges-from-restructuring-strategy-for-focused-brand.

16. Franz van Houten (CEO of Philips), interview with the author's research team, December 16, 2021.

17. General Stanley A. McChrystal (former commander of the Joint Special Operations Command), interview with the author's research team, December 13, 2021.

18. Ben Lockhart, "Intermountain Leaders Meet to Discuss Changes; Uncertainty Remains over Affected Jobs," *KSL*, March 23, 2018, https://www.ksl.com/article/46286292/intermountain-leaders-meet-to-discuss-changes-uncertainty-remains-over-affected-jobs.

19. "Intermountain Healthcare Announces New Clinical Structure," *Intermountain Healthcare*, accessed May 17, 2022, https://intermountain healthcare.org/about/who-we-are/trustee-resource-center/newsletter/ newsletter-archive/intermountain-healthcare-announces-new-clinical -structure/; "Intermountain's Reorganization Is About Providing Better Care More Consistently and More Affordably," *LinkedIn*, March 26, 2019, https:// www.linkedin.com/pulse/intermountains-reorganization-providing-better -care-more-robert-allen?articleId=6513865692935258112.

20. Dr. Chad A. Spain (family medicine physician at Intermountain), interview with the author's research team, November 5, 2021.

21. "Intermountain Announces New Company to Elevate Value-Based Care Capabilities," *Intermountain Healthcare*, accessed May 17, 2022, https:// intermountainhealthcare.org/about/who-we-are/trustee-resource-center/ newsletter/newsletter-archive/intermountain-announces-new-company-to -elevate-value-based-care-capabilities/.

22. "Episode 33: Reimagining Primary Care," Intermountain Healthcare Podcast, accessed May 17, 2022, https://intermountainhealthcare.org/about/podcasts/ intermountain-podcast-episodes/ep-33/.

23. "Fact Sheet: Covid-19 Pandemic Results in Bankruptcies or Closures for Some Hospitals," American Hospital Association, November 2020, 1, https://www .aha.org/system/files/media/file/2020/11/fact-sheet-covid-hospital -bankruptcies-1120.pdf.

24. Sue Robel (senior vice president of clinical operations and chief nursing executive at Intermountain), interview with the author's research team, October 8, 2021.

Chapter 5

1. Erick Ridout and Marissa Ridout, "'Every One of These Babies I've Taken Care of Is a Legacy,'" StoryCorps, accessed May 17, 2022, https://intermountain healthcare.org/about/storycorps/erick-ridout-and-marissa-ridout/. This story also draws on a presentation Dr. Ridout gave to the American Academy of Pediatrics on October 10, 2021. Note that the patient's name is spelled "Maci" in this presentation but is spelled "Macy" elsewhere.

2. Maria Castellucci, "Fewer Tests, Treatments for NICU Babies Reduces Infections, Cuts Costs," *Modern Healthcare*, April 13, 2019, https://www .modernhealthcare.com/care-delivery/fewer-tests-treatments-nicu-babies -reduces-infections-cuts-costs.

3. Dr. R. Erick Ridout (neonatologist at Intermountain), interview with the author's research team, November 11, 2021.

4. See Christopher Cheney, "How Intermountain Reduced NICU Infections, Pain, Blood Loss," *Health Leaders*, April 16, 2019, https://www.healthleaders media.com/clinical-care/how-intermountain-reduced-nicu-infections-pain -blood-loss.

5. Castellucci, "Fewer Tests, Treatments for NICU Babies Reduces Infections, Cuts Costs."

6. Ridout and Ridout, "'Every One of These Babies I've Taken Care of Is a Legacy.'"

7. Marc Harrison and Thomas H. Lee, "Short-Term Loss, Long-Term Gain: Encouraging Bottom-up Ideas That Revise the Value Equation," *NEJM Catalyst*, Innovations in Care Delivery, February 11, 2020, https://catalyst.nejm .org/doi/full/10.1056/CAT.20.0046.

8. "Intermountain Operating Model: A Guide for Caregivers and Leaders," Intermountain Healthcare, 2021, p. 1.

9. Dr. Erick Ridout (neonatologist at Intermountain), interview with the author's research team, November 11, 2021.

10. Guido Bergomi (executive director at Intermountain's office of patient experience), interview with the author's research team, December 17, 2021.

11. Mike Woodruff, MD (emergency room physician and senior medical director for the office of patient experience at Intermountain), interview with the author's research team, December 2, 2021.

12. Wes Johnson (paralympic coach and founder of Balanced Art Multisport in Salt Lake City, Utah), interview with the author's research team, December 14, 2021.

13. Orit Gadiesh (chairwoman of Bain & Company), interview with the author's research team, November 29, 2021.

14. In 2019, for instance, we implemented over 54,000. See Matt Pollard and Namita Seth Mohta, "Implementing 54,000+ Ideas in a Culture of Continuous Improvement," *NEJM Catalyst*, July 28, 2020, https://catalyst.nejm.org/ doi/full/10.1056/CAT.20.0455.

15. Matt Pollard, MD (vice president of continuous improvement at Intermountain), interview with the author's research team, November 1, 2021.

16. Pollard and Mohta, "Implementing 54,000+ Ideas in a Culture of Continuous Improvement."

17. Ronald de Jong and Freek Vermeulen, "The Strategic Transformation of Royal Philips," London Business School Case Study, June 2021, p. 1. See also Srikant M. Datar, Rajiv Lal, and Caitlin N. Bowler, "Royal Philips: Designing Toward Profound Change," Harvard Business School Case Study 9-118-017, November 26, 2017.

18. Frans van Houten (CEO of Philips), interview with the author's research team, December 16, 2021.

19. "Philips' Revenue Worldwide from 2009 to 2021," *Statista*, February 2022, https://www.statista.com/statistics/272107/philips-revenue-worldwide-since -2006/.

20. Matt Pollard, MD (vice president of continuous improvement at Intermountain), interview with the author's research team, November 1, 2021.

21. Marc Harrison, "How a U.S. Health Care System Uses 15-Minute Huddles to Keep 23 Hospitals Aligned," *Harvard Business Review,* November 29, 2018, https://hbr.org/2018/11/how-a-u-s-health-care-system-uses-15-minute-huddles-to-keep-23-hospitals-aligned.

22. "Critical Care Transport," *Cleveland Clinic* (brochure), 2012, https://my.clevelandclinic.org/-/scassets/files/org/critical-care/critical-care-transport-brochure.pdf?la=en.

23. Matt Pollard, MD (vice president of continuous improvement at Intermountain), interview with the author's research team, November 1, 2021.

Chapter 6

1. "Protecting Ghana's Election: Instant Agility with Zipline's Autonomous Delivery Network," Zipline, February 2021, https://assets.ctfassets.net/pbn2i2zbvp41/3yrQaMNdJ1u1J2aSEucjzt/4412ea5d12896d15b7eb41a2212d0295/Zipline_Ghana_PPE_Global_Healthcare_Feb-2021.pdf.

2. Keller Rinaudo (founder and CEO of Zipline), interview with the author's research team, January 23, 2022.

3. "Intermountain Healthcare and Zipline Partner," Zipline, November 11, 2021, https://flyzipline.com/press/intermountain-healthcare-and-zipline-partner/.

4. Marc Harrison, "What One Health System Learned About Providing Digital Services in the Pandemic," *Harvard Business Review*, December 11, 2020, https://hbr.org/2020/12/what-one-health-system-learned-about-providing-digital-services-in-the-pandemic.

5. "New Survey Shows Consumers Want Increased Access to Clinical Care at Home," Intermountain Healthcare, December 2, 2021, https://intermountainhealthcare.org/news/2021/12/new-survey-shows-consumers-want-to-access-clinical-care-at-home/.

6. Mike Miliard, "Intermountain Expands Reach, Broadens Offerings of Hospital at Home program," *Healthcare IT News*, August 6, 2021, https://www.healthcareitnews.com/news/intermountain-expands-reach-broadens-offerings-hospital-home-program.

7. "Intermountain Healthcare Opens New Hospital—Without a Building or Walls," Intermountain Healthcare, February 28, 2018, https://intermountainhealthcare.org/news/2018/02/intermountain-healthcare-opens-new-hospital-without-a-building-or-walls/.

8. Brenda Reiss-Brennan, "Mental Health Integration: Normalizing Team Care," *Journal of Primary Care & Community Health*, November 7, 2013, https://doi.org/10.1177/2150131913508983.

9. Brenda Reiss-Brennan et al., "Achieving Population Health Through Mental Health Integration and Team-Based Care," *Intermountain Healthcare* (brochure),

accessed May 23, 2022, https://www.jefferson.edu/content/dam/academic/population-health/hearst-health-prize/Intermountain-poster%20f.pdf.

10. In May 2022, we announced a partnership with General Catalyst to explore the creation of a "clicks and mortar" ecosystem for healthcare: "Intermountain Healthcare and General Catalyst to Collaborate on Innovation," *Global News Wire*, May 9, 2022, https://www.globenewswire.com/news-release/2022/05/09/2438830/23694/en/Intermountain-Healthcare-and-General-Catalyst-to-Collaborate-on-Innovation.html.

11. Hemant Taneja (managing director of General Catalyst), interview with the author's research team, January 5, 2022.

12. Jonathan Shieber, "Plume Is Building a Healthcare Service Specifically for the Transgender Community," *TechCrunch*, June 18, 2020, https://techcrunch.com/2020/06/18/plume-is-building-a-healthcare-service-specifically-for-the-transgender-community/.

13. Dr. Derrick Haslem (oncologist at Intermountain), interview with the author's research team, November 18, 2021.

14. Haslem, interview.

15. "Does Tele-oncology Work?" Intermountain Healthcare (podcast), https://intermountainhealthcare.org/about/podcasts/thanks-for-asking-podcast-episodes/2-ep-16/.

16. Derrick S. Haslem et al., "Using a Tele-oncology Service Provides a Direct Benefit to Patients and Caregivers in Rural Communities in the Intermountain West," *Journal of Clinical Oncology* 38, no. 15 (2020), https://ascopubs.org/doi/abs/10.1200/JCO.2020.38.15_suppl.e14153?af=R.

17. "Does Tele-oncology Work?" Intermountain Healthcare (podcast).

18. Nickolas Mark (managing director of Intermountain Ventures), interview with the author's research team, February 10, 2022.

19. "Intermountain Ventures Fund," Intermountain Health, accessed May 23, 2022, https://intermountainhealthcare.org/about/transforming-healthcare/innovation/business-development/ventures/innovations-fund/; "Our partners see the potential to redefine what great healthcare can be," Intermountain Ventures, accessed May 23, 2022, https://intermountainventures.com/portfolio/#undefined.

20. Mandy Roth, "6 Things You Can Learn About Innovation from Intermountain Ventures," *Health Leaders*, November 26, 2019, https://www.healthleadersmedia.com/innovation/6-things-you-can-learn-about-innovation-intermountain-ventures.

21. Makenzie Holland, "Intermountain Ventures: A Look Inside a Healthcare Venture Fund," *TechTarget*, March 27, 2019, https://searchhealthit.techtarget.com/feature/Intermountain-Ventures-A-look-inside-a-healthcare-venture-fund.

22. Roth, "6 Things You Can Learn About Innovation from Intermountain Ventures."

23. "Alluceo," Intermountain Healthcare, accessed May 24, 2022; Greg Slabodkin, "Intermountain Launches Company to Integrate Mental Health Services," *Health Data Management*, March 12, 2018, https://www.healthdata management.com/articles/intermountain-launches-company-to-integrate -mental-health-services.

24. Jasmine Pennic, "Intermountain to Deploy AI-Powered Digital Assistants Across Clinically Integrated Network," *HIT Consultant*, October 6, 2020, https://hitconsultant.net/2020/10/06/intermountain-healthcare-notable -partnership/.

25. "My Health+," Intermountain Healthcare, accessed May 24, 2022, https:// intermountainhealthcare.org/patient-tools/my-health-plus/.

Chapter 7

1. Sydney Lupkin, "A Decade Marked by Outrage over Drug Prices," NPR, December 31, 2019, https://www.npr.org/sections/health-shots/2019/ 12/31/792617538/a-decade-marked-by-outrage-over-drug-prices.

2. Michael R. Sisak and Jennifer Peltz, "Shkreli Ordered to Return $64M, Is Barred from Drug Industry," AP, January 14, 2022, https://apnews.com/ article/martin-shkreli-daraprim-profits-fb77aee9ed155f9a74204cfb13 fc1130.

3. Zoe Thomas and Tim Swift, "Who Is Martin Shkreli—'The Most Hated Man In America'?" BBC, August 4, 2017, https://www.bbc.com/news/world-us -canada-34331761.

4. Dan Liljenquist (chief strategy officer at Intermountain), interview with the author's research team, November 12, 2021.

5. Civica Rx, "Not-for-Profit Generic Drug Company Officially Established, Attracts Interest of More Than 120 Health Organizations," news release, September 6, 2018, https://civicarx.org/wp-content/uploads/2020/02/ Civica_Rx_News_Release_9-4-18.f8fecc3d.pdf.

6. See, for example, Reed Abelson and Katie Thomas, "Fed up with Drug Companies, Hospitals Decide to Start Their Own," *New York Times*, January 18, 2018, https://www.nytimes.com/2018/01/18/health/drug-prices-hospitals .html; Liljenquist, interview.

7. Liljenquist, interview.

8. Civica, internal presentation; Liljenquist, interview.

9. CivicaScript, "CivicaScript," June 16, 2021, news release, https://civicarx.org/ wp-content/uploads/2021/06/CivicaScript-FINAL_June.16.2021.pdf.

10. Adam Brandenburger and Barry Nalebuff, "The Rules of Co-opetition," *Harvard Business Review*, January-February 2021, https://hbr.org/2021/01/ the-rules-of-co-opetition; https://knowledge.insead.edu/strategy/managing -the-paradoxes-of-coopetition-10466; Joe DiVanna, "Coopetition in the New Economy," *Duke* (corporate education), September 2020, https:// www.dukece.com/insights/coopetition-in-the-new-economy/; Yunzhong Cheng, "What Is 'Coopetition' and How Can International Organizations

Help?" World Economic Forum, May 6, 2021, https://www.weforum.org/agenda/2021/05/what-is-coopetition-and-how-can-international-organizations-help/.

11. "Northern Ohio Trauma System," Annual Report (2010): 8, https://www.northernohiotraumasystem.com/media/1053/2010-annual-report.pdf.

12. "About NOTS," Northern Ohio Trauma System, accessed May 24, 2022, https://www.northernohiotraumasystem.com/about-nots/.

13. "Cycle for Health UAE," Cleveland Clinic Abu Dhabi, https://www.clevelandclinicabudhabi.ae/en/about-us/pages/cycle-for-health.aspx.

14. "Huntsman Cancer Institute and Intermountain Healthcare Launch Join Cancer Care Program for Adolescents and Young Adults," Huntsman Cancer Institute, https://healthcare.utah.edu/huntsmancancerinstitute/news/2017/05/huntsman-cancer-institute-and0intermountain-healthcare-launch-aya.php.

15. Cornelia Ulrich, "Development, Implementation, and Evaluation of a Joint Research Funding Mechanism Addressing Cancer Control Needs of the State: The Utah Grand Challenges," Huntsman Cancer Institute, https://drexel.edu/~/media/Files/medicine/drexel-pdfs/programs/program-elam/2020-leaders-forum/ELAM-leaders-forum-2020-Ulrich.ashx?la=en.

16. "ARUP and Intermountain Healthcare Collaborate to Meet COVID-19 Testing Needs," ARUP and Intermountain Healthcare, March 31, 2020, https://www.aruplab.com/news/3-31-2020/arup-intermountain-collaborate-covid-19.

17. Intermountain Healthcare, "Medical Leaders from Utah's Major Health Systems to Address Utah's COVID Spike and Potential Impact on State's Hospitals and Caregivers," news release, July 6, 2021, https://intermountainhealthcare.org/news/2021/07/medical-leaders-from-utahs-major-health-systems-to-address-covid-spike-and-potential-impact-on-states-hospitals-and-caregivers/.

18. Becky Jacobs, "Utah Health Care Leaders Declare Systemic Racism a Public Health Crisis," *Salt Lake Tribune*, January 12, 2021, https://www.sltrib.com/news/2021/01/13/utah-health-care-leaders/.

19. Kathy Wilets, "Intermountain Healthcare Partners with the University of Utah to Create Academic Program to Help Keep People Healthy," University of Utah (Health), April 8, 2021, https://healthcare.utah.edu/publicaffairs/news/2021/04/intermountain-population-health.php.

20. Ginni Rometty (former CEO at IBM), interview with the author's research team, January 19, 2022. In crafting this narrative, I also rely on Tony's own account available at the following: "From Serving Coffee to Writing Code—How One IBMer Changed the Future of this Apprentice," IBM (Careers blog), November 12, 2019, https://www.ibm.com/blogs/jobs/2019/11/12/from-serving-coffee-to-writing-code-how-one-ibmer-changed-the-future-of-this-apprentice/.

21. "From Serving Coffee to Writing Code—How One IBMer Changed the Future of This Apprentice," IBM (Careers blog), November 12, 2019, https://www.ibm.com/blogs/jobs/2019/11/12/from-serving-coffee-to-writing-code-how-one-ibmer-changed-the-future-of-this-apprentice/.

22. Please explore the New Collar jobs and the apprenticeship program at https://www.ibm.com/us-en/employment/newcollar/.

23. Rometty, interview.

24. Rometty, interview.

25. Rometty, interview.

26. "P-Tech," IBM, accessed May 24, 2022, https://www.ibm.org/initiatives/p-tech.

27. "Merck Executive Chairman Ken Frazier on Equity in Healthcare," A Healthier Future (podcast), 35.00, https://podcasts.apple.com/us/podcast/a-healthier-future/id1612299596?i=1000557070365.

28. "Measurable actions. Immeasurable possibilities." One Ten, accessed May 24, 2022, https://oneten.org/about/mission/.

29. Anuja Vaidya, "Graphite Health Launches with Plans to Create a Marketplace for Digital Tools," *MedCity News*, October 5, 2021, https://medcitynews.com/2021/10/graphite-health-launches-with-plans-to-create-a-marketplace-for-digital-tools/.

30. Please see Larry Gabriel's remarkable testimonial video: "Patient Stories," Intermountain Healthcare, May 25, 2022, https://intermountainhealthcare.org/services/genomics/patients/patient-stories/.

31. "A Genetic Link to Vertigo? Discussion with Dr. David Jones," January 13, 2022, https://hearinghealthmatters.org/thisweek/2022/genetics-vertigo-dizziness/; Dr. Lincoln Nadaud (oncologist at Intermountain and director of Precision Genomics), interview with the author's research team, October 29, 2021.

32. Jonathan Byrnes and John Wass, "'Showcase Projects' Can Deepen Your Relationships with Profitable Customers," *Harvard Business Review*, October 5, 2021, https://hbr.org/2021/10/showcase-projects-can-deepen-your-relationships-with-profitable-customers.

33. "In Business to Improve Lives," TOMS Impact Report 2021, https://www.toms.com/us/impact/report.html.

Chapter 8

1. "Helping Our Clients and Communities Thrive," 2011 KeyCorp Corporate Social Responsibility Report, https://www.key.com/kco/images/2011-CR-report-053018.pdf.

2. Jenna Goudreau, "From Secretary to CEO: Beth Mooney Makes Banking History," *Forbes*, September 6, 2011, https://www.forbes.com/sites/jennagoudreau/2011/09/06/key-corp-ceo-beth-mooney-makes-banking-history-power-women/?sh=457cfd953e43.

3. Beth Mooney (former CEO of KeyCorp), interview with the author's research team, January 12, 2022.

4. KeyCorp, "KeyCorp to Acquire First Niagara Financial Group," *PR Newswire*, press release, October 30, 2015, https://www.prnewswire.com/news-releases/keycorp-to-acquire-first-niagara-financial-group-300169466.html.

5. "Key Bank," *Mergr*, accessed May 25, 2022, https://mergr.com/keycorp.-acquisitions.

6. "KeyCorp Total Assets 2010-2022," *Macrotrends*, accessed May 25, 2022, https://www.macrotrends.net/stocks/charts/KEY/keycorp/total-assets.

7. "KeyCorp—35 Year Stock Price History," *Macrotrends*, accessed May 25, 2022, https://www.macrotrends.net/stocks/charts/KEY/keycorp/stock-price-history.

8. Michael E. Porter and Mark R. Kramer, "Creating Shared Value," *Harvard Business Review*, January-February 2011, https://hbr.org/2011/01/the-big-idea-creating-shared-value.

9. "Intermountain to Acquire HealthCare Partners Nevada," Intermountain Healthcare, accessed May 25, 2022, https://intermountainhealthcare.org/about/who-we-are/trustee-resource-center/newsletter/newsletter-archive/intermountain-to-acquire-healthcare-partners-nevada/.

10. "Intermountain Healthcare Reaches Agreement to Acquire HealthCare Partners Nevada," Intermountain Healthcare, June 21, 2019, https://intermountainhealthcare.org/news/2019/06/intermountain-healthcare-reaches-agreement-to-acquire-healthcare-partners-nevada/.

11. Adriana Gardella, "Will Your Company Grow Itself to Death?" CBS News, April 19, 2010, https://www.cbsnews.com/news/will-your-company-grow-itself-to-death/.

12. Rob Allen (chief operating officer at Intermountain), interview with the author's research team, January 18, 2022.

13. Marc Harrison, "Intermountain Healthcare Quarterly CEO Update 9/9/20," YouTube video, 43.40, published September 20, 2020, https://www.youtube.com/watch?v=woqpr_YkllA&t=28s.

14. "3 Years at the Top: Moving Intermountain to Wellness and Value," MAG.com, https://www.managedcaremag.com/archives/2019/9/3-years-top-moving-intermountain-wellness-and-value/.

15. Dan Liljenquist (chief strategy officer at Intermountain), interview with the author's research team, January 26, 2022.

16. Bob Bradway (CEO at Amgen), interview with the author's research team, January 21, 2022; "Mission and Values," Amgen, accessed May 25, 2022, https://www.amgen.com/about/mission-and-values.

17. Amgen, "Amgen to Acquire Five Prime Therapeutics for $1.9 Billion in Cash," press release, March 4, 2021, https://www.amgen.com/newsroom/press-releases/2021/03/amgen-to-acquire-five-prime-therapeutics-for-$1-9-billion-in-cash.

18. Liljenquist, interview.
19. Bradway, interview.

Chapter 9

1. Intermountain Healthcare, "Social Determinants of Health," December 2020, 1, https://intermountainhealthcare.org/ckr-ext/Dcmnt?ncid=529732182.
2. Alliance for the Determinants of Health, "Update 2021," https://alliance fordeterminantsofhealth.org/wp-content/uploads/2022/03/2021-Alliance -Report.pdf; Eli Kirshbaum, "United Way of Salt Lake Partners with Intermountain Healthcare to Address Social Determinants of Health," November 23, 2020, https://stateofreform.com/news/2020/11/united-way -of-salt-lake-partners-with-intermountain-healthcare-to-address-social -determinants-of-health/.
3. Seth Southwick (assistant vice president of kidney services at Intermountain), and Nannette Berensen (vice president and chief operating officer of clinical shared services at Intermountain Healthcare), interview with the author's research team, March 24, 2022.
4. Lauren Taylor, "Housing and Health: An Overview of the Literature," *HealthAffairs*, June 7, 2018, https://www.healthaffairs.org/do/10.1377/ hpb20180313.396577/.
5. Nick Fritz (director of impact investing at Intermountain), interview with the author's research team, November 4, 2021.
6. Intermountain Healthcare, "Social Determinants of Health."
7. Intermountain Healthcare, "Community Health Impact Report 2020," 11–13 passim, https://intermountainhealthcare.org/-/media/files/community -benefit/community-health-impact-report-2020.pdf.
8. Intermountain Healthcare, "Intermountain Healthcare Sets Goal to Reduce Opioid Prescribing by 40 Percent," August 22, 2017, https://intermountain healthcare.org/news/2017/08/intermountain-healthcare-sets-goal-to-reduce -opioid-prescribing-by-40-percent/.
9. Mikelle Moore (chief community health officer at Intermountain), interview with the author's research team, November 18, 2021.
10. United States Congress Joint Economic Committee, "The Epidemic Preceding the Pandemic: Will Utah's Progress Hold?," February 19, 2021, https:// www.jec.senate.gov/public/index.cfm/republicans/2021/2/the-epidemic -preceding-the-pandemic.
11. Shannon Clegg (senior strategy consultant and neonatal intensive care nurse), interview with the author's research team, February 17, 2022.

Chapter 10

1. I draw these comments from Intermountain's internal Yammer social media site, as well as from responses to a survey we field to caregivers to gauge their experience on the job.

2. Intermountain's internal Yammer site and responses to caregivers survey.
3. Katie Welkie (CEO of the Primary Children's Hospital at Intermountain Healthcare), interview with the author's research team, October 6, 2021.
4. Brad Gillman, "Building Healthy Eating Environments at Intermountain," Intermountain Healthcare, January 27, 2017, https://intermountain healthcare.org/blogs/topics/live-well/2017/01/building-healthy-eating -environments-at-intermountain/.
5. Intermountain's internal Yammer site as well and responses to caregivers survey.
6. Heather Brace (chief people officer at Intermountain), interview with the author's research team, October 6, 2021.
7. Mikelle Moore (chief community health officer at Intermountain), interview with the author's research team, December 7, 2021.
8. Governor Spencer J. Cox, "Utah Covid-19 Briefing," YouTube video, 1:06:44, https://www.youtube.com/watch?v=mhiRWp--Tc8.
9. Sean P. Means, "Intermountain's CEO Makes a Plea to Utahns: Wear a Mask," *Salt Lake City Tribune*, August 31, 2021, https://www.sltrib.com/news/2021/08/31/intermountains-ceo-makes/.
10. Intermountain Healthcare, "Intermountain Healthcare Is Closing 25 Community Pharmacies in August 2021," accessed May 25, 2022, https://intermountainhealthcare.org/services/pharmacy/community-pharmacies/.
11. Scott D. Pierce, "Intermountain Is Closing 25 Retail Pharmacies and Looking for New Jobs for 250 Employees," *Salt Lake City Tribune*, July 13, 2021, https://www.sltrib.com/news/2021/07/13/intermountain-is-closing/.
12. Todd B. Kashdan, *The Art of Insubordination: How to Dissent & Defy Effectively* (New York: Avery, 2022), 10 passim.

Chapter 11

1. "Suicide and Firearm Injury in Utah: Linking Data to Save Lives," research report, Harvard T. H. Chan School of Public Health, October 2018, https://dsamh.utah.gov/pdf/suicide/Suicide%20and%20Firearm%20Injury%20in%20Utah%20-%20Final%20Report.pdf; you can find more recent data at "Gun Ownership by State," World Population Review, 2022, https://worldpopulationreview.com/state-rankings/gun-ownership-by-state.
2. Morissa Henn (former community health director at Intermountain and current associate commissioner at New Hampshire's Department of Health and Human Services), interview with the author's research team, November 18, 2021.
3. Noah Leavitt, "Uncommon Ground," *Harvard Public Health: Magazine of the Harvard T. H. Chan School of Public Health* (special report), Fall 2018, https://www.hsph.harvard.edu/magazine/magazine_article/uncommon-ground/.
4. Henn, interview.
5. For these details and others in this story, I rely on Leavitt, "Uncommon Ground."

6. Leavitt, "Uncommon Ground."

7. Leavitt, "Uncommon Ground."

8. Henn, interview.

9. Surae Chinn, "Safe Storage of Guns to Prevent Suicides," ABC4, updated August 23, 2019, https://www.abc4.com/sponsored/4pm-sponsored/safe -storage-of-guns-to-prevent-suicides/.

10. Katie McKellar, "Two Utah Gun Bills—Including 'Lauren's Law'—Stall, While 2 Others Advance to House Floor," *Deseret*, February 20, 2019, https://www. deseret.com/2019/2/20/20666372/two-utah-gun-bills-including-lauren -s-law-stall-while-2-others-advance-to-house-floor; Bethany Rodgers, "Utahns Could Temporarily Give up Their Right to Buy Guns Under Bill Before State Lawmakers," *Salt Lake Tribune*, February 17, 2021, https://www .sltrib.com/news/politics/2021/02/17/utahns-could-temporarily/.

11. Lindsay Woolman, "Intermountain Working to Prevent Suicides by Firearms," Intermountain Healthcare, October 8, 2019, https://intermountain healthcare.org/blogs/topics/transforming-healthcare/2019/10/preventing -suicides-by-firearms/.

12. Emma Johnson, "Blue Plate Diner in Salt Lake City Announces Closure," ABC4, updated May 4, 2021, https://www.abc4.com/news/wasatch-front/ blue-plate-diner-in-salt-lake-city-announces-closure/.

13. Of Intermountain's caregivers, 75 percent had been fully vaccinated and 82 percent had received at least one dose.

14. Katie McKellar, "Utah Homeless Spending Is up by 600%, but the Problems 'Continue to Grow.' Here's What an Audit Says Leaders Should Do," *Deseret*, November 16, 2021, https://www.deseret.com/utah/2021/11/16/22785513/ audit-utah-homelessness-spending-rose-but-problems-continue-to-grow-salt -lake-city-homeless; Gregory Scruggs, "Once a National Model, Utah Struggles with Homelessness," Reuters, January 10, 2019, https://www .reuters.com/article/us-usa-homelessness-housing/once-a-national-model -utah-struggles-with-homelessness-idUSKCN1P41EQ.

15. Clark Ivory (chief executive officer of Ivory Homes), interview with the author's research team, March 1, 2022.

16. Kem C. Gardner, "Utah Homeless Services," University of Utah (Policy Institute), November 2020: 5 passim, https://gardner.utah.edu/wp-content/ uploads/HomelessReport-Nov-2020.pdf?x71849.

17. Mike Leavitt (former Utah governor and US secretary of health and human services), interview with the author's research team, December 1, 2021.

18. Bert Zimmerli (chief financial officer at Intermountain), interview with the author's research team, January 26, 2022.

INDEX

Marc Harrison, MD, will run a healthcare platform business for the venture capital firm General Catalyst. The former president and CEO of Intermountain Healthcare, he is a pediatric critical care physician with a proven track record as a top operations executive on a global scale. He is a national and international thought leader on transformation and innovation, ranking among *Fortune*'s Top 50 World's Greatest Leaders in 2019. Dr. Harrison also ranked second among Modern Healthcare's Most Influential Physician Executives and Leaders and tied for second on its list of the 100 Most Influential People in Healthcare in 2018.

Dr. Harrison embraces strategic partnerships and novel collaborations to solve systemic problems and improve lives. Together with Intermountain's 60,000 caregivers, he has implemented bold new approaches to improve health, redefine value-based care, and serve people in new ways. Intermountain's partnerships, pioneering initiatives, and commitment to service are transforming healthcare and bearing fruit for patients and communities.

Previously, Dr. Harrison served as CEO of Cleveland Clinic Abu Dhabi, chief of international business development at Cleveland

Clinic, and chief medical operations officer. He received his undergraduate degree from Haverford College, his medical degree from Dartmouth Medical School, completed a pediatric residency and pediatric care fellowship at Intermountain's Primary Children's Hospital, and a Master of Medical Management at Carnegie Mellon University.

Dr. Harrison is an all-American triathlete and represented the United States at the 2014 World Championships.